SEXUAL CULTURE IN THE LITERATURE OF MEDIEVAL BRITAIN

SEXUAL CULTURE IN THE LITERATURE OF MEDIEVAL BRITAIN

Edited by
Amanda Hopkins, Robert Allen Rouse
and Cory James Rushton

D. S. BREWER

© Contributors 2014

All Rights Reserved. Except as permitted under current legislation
no part of this work may be photocopied, stored in a retrieval system,
published, performed in public, adapted, broadcast,
transmitted, recorded or reproduced in any form or by any means,
without the prior permission of the copyright owner

First published 2014
D. S. Brewer, Cambridge
Paperback edition 2016

ISBN 978 1 84384 379 5 hardback
ISBN 978 1 84384 444 0 paperback

D. S. Brewer is an imprint of Boydell & Brewer Ltd
PO Box 9, Woodbridge, Suffolk IP12 3DF, UK
and of Boydell & Brewer Inc.
668 Mt Hope Avenue, Rochester, NY 14620–2731, USA
website: www.boydellandbrewer.com

The publisher has no responsibility for the continued existence or accuracy
of URLs for external or third-party internet websites referred to in this book,
and does not guarantee that any content on such websites is,
or will remain, accurate or appropriate

A CIP catalogue record for this book is available
from the British Library

This publication is printed on acid-free paper

Contents

	Introduction A Light Thrown upon Darkness: Writing about Medieval British Sexuality ROBERT ALLEN ROUSE AND CORY JAMES RUSHTON	1
1	'Open manslaughter and bold bawdry': Male Sexuality as a Cause of Disruption in Malory's *Morte Darthur* KRISTINA HILDEBRAND	13
2	Erotic (Subject) Positions in Chaucer's *Merchant's Tale* AMY S. KAUFMAN	27
3	Enter the Bedroom: Managing Space for the Erotic in Middle English Romance MEGAN G. LEITCH	39
4	'Naked as a nedyll': The Eroticism of Malory's Elaine YVETTE KISOR	55
5	'How love and I togedre met': Gower, Amans and the Lessons of Venus in the *Confessio Amantis* SAMANTHA J. RAYNER	69
6	'Bogeysliche as a boye': Performing Sexuality in *William of Palerne* HANNAH PRIEST	85
7	Fairy Lovers: Sexuality, Order and Narrative in Medieval Romance AISLING BYRNE	99
8	Text as Stone: Desire, Sex, and the Figurative Hermaphrodite in the *Ordinal* and *Compound of Alchemy* CYNTHEA MASSON	111
9	Animality, Sexuality and the Abject in Three of Dunbar's Satirical Poems ANNA CAUGHEY	127
10	The Awful Passion of Pandarus CORY JAMES RUSHTON	147
11	Invisible Woman: Rape as a Chivalric Necessity in Medieval Romance AMY N. VINES	161
	Notes on Contributors	181
	Index	183

Introduction
A Light Thrown upon Darkness: Writing about Medieval British Sexuality

ROBERT ALLEN ROUSE and CORY JAMES RUSHTON

THE hit HBO cable series *Game of Thrones* (2011–14) – the fantasy-medieval saga based on George R. R. Martin's *Song of Ice and Fire* novels – has provided more than its fair share of salacious sex scenes. Rape, marital rape, attempted rape, prostitution, group sex, sodomy (of both heterosexual and homosexual forms), incest, sex leading to castration, sex leading to leech-application, and even – occasionally – vanilla consensual sex, have appeared on the screen in the first four seasons of the show. The show, while generally well reviewed, has come under sustained criticism from certain sectors of the media for its depiction of a brutal medieval sexuality, a misogynous sexual culture replete with the threat of violent coercion. This popular (mis)representation of sex in what passes for the Middle Ages in the popular mind is, of course, far from a new phenomenon, and can be traced back through a long genealogy of such representations. One much dissected recent moment in this genealogy is found in Quentin Tarantino's *Pulp Fiction* (1994), where the African-American gangster Marsellus (Ving Rhames), having been saved from looming sodomitic rape by Bruce Willis's character Butch, vows his own distinct form of violent sexual revenge: 'What now? Let me tell you what now. I'ma call a coupla hard, pipe-hittin' niggers, who'll go to work on the homes here with a pair of pliers and a blow torch. You hear me talkin', hillbilly boy? I ain't through with you by a damn sight. I'ma get medieval on your ass.'[1]

For modern western culture, 'medieval' often acts as unsophisticated shorthand for 'barbaric' or 'backward', as is witnessed by the common use of the term to describe the place of women in, for example, Islamic-dominated societies such as Afghanistan and Saudi Arabia. This transtemporal deployment of the medieval to describe modern misogynistic societies partakes

---

[1] See Carolyn Dinshaw, *Getting Medieval: Communities and Sexualities, Pre- and Postmodern* (Durham, NC, 1999), pp. 183–206.

of a long tradition of developmental geo-temporalist thought, characteristic of nineteenth-century anthropology, but showing no signs of disappearing from the popular western world-view.[2] This pejorative sense of 'medieval' also colours the understanding of sex and sexuality in a similar transtemporal manner; western society views such cultures as sexually repressive and misogynistic, thus labelling them as 'medieval'. This then inflects the popular understanding of the western medieval itself. It should hardly come as a surprise, then, to see the harsh sexual landscape of Martin's fiction – and the television series that it has spawned – being conflated with, and confused for, the sexual culture of the 'historical' Middle Ages.

'For love that tyme was nat as love ys nowadayes'[3]

When Thomas Malory tells the readers of his *Morte Darthur* that he cannot be certain just what Lancelot and Guinevere were doing in her chambers late at night – 'whether they were abed other at other maner of disportis' – he means that he simply won't say whether they were having sex or not. Malory scholars have duly argued over this exact issue, how it seems to contradict earlier passages where they do sleep together, and just what it says about Malory as an author (incompetent, sly or elusive). The word he uses, 'disportis' or 'amusements', seems to justify an either/or question: they were having sex, or they were engaged in other – non-sexual – activities. Chaucer uses the phrase 'greet desport' to describe the dignified appearance of the Prioress (Prol., I. 137), but also uses it when the Wife of Bath suggests how husbands ought to let wives amuse themselves as they wish: 'Thou sholdest seye, "Wyf, go wher thee liste; / Taak youre disport; I wol nat leve no talys. / I knowe yow for a trewe wyf, Dame Alys"' (WoB III. 318–20). Of course, Alys is not exactly a true wife, and her suggested advice is full of erotic ambiguity swirling around the possibility of adultery. Indeed, critics have often noted the latent eroticism of the portrait of the Prioress: 'disport', for Chaucer, is always at least potentially an erotic pun carrying a sense of frisson. The baseline reading of Malory, then, might be misguided. One possibility has to be that their amusements are non-sexual, but another is that a bed might not be physically involved: are Lancelot and Guinevere in bed having sex, or are their sexual games being conducted in some other way? Where would flirting lie on this spectrum? In an era that could see the word 'paternoster' take on 'an amatory coloring' because the murmuring of prayer sounded like love-making to the anonymous author of the Latin *Prisciani regula*, erotic possibility seems a wider category than we have often imagined.[4]

---

[2] For a discussion of the medieval operating in this untimely manner see John Ganim, *Orientalism and Medievalism* (New York, 2005), p. 9.

[3] Sir Thomas Malory, *The Works of Sir Thomas Malory*, ed. Eugène Vinaver, rev. P. J. C. Field, 3 vols (Oxford, 1990), p. 1165.

[4] Jan M. Ziolkowski, 'The Erotic Paternoster', *Neuphilologische Mitteilungen* 88 (1987): 31–4.

Any history of sexuality shares with other histories (social, literary) a tendency towards the unitary; this is doubly so with the Middle Ages, because the historiographies of other periods insist on their unitariness in order to demonstrate the diversity of other eras. Michel Foucault does precisely this in the first volume of his *History of Sexuality*:

> The Middle Ages had organized around the theme of the flesh and the practice of penance a discourse that was markedly unitary. In the course of recent centuries, this relative uniformity was broken apart, scattered, and multiplied in an explosion of distinct discursivities which took form in demography, biology, medicine, psychiatry, psychology, ethics, pedagogy, and political criticism. More precisely, the secure bond that held together the moral theology of concupiscence and the obligation of confession (equivalent to the theoretical discourse on sex and its first-person formulation) was, if not broken, at least loosened and diversified: between the objectification of sex in rational discourses, and the movement by which each individual was set to the task of recounting his own sex, there has occurred, since the eighteenth century, a whole series of tensions, conflicts, efforts at adjustment, and attempts at retranscription.[5]

To a significant extent, Foucault's assertion is demonstrably true: the modern era has seen an intense interest in categorization and disciplinarity that paradoxically worked to form a new master narrative comprised of ever-smaller narrative identities. But as any medievalist knows, much is lost when we accept the forced 'unitarification' of an entire complex period. What David Perkins says concerning literary history holds true of all histories: 'We could argue that the intention organizing a literary history justifies its omissions and its emphases. But whatever the intention, to a reader who knows the material as well as the literary historian and, of course, to the literary historian himself, any narrative will seem incomplete and somewhat arbitrary.'[6] Indeed, if we are now beginning to understand that sexuality is always 'various' – paraphiliac, manifesting in a perhaps infinite number of ways – then to ask for the complete picture is to consciously or unconsciously insist on something teleological, also-ran sexualities lumbering imperfectly towards the heteronormative.

The question of, or insistence on, a difference between sexuality and the 'erotic' has this teleological longing at its heart, and uncomfortably assumes that heteronormativity can somehow paradoxically include variation (apparently through the notion of consent between adults). This distinction is important to a degree, but it a question complicated by modern ideas of the individual's identity, of a sexuality that is also the self. Perhaps the difference is that sexuality contributes to what you are, where your attraction will be directed, but the erotic is about what happens when you feel that attraction:

---

5 Michel Foucault, *The History of Sexuality: An Introduction*, trans. Robert Hurley (New York, 1990), pp. 33–4.
6 David Perkins, *Is Literary History Possible?* (Baltimore and London, 1992), p. 31.

the erotic is about frisson, desire and need. Anything outside the ordinary, in medieval ecclesiastical doctrine, was by definition considered a sin: if this act contributed to your identity, it was to confirm that you were a sinner, not that you were either hetero- or homosexual, a sadomasochist, or someone sexually attracted to people wearing plush animal costumes, or dressed like a fire-fighter or the anime super heroine Sailor Moon. While western culture still maintains a socially useful all-encompassing category, the 'pervert', decisions about what constitutes perversion are no less arbitrary than the acts that might place one within that category.[7] Behavioral patterns that are deemed to be outside the norm depend on a definition of the 'norm' that is itself problematic, even for the supposedly homogenous Middle Ages. Our individual sexualities are, at least in part, the result of our encounters with the world: first crushes, a particular scent associated with one individual, a kind of uniform, an exposure to pornography, would all seem to play a role in what we individually find erotic. Sexuality may be inherent or even genetic; the erotic is learned. In this way, gender and class (among other things) would matter when it comes to erotic moments, and the same moment could be fundamentally different to the people involved (as in moments of rape or the voyeuristic, discussed in some of this collection's essays). For all the differences between how we see love and how Malory saw love, it was likely always true that our environments modified our individual sense of what was hot and what was not. In another section of Malory's book, three knights come to blows over which queen is the most attractive: Guinevere, Isolde, or Morgause. Morgause's supporter, Lamorak, makes the case that nobody can force somebody else to feel an attraction. All three are heterosexual men, apparently with a shared fetish for royal women, but even within that category the three men value different things. The insistence that we distinguish between sexuality and the erotic, or between who we are and the acts we perform and commit, has uncomfortable connections to the medieval that go beyond popular conceptions of barbarity, intolerance and gender inequality. These connections are rooted in the idea of the heteronormative itself.

Louis-Georges Tin's recent monograph, *The Invention of Heterosexual Culture*, encapsulates the problem by first raising a very good question and then, second, steadfastly refusing to read anything by a medievalist that might help answer it: historical criticism assumes that heterosexuality is 'ever-present' and 'transparent to itself', evading critique because it presents itself as 'a self-evident point of departure'.[8] Making a necessary distinction between reproduction and the culture of romantic love, Tin reminds us that the latter is worth considering:

> heterosexual practices are universal, whereas the culture of heterosexuality is not. Although human nature is manifestly heterosexual, which allows the

---

[7] In the twenty-first century, psychiatric diagnosis may have replaced canon law in the designation of paraphilia and other sexual perversion, but these categories are equally arbitrary.
[8] Louis-Georges Tin, *The Invention of Heterosexual Culture* (Cambridge, MA, 2008; 2012), p. vii.

reproduction of the species, human cultures are not necessarily heterosexual – that is, they do not always give symbolic primacy to the man–woman couple and to love in its cultural, literary, or artistic representations, as close study of ancient and archaic civilizations reveals.[9]

This is one way to isolate the difference between sexuality and the concept of the erotic, but it also testifies to the way in which cultures resist making that distinction. Tin's thesis is that the culture of courtly love testifies to a new heterosexuality, an insistence on companionate love between men and women in opposition to the homosocial culture that came before and was more interested in the relationship between men. It is difficult to say who would have been responsible for this sea-change, given that Tin outlines the extensive ecclesiastical, noble and medical opposition to the new heterosexuality. Surely there is nobody left to blame. But something does seem to change between the *Song of Roland* – where Aude only matters as the woman who will bind her brother and his best friend together – and Andreas Capellanus, who says that passionate love cannot exist between people of the same sex.[10] While Tin makes little reference to Christine de Pizan, she would appear to confirm, in her *Book of the City of Ladies*, that by the end of the Middle Ages, attraction between the sexes appears so natural to the culture that its mystery can be assumed rather than explained:

> 'My lady, there's a kind of natural attraction at work on earth which draws men to women and women to men. This isn't a social law but an instinct of the flesh: stimulated by carnal desire, it makes the two sexes love each other in a wild and ardent way. Neither sex has any idea what it is that causes them to fall for each other like this, but they succumb in droves to this type of emotion, which is known as passionate love.'[11]

By the twentieth century, Tin argues, the struggle to valorize homosexuality is a struggle against a heterosexuality so normative that it can barely be questioned. But it could be argued that Tin does not go far enough, that what he sees as a pre-heterosexual homosocial culture is in fact a pre-heterosexual paraphiliac culture, a world of sexual experiences and desires as potentially infinite as the number of existing individuals (and the combinations between those individuals).

However, this is not to say that there are no points of connection between modern and pre-modern sexualities. Slavoj Žižek observes that:

> We are thus dealing with the structure of a temporal loop: there is sexuality not only because of a gap between adult sexuality and the child's unprepared gaze traumatized by its display, but because this child's perplexity

---

9 Tin, *The Invention of Heterosexual Culture*, p. ix.
10 Tin, *The Invention of Heterosexual Culture*, pp. 6–9, 28–9.
11 Christine de Pizan, *Book of the City of Ladies*, trans. Rosalind Brown-Grant (Harmondsworth, 1999), p. 171.

continues to sustain adult sexual activity itself. This paradox also explains the blind spot of the topic of sexual harassment: *there is no sex without an element of 'harassment'* (of the perplexed gaze violently shocked, traumatized, by the uncanny character of what is going on). The protest against sexual harassment, against violently imposed sex, is thus ultimately *the protest against sex as such*: if one subtracts from the sexual interplay its painfully traumatic character, the remainder is simply no longer sexual. 'Mature' sex between the proverbial consenting adults, deprived of the traumatic element of shocking imposition, is by definition *desexualized*, turned into mechanical coupling.[12]

Žižek's point is quite close to Leo Bersani's oft-repeated claim that sexuality, for our culture as for others, is wrapped in comfortable lies: 'the redemptive reinvention of sex' as one of mutual tenderness and emotional depth rather than penetration and power.[13]

> Romantic love has been one of our more effective myths for making sense out of our sensations. It organizes bodily intensities around a single object of desire and it provides a more or less public theater for the enactment of the body's most private life. In love, desires and sensations are both structured and socialized.[14]

While Bersani's case may be overstated and modern society may have good reason (even if Bersani were absolutely right) to redefine sex along more constructive lines, it remains true that the Middle Ages saw sex exactly as Bersani sees it.[15] If there is a depiction of mutual and emotionally resonant sexual activity, it usually comes as a result of negotiation. Where we see loveliness, the texts often see things otherwise: the poem is correct in judging that Erec's fall into uxoriousness is wrong, even if we do not necessarily agree; Chaucer's one depiction of beautifully equal sex is Alison and Nicholas, but they are committing adultery. In fact, as Allman and Hanks have argued, even Chaucer (traditionally viewed as medieval literature's great liberally progressive hope) sees sex as something inherently violent and competitive. In their opinion, 'the English canon's favorite "wayside drama" has this specific, jaundiced bodily economy of the erotic: males pierce; women bleed'.[16] This is undoubtedly a dark view of medieval sexuality, and it is almost certainly the one that Martin and HBO responded to in crafting the *Game of Thrones* franchise. Indeed, the one 'pleasant' depiction of a sexual relationship in Martin's books

---

[12] Slavoj Žižek, *Ticklish Subject: The Absent Centre of Political Ontology* (New York, 2009), pp. 343–4.
[13] Leo Bersani, *Future for Astyanax: Character and Desire in Literature* (New York, 1984), pp. 214–15.
[14] Bersani, *Future for Astyanax*, p. 89.
[15] *The Erotic in the Literature of Medieval Britain*, ed. A. Hopkins and C. J. Rushton (Cambridge, 2007), pp. 9–11.
[16] W. W. Allman and D. Thomas Hanks, 'Rough Love: Notes Towards an Erotics of *The Canterbury Tales*', *The Chaucer Review* 38:1 (2003): 36–65 (53).

is the careful, negotiated beginning of Daenerys Targaryen's marriage to Khal Drogo – unfortunately turned into another brutal encounter in the series.

Yet this 'harassment' is not the only, or perhaps even the most important, point of connection between Žižek and the medieval. Žižek's mechanical, desexualized coupling is intended to sound like a nightmare, but it was precisely this that Augustine argued humanity had lost in the Fall: sexuality for procreation without the inconvenient lusts that accompany sex in the fallen world. Augustine's vision was one of perfect male control: instead of feeling 'the morbid condition of lust', the 'sexual organs would have been brought into activity by the same bidding of will as controlled the other organs'.[17] On this account, there is no fear of sex, but explicitly a fear of the erotic, of frisson itself. Augustine's vision of a mechanical, necessary sexual act is also a vision of sex as de-individualized: if the sexual act can occur without arousal, it follows that anyone could breed with anyone else at any time as long as the reason to do so was compelling enough. Individual attraction, the necessity of seduction with its attention to the other individual, becomes unnecessary, not only sinful but an unfortunate distraction. For Augustine, as for Žižek, the erotic is found in the uncanny, the disturbing. Even on the issue of 'harassment', there is a connection: Augustine argues that in the absence of male lust there would be 'no loss of the wife's integrity, just as the menstrual flux can now be produced from the womb of a virgin without loss of maidenhead'.[18] Augustine's vision is that of a procreative sexuality free of shock, trauma, the unexpected, the unlooked-for: the contingent lives of individuals interacting in an unpredictable world. It is this vision that leads to the medieval Church's attempts to regulate sexuality, to determine what is bad and less-bad when it comes to sexual behaviour. To follow Foucault in assuming that the European Middle Ages, across a millennium and a continent, fell easily and comfortably in line with the Church's efforts is to ignore the basic fact that those efforts were continuous and repeated – in short, they were ineffective.

This collection of essays will suggest that to offer a sampling of possibilities is both a better assessment of the past, and perhaps a more optimistic model for the future. *The Erotic in the Literature of Medieval Britain* (2007) was intended as a snapshot (or a series of snapshots) of the situation obtaining in the broad geographical and chronological boundaries of the medieval British Isles, but could well be criticized for not containing enough Chaucer, or enough Gower, or enough *fabliaux*, as in Tison Pugh's review: 'The Lanval legend receives too much coverage; Chaucer's fabliaux too little. Many notable authors of medieval Britain – John Gower, William Langland, Robert Henryson, Thomas Hoccleve – are mentioned only in passing, if at all.'[19] While this would seem to privilege the literary canon over issues of the erotic – is there anything in Langland to

---

[17] Augustine, *City of God* III.14.26, in *Love, Sex and Marriage in the Middles Ages*, ed. Conor McCarthy (London and New York, 2004), p. 40.
[18] Augustine, *City of God* III.14.26.
[19] Tison Pugh, review in *English Studies in Canada* 34:2/3 (2008): 271–4 (274).

match the voyeuristic pleasures of *Lanval*? – this current volume sees more essays on Chaucer and Gower. The first volume could also be critiqued for not being able to offer a firm definition of the erotic at the end, as in Kathleen Coyne Kelly's perceptive review:

> While the essays in this collection offer many fine readings of texts, we are not that further along to defining what a medieval erotic *is* at the end of it. Still, given that scholars of medieval sexuality, sexual practices, and desire have had to contend with a shifting, oblique, or missing vocabulary, the contributors to *The Erotic in the Literature of Medieval Britain* address this problem in what is, perhaps, the only reasonable way to do so; that is, to read for the erotic in narratives of acts or instances of identity-formation, and to read for acts or instances of identity-formation in the erotic.[20]

Kelly's comment echoes, and in part helps to inaugurate, the conversation in the introduction above. The point remains that neither volume is intended as a complete examination of medieval sexual culture as it is represented in the British Isles, even should such a thing be possible. There can be no such thing as 'a medieval erotic' – the 'erotic' is always a category of multiplicity, unified by effect ('are you aroused?') rather than cause ('what are the distinct things which can arouse someone born between, for example, the Fall of Rome and the Fall of Constantinople in a particular continental space?'), for exactly the reasons Kelly astutely suggests.

The sexual culture of medieval Britain was diverse and complex, both in its manifestation in theory and practice, and in the uses to which it was deployed in the literary remains from the period. The essays in this collection reflect this variety of form and function, considering representations of sexualities gendered masculine, feminine, and other, behaviours normative and non-normative, and deployments of sexual culture that structure texts, social and physical spaces, and power relationships. These representations, like all such literary articulations, simultaneously reflect and refract historical social practice, illuminating both the realities and the ideologies of medieval British sexuality.

This volume begins in the dark, with the problematic nature of unconstrained male sexual desire. Kristina Hildebrand examines the anxiety surrounding the disruptive power of violent masculine sexuality in Malory's Arthurian world, threatening both social and spiritual disorder. Hildebrand reads the chief articulation of this anxiety in the Pentecostal oath, foregrounding the necessity of sexual regulation to the success of Arthur's perfect society. In her discussion of the sexual dynamics of Malory's text, Hildebrand examines first the disruptive sexual acts that break or threaten the bonds and hierarchies of feudal society, and second the incestuous desire that lies hidden behind the concern for the chastity of female relatives. This second theme of male control of female chastity, or sexuality, forms the ground for Amy S. Kaufman's essay.

[20] Kathleen Coyne Kelly, review in *Studies in the Age of Chaucer* 30 (2008): 372–5 (374).

In a striking reassessment of the sexual dynamics of Chaucer's *Merchant's Tale*, Kaufman makes a compelling case for May's subversion of Januarie's normative masculine attempt to literally wall up her sexuality through the construction of the pleasure garden. In the figure of the courtly lover, Damyan, Kaufman deploys feminist theory to reveal a receptive alternative masculinity 'through which the silently oppressed learns to express her desire', providing a rare glimpse into a female-orientated erotic.

From Januarie's failed attempt to control female sexuality in the space of the garden, we move to the consideration of another erotic space, that of the bedroom or chamber. Megan G. Leitch examines the architecture of the erotic in medieval romance through the lens of spatial theory, focusing 'on moments of conflict concerning fulfilment or frustration of desire wherein spaces receive more attention than bodies, or compete with bodies for textual attention'. Spaces, we are reminded, are products of power relations, and the bedroom emerges as a complex site of the projection and negotiation of sexuality and eroticism. Yvette Kisor also begins in the bedroom, observing that when Malory's Elaine 'skypped oute of her bedde all naked' (2.795) and kneels to beg for her life, her nudity and her vulnerability combine to produce a powerful effect upon Lancelot. Kisor identifies a complicated frisson in this scene of passivity and nakedness, allowing us to read erotic figures such as the naked Elaine as instruments wielded by other, more aggressive, women such as Morgan le Fay, the queen of North Galys or Dame Brusen. Here we find an active and transgressive female sexuality, disguised in the normative body of the passive female subject, which targets Lancelot in both Malory and the *Lancelot-Grail* cycle.

Lancelot famously fails at sexual self-restraint when presented with such alluring temptation, raising the dangers of sexual desire for jejune men in medieval Britain. However, sexuality is not, despite what our current obsession with the cult of youth may suggest, the sole preserve of the young. Samantha J. Rayner turns to the question of the *senex amans* in the *Confessio Amantis*, examining the relationships of Gower's elderly lovers – and of the poet himself – both to female objects of desire and to the figure of Amans himself. Sexual love is a component of most human experience, and Rayner examines how the interplay between Gower's figures of Genius, Venus and Amans articulate a sexuality that holds truths applicable to readers of all ages.

Sexuality, as with much that constitutes human identity, is performative. Hannah Priest's study of sexual behaviour in *William of Palerne*, a text characterized by somatic and gender transformations, identifies the heroine Melior as performing the role of the masculine courtly lover in her pursuit of William, the object of her desire. In a tale of the metamorphosis produced by lycanthropy, the playful performance of opposite gendered sexuality invokes a fluid sexual culture in which masculine and feminine sexualities can be put on, and taken off, as easily as clothed disguises. *William of Palerne* then, for Priest, is a ludic space in which sexual identities can be temporarily dissevered from biological gender in a manner both light-hearted and ironic. Romance also acts as an alternative erotic space in Aisling Byrne's study of the trope of the faerie lover. Tracing the trope through Middle English, Anglo-Norman and Irish narratives, Byrne argues that the adoxic sexual space permits certain types of relationships that would be transgressive in the real medieval world, but also that 'texts like *Lanval* still use the motif to produce plots that highlight distinctly non-transgressive orthodox ideas'. Byrne reads the consequences of complicated sexual relationships with faerie lovers as producing a primarily narratological, rather than ethical, effect, exposing 'the machinery of the plot and the problems that absolute gratification poses for narrative'.

Sex is the coming together of men and women, in all their various paraphiliac heterosexual and homosexual conjunctions, and the erotic is the affect of attraction that structures and articulates desire. While it is common to speak of repression and sublimation as alternatives to the erotic or the sexual, this obscures the way in which the erotic can linger in that which ostensibly replaces it. As such, there is also an erotic of material objects, as Cynthea Masson illustrates in her essay on 'sexual and gendered play within alchemical language and literature'. In the alchemical writings of the fifteenth century, Masson finds that erotic desire is 'redirected from the physical body and material world toward the divinely inspired knowledge of the alchemical corpus'. This is not simply a metaphorical deployment of the language of human desire, but also a rhetorical one, situating not only the practice of alchemy as analogous with desire, but figuring the very knowledge itself as erotic. If the erotic is about intense desire, the longing on display in alchemical texts would seem to qualify.

Anna Caughey discusses the combination of animal and sexual imagery in the satirical poems of William Dunbar. Taking as her starting point Julia Kristeva's concept of the abject, Caughey examines Dunbar's complex intermingling of the abject and the animal with the language of praise and celebration in his poetry, identifying a 'dark *jouissance*' through which the abject becomes a source of the erotic and the humorous. Cory James Rushton continues the theme of such dark pleasures in a reading of *Troilus and Criseyde* that coalesces around the implied 'dark' narratives of incest, possession, force and rape that underlie both the text (and its texts) and the mainstream of male sexuality (medieval or otherwise). Criseyde's status as widow is an important component of her object status under the gaze of men both within the poem and within the academy. Pandarus leads the innocent Troilus (innocent only in guile, not in intent), giving shape and direction to his desires for the 'experienced and non-virginal woman'. These desires manifest in what Rushton reads as 'the trap' where Criseyde is prey, both metaphorically animal and most cruelly human. The subject of rape is also the topic of Amy N. Vines's essay, which asks how we read texts 'where the rapist is also the heroic figure of the text'. Contra to those explicit codes of chivalry that prohibit rape, such as Malory's Pentecostal oath, Vines argues that 'the act of rape is in many cases a foundational aspect of establishing masculine chivalric identity'. Addressing Chaucer's *Wife of Bath's Tale*, the Old French *Percival* Continuation, and the Middle English *Partonope of Blois*, Vines exposes some very uncomfortable possibilities about the fundamental place of male sexual aggression in the implicit expectations of medieval chivalric behaviour.

The essays in this volume speak to the diverse range of erotics and sexualities articulated within the cultures of late medieval Britain. In a volume of this type one can make no claims to comprehensive coverage of time, geography or genre. Rather, we have assembled a range of essays that – we hope – represent to some small degree the diversity of medieval British sexualities. Sexual culture was no more homogenous in medieval Britain than it is today, despite the attempts of canon law and social convention to regulate it. In fact, the very existence of the prohibitions against and penitentials for sexual activities of all types highlights their very presence in the lived practice of medieval people, who were just as invested and interested in sex as we are today.

I

'Open manslaughter and bold bawdry': Male Sexuality as a Cause of Disruption in Malory's Morte Darthur

KRISTINA HILDEBRAND

AS Roger Ascham famously observed, Malory's *Morte Darthur* is primarily concerned with 'open manslaughter, and bold bawdry'.[1] I would not disagree; in fact, I would say that these themes are not only dominant but are inextricably interwoven. Male sexuality, in Malory, is consistently portrayed as potentially violent and disruptive, dangerous not only to individuals but to the whole structure of society, and therefore in need of controlling measures. The medieval world did not, of course, often portray any form of sexuality positively. Sexual desire leads both men and women to sin: both directly in committing fornication, incest and adultery, and indirectly in committing treason or disregarding their duties. It could easily be assumed that this is a divide between the clergy on the one side, themselves compelled to live in celibacy and thus suspicious of sexual desire, and the more relaxed nobility and commons on the other, cheerfully ignoring the rules when it suited them. However, this is too simple a dichotomy. Malory himself, despite the bold bawdry, shares in the suspicion of unregulated desire, in his nostalgia for a chaster time,

> nowadayes men can nat love sevennyght but they muste have all their desyres ... But the olde love was nat so. for men and women coulde love togydirs seven yerys, and no lycoures lustis was betwyxte them, and than was love trouthe and faythefulnes.[2]

David Benson points out that 'human love is highly valued by Malory, but not erotic passion', and that 'Malory is more interested in friends and comrades

---

[1] Roger Ascham, *The Schoolmaster* (1570), in *English Works*, ed. William A. Wright (Cambridge, 1904), p. 231.
[2] Sir Thomas Malory, *Works*, ed. Eugene Vinaver, 2nd edn (1971; Oxford, 1977), p. 649. Further references will be to this edition.

than in sexual relationships': compared to his sources he tones down the sexual component of Lancelot's and Guinevere's relationship.[3] However, I would argue that the text is not so much uninterested in as highly suspicious of sexual relationships, especially those that occur – as do the majority of sexual relationships portrayed in the text – outside wedlock. Sexuality is best when regulated, even in Malory's world of heroic lovers. A noble man or woman will love someone, but desire should be moderated. Control over male sexuality is a social and communal issue: it is exerted through recognized channels such as the concepts of chivalry and courtly love. This control is one of the central concepts in the Pentecostal oath: 'allwayes to do ladyes, damesels, and jantillwomen and wydowes socour: strengthe hem in hir ryghtes, and never to enforce them, uppon payne of dethe' (75). The most interesting part of this is not the expectation that Arthur's knights will protect women – a reasonably well-established part of chivalry – but that this expectation needs to be enforced with an oath. It cannot be left to the individual knight to live up to his duty towards women, including not committing rape, without the threat of extreme punishment. Other parts of the oath mention punishment 'uppon payne of forfiture of their worship and lordship of kynge Arthur for evirmore' (75), but no other part is enforced with the threat of execution. Dorsey Armstrong has pointed out that 'the ideals of the Oath serve as a guide to proper behaviour *throughout the narrative*', making the control of male sexuality one of the central themes of Malory's text.[4]

Malory's concern appears to be with the havoc wreaked by sexual desire when it is not controlled by the will, either of the desiring subject or of the desired object. Many of his primary villains exhibit this lack of control over their desire: Breunis sans Pité is not only a treacherous opponent, fond of riding down knights afoot, but also a rapist; Morgan le Fay is repeatedly depicted as sexually rapacious – she is one of the queens who offer Lancelot a choice between taking one of them for a paramour or being imprisoned; Meleagant – whose cowardice is shown in his attacking unarmed knights yet hesitating to fight Lancelot – abducts Guinevere, clearly intending rape. However, in addition to such obviously negatively portrayed characters, many of the otherwise positively depicted knights exhibit a disruptive and violent sexuality. In the light of this, I would argue that Malory's depiction of male sexuality is no less complex and ambiguous than his portrayal of female sexuality.

When female sexuality is transgressive, it tends to be obvious to the reader: the ideal of the sexually demure woman, such as Igrayne, who is mutely traded between men, is sharply contrasted against women who aggressively pursue the object of their desire, such as the woman with a necrophiliac lust for

---

[3] C. David Benson, 'The Ending of the *Morte Darthur*', in *A Companion to Malory*, ed. Elizabeth Archibald and A. S. G. Edwards (1996; Cambridge, 2000), pp. 203–20 (p. 228).
[4] Dorsey Armstrong, *Gender and the Chivalric Community in Malory's* Morte d'Arthur (Gainesville, FL, 2003), p. 31.

Lancelot. However, transgressive male sexuality is more difficult to identify: male sexuality is typically depicted as aggressive, thus the portrait of male sexuality as violent and disruptive becomes invisible due to its normalization. Transgressive male sexuality in Malory concerns both sexual acts and desires: it breaks boundaries not only of permitted acts but also of permissible desires. In this essay, I intend to look more closely at two forms of transgressive male sexuality, hoping to bring them out of the invisibility of normalization: the disruptive sexual acts that break or threaten the bonds and hierarchies of feudal society, and the incestuous desire hidden behind a concern for the chastity of female relatives.

Medieval society, while by no means inherently hostile to social mobility, was primarily structured through male hierarchal relationships and mutual bonds. Sexual acts that disrupt such a hierarchy and mutuality include adultery, and it is in this form that the two primary examples of transgressive desire appear in Malory's text. These sexual encounters affect not only the participants but also the whole of Malory's Arthurian society, as witnessed by Uther Pendragon's desire for Igrayne, and Arthur's for Morgawse. These two stories are curiously parallel: in both cases, the affair involves the sovereign and an opponent with the potential to become a vassal and ally, and articulates the conception of a significant male character. This parallelism been discussed before, but here I would like to consider them in the wider Malorian context of male sexuality as disruptive unless it is controlled by a woman's presence – active or passive. These are not isolated incidents of destructive male desire: they are parts of a larger picture.

Uther Pendragon's desire for Igrayne, duchess of Cornwall, disrupts society in several ways. It is of course an illicit desire – not only adulterous but also aimed at the wife of his vassal, whose interests he has a duty to protect.[5] The most immediate disruption is the return to war: after making peace with the duke of Cornwall, 'that helde warre ageynst hym long tyme' (3), Uther Pendragon's attempts at seduction result in the duke removing himself from court and refusing to return, and thus is the peace undone. With Igrayne out of reach, Uther Pendragon's immoderate desire and his anger at having it thwarted make him fall ill. This illness is not only a threat to the stability of the country, ruled by a king without an heir, but is the direct cause of Merlin's intervention. Through magic, Merlin gives Uther access to Igrayne and makes sure that Arthur is conceived. As we shall see, this clandestine meeting will have consequences, positive and negative, long after Uther has taken his immoderate desire to his grave.

As has been pointed out by Victoria Guerin, Uther's immoderate desire for Igrayne leads to Arthur's incest: the price demanded by Merlin for disguising Uther as Igrayne's husband is the rearing of Arthur in secrecy, and this leads to

---

5 They would appear to be enemies about to be reconciled, but the fact that Uther can command the presence of the duke of Cornwall at his court, and go to war against him if he does not obey, indicates that they are feudal lord and vassal.

Arthur's ignorance of the incest he commits with Morgawse.[6] Uther's immoderate and sinful desire leads to his son's sin, which in its turn is at least partly responsible for the fall of Arthur and the Round Table: the sins of the fathers are being visited not just on their children but on the entire realm. Despite the illicit nature of the union of Uther and Igrayne, it results in Arthur, whereas that of Arthur and Morgawse results in Mordred. The differing offspring – one the greatest of all kings, the other the unnatural son who brings him down – point to differences between the two affairs, but they are also inextricably linked. Uther's and Igrayne's illicit union is mitigated by a number of factors: firstly that Igrayne is ignorant of any adultery, in her belief that Uther is her husband the duke, and secondly that she is – though neither of them knows it at time – recently widowed and so committing adultery neither in intention nor in fact. In contrast to this, Arthur and Morgawse are fully aware that she is married to Lot of Orkney – she is at Arthur's court seemingly as a messenger of peace. As Armstrong points out, 'Morgawse is an *active* player in the adultery'.[7] Unlike Arthur's other pre-marital lover, the Lady Lyonors, who is unmarried (26), Morgawse knowingly commits adultery, making her an anti-Igrayne and producing offspring warped by this sin. In Malory's text, the blame falls on Morgawse, who defrauds her husband both by cuckolding him and by letting him raise an illegitimate son, and who breaks the rules of the patriarchal society by being an active party in the exchange of her body.[8] Yet this assigning of blame should not make us ignore the social effects of Arthur defrauding his fellow king and potential vassal by sleeping with his wife.

While Arthur's and Morgawse's adulterous affair has direct consequences for the story as a whole, resulting in the birth of Mordred who will, in his turn, be a major cause of the fall of the Round Table, it is perhaps not as obvious that it has immediate effects on society long before Mordred is grown to adulthood. Arthur's desire for Morgawse mirrors Uther's for Igrayne, in that it is a connection that is not only adulterous but also destroys an opportunity to turn an enemy into an ally. It is unclear how the relationship between Arthur and Lot of Orkney progresses: Lot is clearly a trusted vassal of Uther's to be given Igrayne's daughter in marriage, but rebels against Arthur at his coronation. Still, the text clearly identifies the affair of Arthur and Morgawse as one source of his consistent refusal to recognize Arthur as his overlord despite earlier feudal bonds:

> of late tyme before [Lot] had bene a knyght of kynge Arthur's, and wedded a syster of hym. And for because that kynge Arthure lay by hys wyff and gate on her sir Mordred, therefore kyng Lott helde ever agaynste Arthure. (48)

---

6   M. Victoria Guerin, 'The King's Sin: The Origin of the Arthur–David Parallel', in *The Passing of Arthur: New Essays in the Arthurian Tradition*, ed. Christopher Baswell and William Sharpe (New York, 1988), pp. 15–30 (p. 23).
7   Armstrong, *Gender and the Chivalric Community*, p. 52.
8   Armstrong, *Gender and the Chivalric Community*, p. 52.

We do not, in fact, ever see Lot acting as a knight of Arthur's, but the destruction of the potential for a feudal bond and peace between the kings is clearly here ascribed to Arthur's actions. Sexual desire disrupts feudal bonds and endangers the realm by turning powerful allies into enemies.

The sexual desires of Uther and Arthur disrupt society, cause wars and disrupt the largely homosocial bonds of feudal society. Male sexual desire also runs the risk of upsetting the social order, as is evidenced by the episode involving Torre. This young man, later knighted by Arthur at his and his father's request, believes himself to be a cowherd's son. He has grown up in a peasant family but shows no inclination towards farming. His father complains that he has

> thirtene sonnes, and all they woll falle to what laboure I putte them and woll be ryght glad to do laboure; but thys chylde woll nat laboure for nothyng that my wyf and I may do, but allwey he woll be shotynge, or castynge dartes, and glad for to se batayles and to beholde knyghtes. (61)

The young cowherd's son, who also looks nothing like the rest of his family, turns out to be the son of King Pellinore, and his abilities and inclinations are accordingly martial. Pellinore, carried away by his desire, has fathered him on a young maiden 'half be force' (62) and then, it appears, has forgotten the whole episode. This comes before the introduction of the Pentecostal oath, so at the time Pellinore was not bound by any oath 'never to enforce' women. While this story is presented as a rather charming tale of the peasant who is secretly a knight and wins recognition for both his parentage and his deeds, it is easy to see the disruptive effects of knights casually raping young women and fathering sons who do not fit in at the level of society into which they are born. The very need to turn this reasonably realistic story into a fairy tale of noble lineage recognized implies its ability to destabilize the hierarchies of society.

Malory's text, as we have seen, is concerned with controlling male sexuality in order to diminish its potential for disruption. The primary control of male sexuality is through marriage: the passive presence of a desired woman. In all these cases, the illicit desire of the knights and kings is directed hierarchically 'downwards', in a desire for the wives of their vassals or potential vassals, or peasant women. This desire is brought under control by marriage: in Uther's case to the woman he so ardently desires, in Arthur's case by marriage to another, but also ardently desired, woman. While we do not see Pellinore married, the existence of legitimate sons indicates that his desire has also been thus tamed. It might seem paradoxical to argue that the presence of a woman regulates male desire, since the presence of a woman is generally what incites desire. However, the presence of Igrayne as Uther's wife, to whom he has a legal right, functions to moderate the dangerous desire: at no other point does Uther put his kingdom at risk for sexual desire. Similarly, Arthur's marriage to Guinevere appears to prevent him from committing adultery with the wives of vassals: the presence, though passive, of a desired woman to whom the man has legal access, can be seen to prevent disruptive extramarital desire. Armstrong observes that 'Igrayne is the gift, an object that is exchanged for peace, property, and a means of establishing male homosocial bonds within this patriarchal, kin-based social order',[9] but even more, she is the means to prevent further disruption to the social order and its homosocial bonds by regulating Uther's desire.

Male desire that is socially 'upward' – an impossibility for Uther and Arthur – is also controlled by women in that it is moderated by the rules of courtly love. Examples here are Lancelot, Tristram and Lamorak, who all love queens; the desired woman controls the man's desire, which is thus rendered less socially destructive. While Guinevere blames Lancelot and her love for the fall of the Round Table, I cannot read the text as fully endorsing that standpoint, and the love of Tristram and Isolde, and that of Lamorak and Morgawse, seem to have the text's full approval. However, there is one occurrence in Malory of a knight's 'upward' desire that does not remain in this comfort zone: Meleagant's desire for Guinevere. Meleagant's desire threatens the community of the Round Table, and, characteristically, it differs from other instances of unrequited courtly love, such as Palomides' for Isode, in that the man ignores the boundaries set by the woman.[10]

Armstrong has shown that Guinevere, as Arthur's wife, is an essential party to the legitimization of Arthur's reign.[11] In the light of this, a threat to Guinevere can be read as a threat to the entire Arthurian social order. Meleagant's abduction is thus not simply a threat to Guinevere personally but an attempt to remove from Arthur that which, above all, validates his position: his queen and the feudal bonds, including the actual Round Table, that marriage gave him. Meleagant appears as a villain in Malory's text, but he is not like Breunis sans Pité or Morgan le Fay, who are introduced as villains and largely maintain that role, and a distance from Arthur's court, for the vast majority of the narrative. Meleagant, on the other hand, is a knight of the Round Table and a vassal of Arthur. Like Uther Pendragon, Arthur, and Pellinore, he has appeared previously in the text as a normative character, yet his desire for Guinevere causes him to abduct and imprison her, attacking unarmed knights in the procedure. His desire crosses the boundaries of courtly love, as well as the social bounds set by his position as Arthur's knight; as Guinevere points out to him, he is 'aboute to dishonoure the noble kyng that made the knyght! Thou shamyst all knyghthode and thyselffe and me' (651). Meleagant's desire is not controlled by obedience to the object of desire, by the Pentecostal oath, nor by his obligations towards his king, and thus runs the risk of disrupting society. It also destroys him: far from the honour brought

---

[9] Armstrong, *Gender and the Chivalric Community*, p. 48.
[10] Palomides does, at one point, carry off Isolde against her will, but he follows normal courtly rules in doing so, challenging Mark to retrieve her. After this episode, he acts towards her as the correct, if rejected, courtly lover and ascribes all his 'worship' to her influence.
[11] Armstrong, *Gender and the Chivalric Community*, pp. 55–6.

upon a knight by service to a lady and to a noble king, Meleagant's desire brings him shame, death and destruction.

Desire that is uncontrolled and uncontrollable is frequently referred to as being 'out of measure'. Love out of measure appears in several instances: Morgaine and Accolon love each other this way (88); so does Palomides love Isolde (440); Lancelot is loved 'oute of mesure' by both Elaine of Carbonek (486) and Elaine of Astolat (639, 641), and he confesses to loving Guinevere this way (539). In addition, while Uther's love for Igrayne is not described as being out of measure, such an excess of emotion is suggested by Uther showing her and her husband 'grete chere out of mesure' (3). All of these loves lie outside marriage and are in several cases adulterous, and none has an unmitigated happy ending. What these loves out of measure have in common is that they cause social disruption rather than regulate male desire. Morgaine's and Accolon's love, though mutual, is disruptive in that it is not only adulterous but also leads to treason and attempted murder (88). Lancelot's love for Guinevere leads him to ignore normative chivalric behaviour: 'for hir sake wolde I do batayle were hit ryght other wronge'(539). This is in direct contradiction of his Pentecostal oath 'that no man take no batayles in a wrongfull quarrell for no love ne for no worldis goodis' (75). Palomides, in his turn, is led by his love for Isolde to seek to harm Tristram and to behave unchivalrously at the tournament at Lonezep (440, 448–9). Like Palomides' love, the loves of Elaine of Carbonek and Elaine of Astolat are unrequited, and prevent them from exercising proper control over male desire. Though they are both sympathetically treated by the text, their love is socially ineffective: Lancelot loves Guinevere, who controls his desire, and these out of measure loves preclude the possibility of marriage, and the homosocial bonds and regulated male desire that marriage could produce. Were they content to love within measure, they could marry someone else: instead Eaine of Astolat dies of her love (639). We can see that while men who love out of measure are brought by their desire to commit unchivalrous acts and break their oaths, women who love out of measure are failing in their duty to control men's desire, as wives or as courtly lovers.

Notably there is also one case of intense desire which is never referred to as out of measure: that of Gareth and Lyonesse. Having plighted their troth, they twice attempt to anticipate their wedding night because 'they brente bothe in hoote love' and 'were so hoote in brennynge love' (205, 206). Had they succeeded in their design, the sexual contact would have been extramarital; nevertheless, in their case this desire is not out of measure. It is thus not simply the illicit love that is out of measure. It would appear that a love can be out of measure due to its being adulterous, strong enough to cause despair – a deadly sin – at the loved one's death, or unrequited: to love where no return can be expected, as do Palomides, Elaine of Carbonek and Elaine of Astolat, is to love out of measure. Again, controlling one's desire so as not to injure others or oneself, and, if female, to exercise control over potentially disruptive male desire, are virtues in Malory's text.

As we have seen, male desire requires control, though this control can be maintained by an oath or by the desired woman. However, there are two cases of male desire that transgresses boundaries by being deliberately incestuous, as opposed to Arthur's unknowing incest with Morgawse.[12] In these two cases, the need felt by men to control women's sexuality seems to hide an incestuous desire for the mother, a desire which is in one case openly acted upon and in the other hidden. Although it occurs later in the narrative, I will deal with Mordred's desire first. At the beginning of the final book of the *Morte Darthur*, Agravayne and Mordred claim to be outraged at the thought of Guinevere in an adulterous sexual relationship. Agravayne states openly that

> 'I mervayle that we all be nat ashamed bothe to se and to know how sir Launcelot lyeth dayly and nyghtly by the quene. And all we know well that hit ys so, and hit ys shamefully suffird of us all that we shulde suffir so noble a kynge as kynge Arthur ys to be shamed.' (673)

The argument here is that their feudal lord is shamed by his wife's adultery. Speaking to Arthur, Agravayne refers to their kinship ties as giving them an interest in the matter: 'we know all that sir Launcelot holdith youre queene, and hath done longe; and we be your syster sunnes, we may suffer hit no longer' (674). The adultery of Guinevere and Lancelot is here presented as shaming not just Arthur but all his kin. However, the other members of their family – Gawaine, Gaheris and Gareth – will have nothing to do with any plans to catch the lovers. Gawaine lists their obligations to Lancelot, but, first, he states the potential disruption of the quarrel: 'and there aryse warre and wrake betwyxte sir Launcelot and us, wyte you well, brothir, there woll many kynges and grete lordis holde wyth sir Launcelot' (673). Gawaine and Gareth, on being unable to talk their brothers out of the plan, comment that 'now ys thys realme holy destroyed and myscheved, and the noble felyshyp of the Rounde Table shall be disparbeled' (674). Again, the primary concern of those Orkney brothers who are not participating in the conspiracy is the realm and the civil war that will inevitably ensue. This again points to the dangers inherent in desire: that of Lancelot and Guinevere or, as we shall see, of Mordred.

It may seem that this supports the reading that Lancelot's and Guinevere's adulterous love is the downfall of the Round Table, but this fails to take Mordred's desire into account. The tale begins by stating that 'sir Aggravayne and sir Mordred had ever a prevy hate unto the quene, dame Gwenyver, and to sir Launcelot' (673). This secret hate might seem a sufficient explanation for Mordred's action, but the reader must then be surprised at his later relationship with the queen, which seems to be structured around desire, not hatred. As Arthur leaves to go to war against Launcelot, he 'made sir Mordred chyeff ruler

---

[12] Tristram's desire for Isolde is technically incestuous as she is his uncle's wife. However, their love dates to well before that union took place, and also differs in other ways from the standard courtly love: it is often openly displayed and approved of at Arthur's court.

of all Ingelonde, and also he put the quene undir hys governaunce: bycause sir Mordred was kynge Arthurs son, he gaff hym the rule off hys londe and off hys wyff' (709). The phrasing here emphasizes both Mordred's blood ties and Guinevere's legal ties to Arthur. However, Mordred proceeds to usurp both throne and queen. He does so with some caution when it comes to the throne: 'he lete make lettirs as thoughe that they had come fromme beyonde the see, and the lettirs specifyed that kynge Arthur was slayne in batayle with sir Launcelot. Wherefore sir Mordred made a parlemente, and called the lordis togydir, and there he made them to chose hym kynge' (707). With the throne Mordred is cautious enough to get the support of the barons. For the queen, he is more straightforward: 'and there he toke quene Gwenyver, and seyde playnly that he wolde wedde her (whych was hys unclys wyff and hys fadirs wyff)' (707).

This intended marriage seems problematic: Mordred has gained the throne with the support of parliament, and if he perceives Guinevere as any kind of threat, he would be most easily rid of her by having her killed, as it seems unlikely that a man who ignores his duties to his father and feudal overlord would stint at a discreet poisoning. The only feeling we have so far seen Mordred exhibit towards Guinevere is a 'privy hate'. As Armstrong points out, Guinevere's dowry is already his, and she is not likely to bear him children, having been barren throughout her marriage to Arthur.[13] Both Armstrong and Elizabeth Archibald diagnose Mordred's desire for Guinevere as an aspect of his relationship with his father – 'Mordred's story is not about a son's emotional relationship with his step-mother but rather about his political relationship with his father'[14] – and with Lancelot: her value to Mordred is that Arthur and Lancelot value her. Armstrong argues that Mordred's desire for Guinevere 'has little to do with sex and everything to do with power'.[15] While I do not disagree with the importance of political power in this attempted marriage, there would also appear to me to be a degree of genuine desire for Guinevere operating in this. The desire Mordred feels for her might be based on her importance to Arthur and Lancelot rather than any personal attraction but it is, nevertheless, desire. The strength of this desire is indicated in the language used about Mordred's feelings.

Initially nothing is said of Mordred's emotions. His intentions are seen in his actions: 'he toke quene Gwenyver and seyde playnly that he wolde wedde her. And so he made redy for the feste and a day prefyxte that they shulde be wedded' (707). He possesses himself of the queen's person, rejects the advice of the bishop of Canterbury despite the threat of excommunication, and attempts 'by fayre meanys and foule meanys' to entice Guinevere back into his presence (708). These actions all indicate a desire for Guinevere strong enough to make him willing to risk excommunication and which distracts him from other concerns. Once the text refers to his emotions, however, they are not those of

---

13 Armstrong, *Gender and the Chivalric Community*, pp. 193–4.
14 Elizabeth Archibald, *Incest and the Medieval Imagination* (Oxford, 2001), p. 213.
15 Armstrong, *Gender and the Chivalric Community*, p. 194.

love or desire but of anger. When Guinevere escapes him, Mordred is 'passynge wrothe oute of mesure' (707). As we have seen, love can be out of measure, but the term is also applied to sorrow and anger, and often refers to not just excessive but unjustified emotion. Mordred's excessive anger might well be a reaction to the embarrassment of having had the queen cleverly thwart his will, but the phrase 'oute of mesure', though by no means exclusively used to indicate sexual desire, frequently appears in connection with it. Out of measure sorrow may be for an injury dealt or received, or for envy, but, interestingly, it is also connected to excessive love: Pelleas makes 'grete mone oute of mesure' over his love for the unworthy Ettarde (101) and there are two suicides due to excessive sorrow caused by love (43, 55) both involving Balyn. Anger out of measure, like Mordred's, appears in various parts of the text. Several characters, both positive and negative, are portrayed as angry out of measure, often at a perceived slight to them or their friends.[16] While there are instances of anger out of measure which are not connected with desire, such as Arthur's anger at his knights losing (644, 647) and later at their deaths in battle (713), and Lamorak's at his brothers for not doing well in the tournaments (408), the anger that is out of measure is often, though not always, connected to love and desire, as when Corsabryne is 'wrothe oute of mesure' fighting Palomides over a damsel he desires (407). It frequently involves the great lovers of Malory's text, Lancelot, Tristram, Lamorak, Guinevere and Isolde: Lancelot is described as 'wrothe oute of mesure' over threats to Guinevere (655, 718); Tristram is 'wrothe oute of mesure' when he learns that Palomides has carried off Isolde (266) and when he later fights Palomides (318, 474, 509); Isolde in her turn is angry out of measure with Palomides for cheating (459); King Mark's quarrel with Tristram and his slander of Guinevere causes anger out of measure in a number of characters (364, 375, 381). Most of these examples are from *The Book of Sir Trystram de Lyones*, which deals perhaps more extensively with desire than any other part of Malory's text. While the connection between anger out of measure and desire is not entirely clear-cut, it is present and firmly established, particularly in the story of Tristram: thus, when Mordred reacts to Guinevere's escape with anger out of measure, the use of that phrase implies desire.

Like Uther and Arthur, Mordred does not consider the consequences of his single-minded desire for Guinevere. The desire of Uther and Arthur for the wife of a potential ally damages their kingdom. Mordred, as the product of an incestuous union, is now repeating the pattern started by Uther's desire for another man's wife. This repeated pattern has grown more serious with every step: Uther's desire is adulterous, Arthur's adulterous and incestuous, Mordred's is adulterous, incestuous and treacherous. Mordred's desire is strong enough to make him disregard the bishop of Canterbury threats of excommunication;

---

[16] For examples, see Malory 37, 266, 318, 364, 375, 379, 381, 385, 392, 407, 408, 413, 459, 474, 509, 644, 647, 655, 713 and 718.

Mordred pays him no heed, being too intent on getting the queen out of the Tower, where she has ensconced herself, and to the altar. Following what seems to be a Pendragon family tradition, the effects on his kingdom of this excessive desire seem to concern him very little. There is also the question of why Mordred is intent on a wedding: if his desire was for the woman that Arthur and Lancelot desire, and for proving his power over her, rape would do, and would be considerably simpler to perpetrate than a wedding which would not be celebrated by any priest in the land, and which would necessarily be a public affair. It is difficult to assign this unreasonable desire only to a wish to possess a woman valued by his two rivals; the reading that makes sense is that his 'prevy hate' of the queen is in fact desire and jealousy. His earlier concern for King Arthur's honour and undefiled marriage bed now appears as jealousy of Lancelot rather than a genuine opposition to Guinevere's adultery.

The openly incestuous desire of Mordred for his stepmother has a parallel at an earlier point in the narrative: the story of Lamorak and Morgawse, and their deaths at the hands of Morgawse's sons, specifically Gaheris. If we read Mordred's actions as springing from desire, then it is also possible to read Gaheris's actions in a similar way. All the sons of King Lot are distressed when finding out that their mother, Morgawse, is having a love affair with Lamorak. This would appear to be a love affair following the rules of courtly love: Lamorak is found lamenting – presumably before he has gained the love of Morgawse – 'O thou fayre quene of Orkeney, kynge Lottys wyff and modir unto sir Gawayne, and to sir Gaherys, and modir to many other, for thy love I am in grete paynys!' (354). Their love is by no means unsuitable: Morgawse is a widow, and Lamorak is close enough to being her social equal. Arthur states that 'hit had bene muche fayrer and bettir that ye hadde wedded her, for ye are a kynges sonne as well as [Morgawse's sons]' (406). In the light of the suitability of this love – Lamorak is listed, with Lancelot and Tristram, as one of the three great lovers – what is the source of the Orkney brothers' distress? The initial argument is one of an existing blood feud. Gawaine argues:

> 'wyte you well, my fayre brethrerne, that this sir Lamerok woll nevyr love us, because we slew his fadir, kynge Pellynor, for we demed that he slew oure fadir, kynge Lotte of Orkenay; and for the deth of kynge Pellynor, sir Lameroke ded us a shame to oure modir. Therefore I woll be revenged.' (375)

Gawaine here seems to indicate a certain doubt about the identity of their father's killer, but also claims that Lamorak does not love their mother, but instead uses her as an instrument of revenge on her sons. This is contradicted by the text, which states that 'aythir loved othir passynge sore' (377).[17] While Gawaine states his intention to have revenge on Lamorak, he seems not to express any anger against his mother. This is not, however, the case with his brother Gaheris.

---

[17] Though not, we might note, out of measure.

In a move very similar to that later used to trap Guinevere and Lancelot together, the Orkney brothers 'sente for her moder there besydes, fast by a castle besyde Camelot, and alle was to that entente to sle sir Lamorak' (377). However, Gaheris, on finding Morgawse and Lamorak in bed together, kills his mother: 'he cam to there beddis syde all armed, with hys swerde naked, and suddeynly he gate his modir by the heyre and strake off her hede' (377). In a rather belated concern for knightly behaviour, he lets Lamorak go, as he is unarmed and, indeed, undressed (378). The fact that he can restrain himself from killing an unarmed man but not his mother – despite his being sworn to protect women – indicates that his anger is primarily directed towards her. The killing is not sanctioned by the other Orkney brothers, though it is unclear what Gawaine is more upset about: 'Gawayne was wroth that sir Gaherys had slain his modir and lete sir Lamerok ascape' (378). As with the discussion preceding the trapping of Lancelot and Guinevere, the whole conversation between Lamorak and Gaheris focuses on shame: Lamorak states that Gaheris's behavior is 'fowle and evyll ... and to you grete shame! Alas, why have ye slayne youre modir that bare you?' Gaheris, however, redirects the shame of his deed onto his mother and Lamorak: 'thou hast put my bretherne and me to a shame: and thy fadir slew oure fadir, and thou to ly by oure modir is to muche shame for us to suffir' (378). Gaheris does not kill Lamorak: 'bycause thou arte naked I am ashamed to sle the.' Instead, his anger is focused on his mother, and on removing her from the shame he thinks she has exposed herself and her sons to by sleeping with a man they consider themselves in blood feud: 'now is my modir quytte of the, for she shall never shame her chyldryn' (378). This conversation, which occupies some seventeen lines, mentions shame five times, four of those with Gaheris as the speaker. While many knights worry about being shamed, the clustering of that specific emotion here carries sexual connotations: Morgawse's shameful sexual activity, but also Gaheris's intense awareness of the entire situation being shameful.

If we look at the parallel situation – that of Mordred and Agravayne – we see two of the Orkney brothers angry that Guinevere is shaming the family by adultery, an anger that turns out, in Mordred's case, to be a desire to have Guinevere to himself. Here, another Orkney brother is angry that another female relative is shaming the family through a non-licensed sexual liaison: an anger that is explicitly directed at the woman, not at her lover, and which seems to be based in a sense of shame. Family honour is, in both cases, used as an argument against the woman, and to advocate their deaths: Guinevere escapes, Morgawse does not. The explicit argument is to control the sexual activity of a kinswoman to prevent her from shaming the family, but at least in Mordred's case that concern is, of course, hypocritical: he has no objection to shaming his father through adultery when he is the one committing it. In the light of this hypocrisy, it is hard not to read Gaheris's actions as springing from a thwarted desire for his mother: she is the primary target of his vengeance, as someone who has betrayed him by being sexually active and – as usual with Morgawse

– exercising her free choice of lover. Gaheris's desire might not be explicitly sexual, like that of Mordred, but he would appear to want his mother to remain only his mother, with no connection to any man other than her sons and her dead husband. His desire for this is strong enough that he is forced to deny her sexual contact with other men, seeing her dead rather than dishonoured, and his passion, although more emotional than sexual, is strong enough that it seems valid to call it incestuous.

Like Uther, Arthur, Pellinore and Meleagant, Gaheris is not generally portrayed as a villain; he does participate in the later killing of Lamorak – though we might note that Mordred strikes the killing blow – but he refuses to participate in the trapping of Lancelot and Guinevere together (673), and also refuses to wear armour to Guinevere's execution (683), where he and his brother Gareth are killed. Apart from this episode, Gaheris seems one of the more peaceable Orkney brothers; this confirms that violent and disruptive desire is a trait appearing even in characters primarily presented as good; it is simply normal for male characters to exhibit this desire. Throughout the text, male sexuality is portrayed as requiring control, even multiple forms of control: through oaths and threats of execution and by the presence of the desired woman, passively through marriage, or actively through the social mechanisms of courtly love. Uncontrolled male sexual desire leads to disruption, threatens the Arthurian community and the society it upholds, and may in the end even become incestuous, trangressing all boundaries. In female characters, transgressive desire often indicates villainy, as with Morgaine's inordinate desire for Lancelot or her out of measure love for Accolon. In male characters, however, transgressive desire appears in characters who are otherwise portrayed as good: Uther Pendragon is a competent king and the father of the hero; Pellinore, Meleagant and Accolon are knights of Arthur's court; Gaheris is opposed to the trapping and execution of Guinevere. Yet all these characters commit acts of disruption and violence due to their sexual desire. If the male characters' desires are viewed not individually, but rather in the context of depictions of such desires across Malory's whole text, a conception of male desire as disruptive and potentially violently destructive appears. There is indeed bold bawdry, but far from being celebrated or even treated as unambiguously positive, instead it inevitable leads to open manslaughter.

2
Erotic (Subject) Positions in Chaucer's Merchant's Tale

AMY S. KAUFMAN

SCHOLARLY assessments of Chaucer's fabliaux seldom acknowledge that these tales are erotic as well as funny; even less frequently do such investigations delve into why fabliaux are a source of pleasure. As Tom Hanks and W. W. Allman note in their article 'Rough Love: Notes toward an Erotics of *The Canterbury Tales*', scholars seem 'to have averted their gaze when Chaucer's characters leap into bed'.[1] Allman and Hanks, as their title implies, study an erotics of violence, mostly of men doing violence to women, and they focus in particular on the *Merchant's Tale* and its 'erotics of stabbing'.[2] A more positive erotic reading of the *Merchant's Tale* appears in Andrew Taylor's 1996 essay 'Reading the Dirty Bits'.[3] Taylor notes the lingering gaze of another scholar, E. Talbot Donaldson, upon a description of young May's body:

> Hir fresshe beautee and hir age tendre,
> Hir myddel smal, hire armes longe and sklendre,
> Hir wise governaunce, hir gentilesse,
> Hir wommanly berynge, and hire sadnesse. (MT 1601–4)[4]

Donaldson writes, 'the Spring of pretty young girls is a permanent thing, and that May in their personas will always warm the masculine heart'.[5] Taylor suggests that pleasure taken in this description and in Donaldson's gloss of it is mimetic: 'For the young college man to share Donaldson's and Chaucer's

---

[1] W. W. Allman and D. Thomas Hanks, Jr, 'Rough Love: Notes Toward an Erotics of *The Canterbury Tales*', *The Chaucer Review* 38:1 (2003): 36–65 (36–7).
[2] Allman and Hanks, 'Rough Love', 50.
[3] Andrew Taylor, 'Reading the Dirty Bits', in *Desire and Discipline: Sex and Sexuality in the Premodern West*, ed. Jacqueline Murray and Konrad Eisenbichler (Toronto, 1996), pp. 280–95.
[4] Citations from Chaucer are taken from Geoffrey Chaucer, *The Canterbury Tales*, ed. Larry D. Benson, *The Riverside Chaucer*, 3rd edn (Oxford, 1987) and are marked by tale abbreviation and line number.
[5] Quoted in Taylor, 'Dirty Bits', p. 280.

pleasure in May is to become, like them, a connoisseur of both good writing and pretty girls, a master of ironic detachment and well-modulated heterosexual desire'.[6] Taylor suggests that we are 'not frank' about dirty reading, and I concur, but what strikes me is not necessarily the privileged male position of this particular reading – Taylor acknowledges this and it is pertinent to his point.[7] It is, instead, that the moment in which Taylor reads Donaldson reading Chaucer is not particularly erotic, especially not compared to some of the explicitly sexual moments in the *Merchant's Tale*. The words that inspire Donaldson are fairly conventional medieval descriptors of a maiden. The most intimate imagery is of May's 'myddel smal' and her 'armes longe and sklendre', and this seems designed to emphasize her youth, likely in comparison to her aged groom-to-be, Januarie. As far as dirty bits go, this one is awfully clean, much more likely to warm the heart than the loins.

The sample reading in Taylor's article, however, provides insight into how today's literary critic negotiates the medieval erotic. Taylor is reading Donaldson reading Chaucer's Merchant reading Januarie's mental image of May, one he conjures while lying alone in bed trying to catalogue the many young women he might select as a bride. The narrator compares Januarie's nightly obsessions, tagged 'Heigh fantasye' and 'curious bisynesse' (MT 1577), with one

> As whoso tooke a mirour, polisshed bryght,
> And sette it in a commune market-place,
> Thanne sholde he se ful many a figure pace
> By his mirour; and in the same wyse
> Gan Januarie inwith his thoght devyse
> Of maydens whiche that dwelten hym bisyde. (MT 1582–7)

Januarie's 'mirour,' as many have noted, is an apt metaphor that indicates his distorted vision of May.[8] Thus, literary criticism aligns its furtive glimpses not with the masterful author Chaucer, or even with the Merchant narrator, but with the cuckolded *senex amans* – the butt of the joke – a character so deluded and obsessive that he hardly can be labelled 'a master of ironic detachment' or of 'well-modulated heterosexual desire'.

Readings that lament the mistreatment of May in the *Merchant's Tale* still empower Januarie's metaphorical mirror as the interpretive lens, rendering May a commodity and a mere reflection of male desires.[9] Regardless of

---

[6] Taylor, 'Dirty Bits', pp. 280–1.
[7] Taylor, 'Dirty Bits', pp. 281–2.
[8] Elaine Tuttle Hansen, *Chaucer and the Fictions of Gender* (Berkeley, 1992), p. 250; and Angela M. Lucas, 'The Mirror in the Marketplace: Januarie through the Looking Glass', *The Chaucer Review* 33:2 (1998): 123–45.
[9] See Paul A. Olson, 'Chaucer's Merchant and January's "Hevene in Erthe Heere"', *English Literary History* 28:3 (1961): 203–14 (205); Deborah S. Ellis, 'The Merchant's Wife's Tale: Language, Sex, and Commerce in Margery Kempe and in Chaucer', *Exemplaria* 2:2 (Oct. 1990): 595–626 (614); Joseph D. Parry, 'Interpreting Female Agency and Responsibility in *The Miller's Tale* and *The Merchant's Tale*', *Philological Quarterly* 80:2 (2001): 133–68 (137–8);

whether one condemns or waxes poetic about her portrayal, May is always figured as an erotic object, determined or overdetermined in some way by masculine narrative. Even when May takes her most active role, leading her lover to their tryst in Januarie's garden and scaling her blind husband's back to reach her pinnacle in the pear tree, Januarie's mirror still distorts her critical reception.

The *Merchant's Tale*'s literary and erotic climax is achieved when May and Damyan consummate their adulterous longings in two brief and candid lines:

> And sodeynly anon this Damyan
> Gan pullen up the smok, and in he throng. (MT 2352-3)

Despite the explicit sexuality of this moment, Damyan's 'thronging' seems to disturb more critics than it titillates. Alcuin Blamires calls Damyan's thrust 'a drastic invasion of May's body by the squire', and adds: 'If we were not persuaded that this precipitousness was something wished for by May after enduring January's protracted labourings, we might wonder how far it is distinguishable from rape.'[10] Those who do find the scene erotic still take a dark view of its sexual nature: Allman and Hanks render Damyan's thrust part of the overall Chaucerian 'eroticism of stabbing' they locate throughout *The Canterbury Tales*, and others believe the action renders May as passive as she was at the beginning of the tale.[11] Still more critics focus on May's silence about the quality or the desirability of the sex act: Elaine Tuttle Hansen argues that 'At the moment of her putative sexual gratification, the narrator closes his eyes; as far as her human creator and his audience know, May's sexual feelings were and are a contradiction in terms, nonexistent and unspeakable'; Sue Niebrzydowski complains that May is emotionally absent and is thus rendered 'the smock to be lifted and the hole to be filled, reduced to the stereotypically voracious vagina that characterizes many a wicked wife'.[12] But is May's internal narrative, or the lack of it, the only way to gauge artistic representations of pleasure? And if there is pleasure to be found in Damyan's throng, is it simply the sadist's pleasure, as Hanks and Allen suggest, or are

---

and Christian Sheridan, 'May in the Marketplace: Commodification and Textuality in The "Merchant's Tale"', *Studies in Philology* 102:1 (2005): 27-44 (32). Holly A. Crocker is a little more optimistic, arguing that 'May's conduct does not shift from passive to active; instead, her behaviour demonstrates that feminine passivity always requires agency' in 'Performative Passivity and Fantasies of Masculinity in the *Merchant's Tale*', *The Chaucer Review* 38.2 (2003): 178-98 (179). See also Crocker, *Chaucer's Visions of Manhood* (New York, 2008), pp. 148-9.

10 Alcuin A. Blamires, *Chaucer, Ethics, and Gender* (Oxford and New York, 2006), p. 96. In a later article, however, Blamires posits intriguingly that May's tryst with Damyan 'stakes a claim' in Januarie's family tree and 'organises there the prospect of offspring from a more attractive source', in 'May in January's Tree', *The Chaucer Review* 45:1 (2010): 106-17 (117).

11 Allen and Hanks, 'Rough Love', 50-1; Ellis, 'Merchant's Wife's Tale', 615.

12 Hansen, *Chaucer and the Fictions of Gender*, p. 265; and Niebrzydowski, '"So wel koude he me glose": The Wife of Bath and the Eroticism of Touch', in *The Erotic in the Literature of Medieval Britain*, ed. Amanda Hopkins and Cory James Rushton (Cambridge, 2007), pp. 18-26 (p. 23).

contemporary readers eliding May's own desire by focusing on language rather than the body?[13]

Susan K. Hagen argues that our discomfort with May's sexuality reveals 'our own society's difficulty in coming to terms with female sexuality in particular and human sexuality in general'.[14] And it may be because we are, as Andrew Taylor suggests, closer to our Victorian ancestors than our medieval ancestors when it comes to matters of desire – especially, I would emphasize, in our failure to theorize female desire.[15] We label ourselves postmodern, post-human, and post-feminist, but we still rely on a Victorian intellectual lineage to define desire for us. Freud begat Lacan, Lacan begat Žižek, and so on. Each springs from each other's head like Athena from Zeus, mystifying to obscurity the erotic potential of the female of the species. I have suggested elsewhere that the female erotic is a locus of crisis for certain ontologies of self-signification: so foreign is women's pleasure from the concept of the formation of the self within patriarchal society that it is rendered invisible in language.[16] But even feminist analyses can fall into the same trap by resisting discussions of the body for fear of biological essentialism. As Elizabeth Grosz argues,

> While materialism has directed our focus to questions of the body, the body still remains elided and covered by representation. Feminist theory has allowed the body to enter discourse, but only, ironically, through its reduction to discourse. The materiality of the body and of discourse only recedes further into the background without being adequately explained.[17]

Feminist discomfort with rendering the body important and communicative may explain the critical focus on May's silence during Damyan's penetration.[18] In this case, to be sure, there is a danger of reducing May to sexual function since, as Niebrzydowski points out, the medieval woman is so often reduced to the body alone in anti-feminist clerical discourse; one might argue that this is precisely what the Merchant narrator intends to do when he places May in the pear tree.[19] But I would suggest that there is also a danger in forgetting about May's body as a medium of agency altogether. For it is May's physical capacity to act within the constraints of her marriage to Januarie, and within

---

[13] For instance, John Pitcher's recent study of female desire in Chaucer, *Chaucer's Feminine Subjects: Figures of Desire in The Canterbury Tales* (New York, 2012), dismisses May from consideration in one sentence because, it claims, she is 'somewhat lacking in dramatic and rhetorical elaboration' (p. 7).

[14] Susan K. Hagen, 'Chaucer's May, Standup Comics, and Critics', in *Chaucer's Humor: The Playful Pilgrimage to Canterbury and Beyond*, ed. Jean Jost (Hamden, CT, 1994), pp. 127–43 (p. 139).

[15] Taylor, 'Dirty Bits', p. 281.

[16] Amy S. Kaufman, 'Guenevere Burning', *Arthuriana* 20:1 (2010): 76–94 (77).

[17] Elizabeth Grosz, 'The Untimeliness of Feminist Theory', *NORA – Nordic Journal of Feminist and Gender Research* 18:1 (2010): 48–51 (50).

[18] See Niebrzydowski, '"So wel koude he me glose"', and Hansen, *Chaucer and the Fictions of Gender*, note 17.

[19] Niebrzydowski, '"So wel koude he me glose"', p. 23.

the constraints of the Merchant's narrative, that exemplifies both her agency and her sexual desire. And it is also within this same agency that the pleasure in the *Merchant's Tale* resides.

In order to share May's pleasure, not only must we theorize the body as a medium of agency, but we must also suspend our anachronistic dismissal of the female erotic. The medieval suspicion of women's interminable lust and greater pleasure makes the erotic landscape of the Middle Ages drastically different from our own. Writers in the Middle Ages suspected that women were capable of levels of sexual fulfilment unattainable by men.[20] From Galen to Gratian to Isidore of Seville, medieval scholars believed that women experienced more pleasure from the act of intercourse than men did.[21] This is not an unqualified boon; to be sure, the stereotype of the lusty woman was used against real women in both literature and life. But nor is it an unqualified cause for condemnation. Medical discourse and anti-feminist clerical discourses are not the same; the former is most frequently frank about women's capacity for pleasure, not pejorative.[22]

Fabliau is intended to be a pleasurable genre. As Martin Stevens argued four decades ago, the world of fabliau 'is crowded by fallible mortals for whom life flows joyfully and for whom sex is a natural and healthy pleasure, enjoyed most salubriously by the young and the free. The offenders are those who threaten this natural order: the arrogant, the vain, the greedy.'[23] In this tale, Stevens suggests, we are meant to side with springtime, fertility, life and the erotic. And in the *Merchant's Tale*, erotic potential is embodied by May herself. Her pursuit of Damyan and her satisfaction through him evokes a female erotic that wreaks havoc on the dominant discourse, giving the reader vicarious pleasure through,

---

[20] See Joyce E. Salisbury, 'Gendered Sexuality', in *Handbook of Medieval Sexuality*, ed. Vern L. Bullough and James A. Brundage (New York and London, 1996), pp. 81–102 (p. 84).

[21] Salisbury, 'Gendered Sexuality', p. 93. Moreover, as Marie Borroff points out, 'it was a widely held tenet of medieval gynecology' that 'conception depended on that woman's experiencing orgasmic pleasure during the sexual act' in *Traditions and Renewals: Chaucer, the Gawain-Poet, and Beyond* (New Haven, CT, 2003), p. 56. Carol Everest agrees and indicates that May's lack of response in sex with Januarie is meant to convey that Januarie cannot get her pregnant: see Carol A. Everest, '"Paradys or Helle": Pleasure and Procreation in Chaucer's "Merchant's Tale"', in *Sovereign Lady: Essays on Women in Middle English Literature*, ed. Muriel Whitaker (New York, 1995), pp. 63–84; and 'Pears and Pregnancy in Chaucer's "Merchant's Tale"', in *Food in the Middle Ages: A Book of Essays*, ed. Melitta Weiss Adamson (New York, 1995), pp. 161–75 (p. 164).

[22] Albrecht Classen also cautions against our presumption that clerical discourse was uniformly anti-feminist, presenting instead a rather complex and varied debate in which women also participated. See his *The Power of a Woman's Voice in Medieval and Early Modern Literatures: New Approaches to German and European Women Writers and to Violence against Women in Premodern Times*, Fundamentals of Medieval and Early Modern Culture 1 (Berlin, 2007), pp. 4–8.

[23] Martin Stevens, 'And Venus Laugheth: An Interpretation of the "Merchant's Tale"', *The Chaucer Review* 7:2 (1972): 118–31 (127). However, c.f. A. S. G. Edwards, 'The *Merchant's Tale* and Moral Chaucer', *Modern Language Quarterly* 51 (1990): 409–26 (412), who accuses Stevens of being a product of 'the swinging sixties, an age temperamentally disposed to optimism' and argues that 'what such readings really demonstrate is a rather desperate resolve to find a comfortable response somewhere in the tale'.

rather than 'upon', May's body. We must therefore entertain the possibility that the *Merchant's Tale* is not always about enjoying reading May, but can sometimes be about enjoying reading *as* May.

We do have some evidence that May's climax titillated readers in the late medieval past. One or more scribal tricksters added lines to the tale in the mid-fifteenth-century Harley MS that remained there for hundreds of years until a scholar finally removed them in 1775.[24] The lines began precisely at the climax in question, directly after 'in he throng'. In addition to describing Damyan's impressive organ, they also speak directly to May's satisfaction:

> A greet tente a thrifty and a long
> She sayde it was the meriest fytte
> That euer in her lif she was at yet
> My lordis tente seruith me nothing thus
> He foldith twifolde be swete Jhesus
> He may not swyue worth a leek
> And yet he is ful gentil and ful meek
> This is leuyr to me than an euynsong.[25]

These words are about Damyan, but the lens through which we read the erotic experience is May's. That the additional lines emphasize Damyan's visual appeal and performance and record May's pleasure suggest that it is the reader's identification with May – a narrative identification that begins in her darkest moments beneath Januarie and culminates in the heady heights of the pear tree – that gives the tale's climax its erotic force. The scribal insertion also suggests that May is only interested in sexual satisfaction from Damyan, not romantic love; for the latter, she prefers her husband Januarie, who is 'ful gentil and ful meek'. The added lines definitively gloss May as a sexual and romantic agent experiencing pleasure rather than a victim or an object of desire.[26]

Chaucer's original May does not have the same opportunity to express her verbal admiration for Damyan's prowess, but her sexual desire for him is packed into metaphor and *double entendre* and there is no reason to believe she does not want that desire satisfied.[27] For instance, her lust simmers beneath the argument she presents to Januarie about climbing the pear tree:

---

[24] These lines were, in fact, in the standard edition of Chaucer until Thomas Tyrwhitt removed them in 1775, and thus were part of the *Merchant's Tale* as received by readers from 1532 to 1775, including Shakespeare, Milton and Pope. For a full discussion of the scribal additions as well as a complete reproduction of them, see Rosalind Field, '"Superfluous Ribaldry": Spurious Lines in the *Merchant's Tale*', *The Chaucer Review* 28:4 (1994): 353–67. Field argues for an individual scribe disappointed by line 2351, 'I cannot glose' (362). See also Edwards, 'Moral Chaucer', 411.

[25] Quoted in Field, 'Superfluous Ribaldry', 354–5. The scribe(s) made additional insertions to two other sections, including January's outrage and his condemnation of May.

[26] C.f. Field, who argues that the lines turn May, 'one of the most inscrutable of Chaucer's women', into a stereotypical unfaithful wife, 'her language ... as low as her behaviour', 'Superfluous Ribaldry', 365.

[27] C.f. Edwards, who argues that 'it is the narrative's refusal to invest the relationship between May and Damian with any definable value, either of condemnation or affirmation, that is

> I moste han of the peres that I see,
> Or I moot dye, so soore longeth me
> To eten of the smale peres grene. (MT 2331–3)

May's desire for 'peres' is a thinly veiled metaphor for her desire for Damyan.[28] If we allow pears to signify Damyan, May's plea smoothly translates into the language of lovesickness: *I moste han, or I moot dye; so soore longeth me*. But this is fabliau, not romance, and the semiotic bar might be a bit lower: 'smale peres grene' contains a latent metaphor, 'grene' also taking its connotative meaning of fertile, young or virginal. Consulting the *Oxford English Dictionary* demonstrates that in the *Cursor Mundi*, Langland and Chaucer's own *House of Fame*, 'grene,' particularly 'When applied to fruits or plants … implies some additional sense: (a) Unripe, immature; (b) young and tender; (c) full of vigorous life, flourishing; (d) retaining the natural moisture, not dried' as well as 'Full of vitality; not withered or worn out'.[29] The pears May desires can be read as a very loaded metaphor for a virginal flourishing Damyan, or stooping even lower, for certain, possibly already exposed parts of Damyan that await May in the tree.[30]

The ripeness of May's lover invokes, by juxtaposition, the withered, dry, plodding advances of May's husband. Januarie must drink a wide variety of spiced wines and potions to prepare for his marital trysts:

> ypocras, clarree, and vernage
> Of spices hoote t'encreessen his corage
> And many a letuarie hath he ful fin. (MT 1807–9)

As Carol Everest explains, the potions are intended to balance Januarie's humours, specifically to warm and moisten the dry, cold constitution of old age.[31] The ripe, moist pears dramatically contrast Januarie's nature, and May's desire for 'pears' is therefore all-consuming:

> I telle yow wel, a womman in my plit
> May han to fruyt so greet an appetit
> That she may dyen but if she of it have. (MT 2335–7)

---

clearly as disconcerting for the modern reader as it was for the medieval scribe who found it necessary to establish that May was enjoying herself', 'Moral Chaucer', 425.

[28] Blamires, *Ethics*, p. 96, and 'January's Tree', 115, though in the latter Blamires suggests multiple other interpretations. Everest argues that the tree also indicates Damyan's fertility in 'Paradys or Helle', p. 80.

[29] *The Compact Edition of the Oxford English Dictionary*, s.v. 'grene'.

[30] Those who note the phallic connotations of the pears and their allusiveness to testicles include Olson, 'Chaucer's Merchant', 208; Hansen, *Chaucer and the Fictions of Gender*, p. 257; and Everest, 'Pears', pp. 170–1.

[31] Carol Everest, 'Sight and Sexual Performance in the *Merchant's Tale*', in *Masculinities in Chaucer: Approaches to Maleness in the Canterbury Tales and Troilus and Criseyde*, ed. Peter G. Beidler (Cambridge, 1998), pp. 91–103 (p. 92). Also see Everest, 'Pears and Pregnancy', p. 162; and Everest, 'Paradys or Helle', pp. 64–5.

If the pears May craves are Damyan, or particular parts of him, then what, precisely, is May's 'plit'? As many critics have pointed out, 'plit' seems intentionally to imply pregnancy.[32] But 'plit' does semiotic double duty by pointing directly to the longing and 'appetit' May expresses, particularly if pears stand for Damyan and/or his procreative parts: in today's terms, we might call her plight sexual frustration. Robert Allen Rouse points out that 'hot-blooded' women, those who were most sexually active, 'owing to their humoural heat and dryness, were thought to be inclined to seek out the carnal act continually, seeking to obtain the moisture contained within male sperm, in order to remedy their own innate dryness'.[33] Following this humoural logic, May's 'plit' should also be construed as real physical urgency, her desire for pears and for Damyan both the prescription for what ails her.

The emphasis on May's lack of pleasure at Januarie's exertions seems to be part of the point of the narrator's disturbing descriptions of their marital sex. Januarie's coital efforts are horrifically prolonged so that he has time to muster the warm, moist humours required to consummate the act. He justifies himself to May, presumably during sex:

> Ther nys no werkman, whatsoevere he be,
> That may bothe werke wel and hastily;
> This wol be doon at leyser parfitly. (MT 1832–4)

The narrative is structured so that the reader endures what May endures, as though we, too, lie beneath Januarie and suffer his dreary ministrations.[34] May is the character through whom we channel our responses, be we 'lief or looth', as Januarie kisses her 'With thikke brustles of his berd unsofte, / Lyk to the skyn of a houndfyssh, sharp as brere' (MT 1824–5). We, along with May, also endure his long apologies for his 'trespass', his lectures justifying his desire for sex, and we endure him the morning after, when

> He was al coltissh, ful of ragerye,
> And ful of jargon as a flekked pye.
> The slakke skyn aboute his nekke shaketh
> Whil that he sang, so chaunteth he and craketh. (MT 1847–50)

all the while with never a glimpse of May's presumably compliant young body.

---

[32] See, for instance, Borroff, *Traditions*, p. 51; and Everest, 'Pears and Pregnancy', pp. 165–70.

[33] Robert Allen Rouse, 'The Medieval Eroticism of Heat', in *The Erotic in the Literature of Medieval Britain*, ed. Hopkins and Rushton, pp. 71–81 (p. 80). Everest also points out that some medieval medical theories held that women who did not have a sexual outlet could suffer from 'suffocation of the womb', 'Paradys or Helle', p. 69.

[34] Borroff, *Traditions*, p. 54, notes that Chaucer seems to position the reader with May intentionally. See also Jill Mann, *Feminizing Chaucer*, Chaucer Studies 30, 2nd edition (Cambridge, 2002), p. 55; Christine M. Rose, 'Women's "Pryvete", May, and the Privy: Fissures in the Narrative Voice in the "Merchant's Tale", 1944–86', *Chaucer Yearbook* 4 (1997): 61–77 (62); and Elizabeth Archibald, "Chaucer's Lovers in Metaphorical Heaven', in *Envisaging Heaven in the Middle Ages*, ed. Carolyn Muessig and Ad Putter (New York, 2007), pp. 222–36 (p. 226).

Instead it is Januarie who, as T. S. Eliot might say, is 'formulated, sprawling on a pin', particularly when we get May's infamous assessment: 'She preyseth nat his pleyyng worth a bene' (MT 1854).

This assessment, along with its implication that May is capable of pleasure with the right partner, disrupts her husband's lengthy discourses on sex as something that offends his bride but that he will impose on her regardless. Plenty of critics identify with May while Januarie belabours her, but once May shows evidence of an appetite and begins to pursue her own desires, many readers report losing sympathy for her, or at least feeling as though a misogynistic narrator wants them to lose sympathy for her.[35] Even those who recognize the awakening of May's voice, such as Elaine Tuttle Hansen and Holly Crocker, identify this as a disturbing turning point in the tale: Hansen considers it a 'terrifying' prospect for the Merchant narrator.[36] But our sympathy for May ends with her sexual innocence only if we continue to privilege Januarie's 'mirour', hoping to catch a glimpse of an innocent, pliable young girl. If we believe in women's erotic inner lives, we might yet sympathize with her boredom, her repressed youth or her wasted vitality.[37] We might, more importantly, read May's journey from empty frustration to burning desire as a story of the birth of the erotic subject.

After May reads a letter from Damyan that professes his love, she tears it to shreds, throws it in the privy and returns to bed, at which point the narrator asks, 'Who studieth now but faire fresshe May?' (MT 1955). This is not the first time the narrator points us toward May's inner life, but it marks a shift from representing her distant disdain to awakening her, and our, erotic curiosity. Just as May begins her study, she is interrupted by Januarie, who wakes up coughing and commands a performance from her in bed:

> Anon he preyde hire strepen hire al naked;
> He wolde of hire, he seyde, han som plesaunce;
> He seyde hir clothes dide hym encombraunce,
> And she obeyeth, be hire lief or looth. (MT 1958–61)

Januarie's interruption serves two important purposes. First, it allows both the reader and May to 'study' the difference between Januarie's coarse command that she 'strepen hire al naked' and the eloquent longings of her potential

---

35 Mann, *Feminizing Chaucer*, p. 55; Ellis, 'Merchant's Wife's Tale', 614; Hagan, 'Chaucer's May', 130; Rose, 'Women's "Pryvete"', 62–3, 70; John Finlayson, '*The Merchant's Tale*: Literary Contexts, the Play of Genres, and Institutionalized Sexual Relations', *Anglia-Zeitschrift für Englische Philologie* 121:4 (2004): 557–80 (573).
36 Hansen, *Chaucer and the Fictions of Gender*, p. 258–9; and Crocker, 'Performative Passivity', 191.
37 As Archibald, 'Chaucer's Lovers', p. 226 argues, though she loses some sympathy for May when she consummates her affair, 'we understand that she has been driven to it not just by lust but also by January's behaviour and attitudes. She is entitled to some paradise too, and this does not mean enduring the pawings of a scratchy-skinned, droopyjowled, lecherous and jealous old man.'

lover, Damyan. Secondly, it allows the reader to contrast May's active pursuit of Damyan with her passive reception of Januarie's advances, during which the narrator implies May's suffering by refusing the reader any access to her emotions: 'How that he wroughte, I dar nat to yow telle, / Or wheither hir thoughte it paradys or helle' (MT 1963–4). Finally, Damyan's letter allows May the choice to initiate sex if she wants it, a prospect that, in the midst of odious marital debts, must seem rather tempting.

May's desires are best understood in stark opposition to her marriage, in which she silently must endure Januarie's one-sided lectures, monologues and songs. Her communications with Damyan, by contrast, offer May a language of erotics in which she can actually participate. May and Damyan communicate by exchanging letters and signs:

> by writyng to and fro
> And privee signes wiste he what she mente
> And she knew eek the fyn of his entente. (MT 2104–6)

By the time Januarie finally loses his eyesight, May is able to use this hidden erotic language to lead her husband, her lover and the reader into her garden for the consummation of her plans. When she spies Damyan hiding in a bush, she relies on the 'privee signes' she has developed with her lover to direct him into the pear tree, 'and up he wente'; the narrator emphasizes how well Damyan knows both May's desires and May herself:

> For verraily he knew al hire entente,
> And every signe that she koude make,
> Wel bet than Januarie, hir owene make. (MT 2212–14)

Damyan is both a receptive partner and a strikingly safe one. He is a mere squire who serves her husband at his table with no land or title of his own; still, she vows that she will 'love hym best of any creature / Though he namoore hadde than his sherte' (MT 1984–5). Damyan's wooing is remarkably passive: he suffers lovesickness, writes a letter to May that he keeps in a silk purse close to his heart, then he hands it to her with a plea not to 'discovere' him only when she comes to his bedside (MT 1942). His passivity enables May's own sexual assertiveness. Consider the scene in which she delivers Damyan her first *billet doux*:

> And sotily this lettre doun she *threste*
> Under his pilwe; rede it if hym leste.
> She taketh hym by the hand and *harde hym twiste*. (MT 2003–5, emphasis mine)

The thrusting and twisting in which May engages belie the seemingly passive 'rede it if hym leste'; May penetrates Damyan's chambers while he sleeps, engaging him in a very physical way, her body telling us what the Merchant denies us by hiding her words. By contrast, as Finlayson points out, Damyan's desire is 'described in the formulaic language of courtly love, "ravysshed", "ny wood", "swelte and swowned", "Venus hurt him". He takes to his bed and laments, as all courtly lovers do.'[38] Of course, this is comedy, and Damyan's passivity makes him a parody of a courtly lover, but that parodic portrayal provides an important literary insight: adulterous lovers can become the vehicles through which wives find their suppressed erotic identities precisely *because* of their passivity. The courtly lover, often mocked in Chaucer as effeminate and read today as 'feminized', inhabits a receptive masculinity that reveals the cracks in the foundation of patriarchal marriage, both the inadequacies and ignorance of the husband and the identity it strips from the wife. The lover becomes a vehicle through which the silent, oppressed wife learns to express her desire. As the shapeshifter in the Wife of Bath's tale teaches us, sovereignty is the ultimate aphrodisiac.

When Januarie goes blind and restricts May's movement completely, insisting that he always be in physical contact with her, the narrator presents us with May's frustrated passion: 'She wayteth whan hir herte wolde breste' (MT 2096). We are teased here, if we have been in tune with May, by erotic anticipation. If we are receptive to our own immersion in May as a character governed by desire, then our longing for Damyan, for escape, for good sex, for anything that makes us feel alive, builds with hers. We, too, have waited when our hearts would burst, or at least our loins, and the moment – the slowly orchestrated, prolonged climax to which the tale has teased us, the moment when Damyan 'Gan pullen up the smok, and in he throng' – is designed to satisfy, not through narrative explication, but through *jouissance*, through pleasure beyond words.

Damyan's throng is the erotic climax both for May and for the reader who employs her as a lens, whether that reader is a sixteenth-century scribe who wishes to prolong the pleasure of the moment or simply a contemporary feminist critic who attempts to find pleasure in an era of patriarchal discourse. And yet, we must be cautious not to ascribe a univocal erotic sensibility to a text as inherently polyvocal as *The Canterbury Tales*. Rough love, as Allman and Hanks point out, exists in Chaucer too: multiple rapes, the mean-spirited *Reeve's Tale*, and even Januarie's own sadistic control of May. Perhaps *The Canterbury Tales* exhibits, most of all, struggles among competing erotic subject positions. May's is the struggle for erotic sovereignty in a world of hierarchies. If we allow May's 'privee signes' to direct our reading instead of gazing at her through Januarie's mirror, her calculated and embodied escape from her husband's monolithic erotic narrative can be the key to our own literary garden of delight.

---

38 Finlayson, *Merchant's Tale*, 571.

3
Enter the Bedroom: Managing Space for the Erotic in Middle English Romance

MEGAN G. LEITCH

IN the late fifteenth-century *Squire of Low Degree*, the incompetent protagonist woos a Hungarian princess in a way that seems to subject the romance genre to derivative, almost parodic, excess. This excess, however, offers particular insight into the representation of wooing in Middle English romance more broadly. While many romance heroines assume their suitors will display knightly prowess to win their love, this princess seems so aware of the Squire's shortcomings that she explains to him precisely what he must do, focusing on the rather boy-scout-like logistics of riding 'Over hylles and dales, and hye mountaines, / In wethers wete, both hayle and raynes', and lodging 'under a tre, / Among the beastes wyld and tame'.[1] Reminiscent here of how a Sir Thopas might understand chivalry, the text continues its overzealous attempt to ape romance when the princess exhaustively details the accoutrements that she expects from a suitor (203–30), and it is equally unable to find the right register when she offers to bankroll his required adventures (251–5). The envious steward's attempts to ruin the Squire by exposing his amorous inclinations are predictable enough; the results, however, have been seen as uncharacteristic of romance, since the king does not object to the Squire courting his daughter,[2] but rather instructs the steward:

> if the squiere come to-night,
> For to speke with that lady bryght,
> Let hym say whatsoever he wyll,
> ...

---

[1] *Squire of Low Degree*, in *Sentimental and Humorous Romances*, ed. Erik Kooper (Kalamazoo, MI, 2006), lines 177–8 and 180–1. The *Squire* is extant in two early sixteenth-century fragments of a de Worde print based on a late fifteenth-century manuscript version; Copland's closely related 1560 print, the base text for the edition cited here, survives complete. The c. 1650 Percy Folio manuscript contains a condensed version. All italics are mine.
[2] Erik Kooper, 'Introduction', in *Sentimental and Humorous Romances*, p. 131.

> *So he come not her chambre within,*
> *No bate on hym loke thou begyn;*
> Though that he kysse that lady fre,
> ...
> *But yf he wyl her chamber breke,*
> *No worde to hym that thou do speke.*
> But yf he come with company
> For to betraye that fayre lady,
> Loke he be taken soone anone,
> And all his meyné everychone,
> And brought with strength to my pryson. (425–43)

As far as the king is concerned, the lowly Squire may speak with and even kiss the princess, provided that he does not seek to enter her chamber. However, this latter stipulation belies the Squire's otherwise surprising liberty, for it shows that this king does – in the essentials – have the expected prohibitive and protective response towards a suitor for his daughter. Yet the *Squire*'s king expresses characteristic patriarchal control over his daughter not by restricting access to her person, but by restricting access to her private space. This essay argues that this is a significant distinction, and one that illuminates a recurring mode in Middle English romance.

The *Squire of Low Degree*'s interest in the erotic is repeatedly conveyed through a focus on the boundaries and possibilities of intimate spaces.[3] When the Squire prepares to leave court to prove himself abroad, it is again a focus on architecture that conveys both the erotic tension and the perils of the situation. Attacked by the steward's thugs as he approaches the princess's bedroom to say farewell, the Squire 'came her chambre to', crying:

> 'Your dore undo!
> Undo,' he sayde, 'nowe, fayre lady!
> I am beset with many a spy.
> ...
> *Undo thy dore*, my worthy wyfe,
> I am besette with many a knyfe.
> *Undo your dore*, my lady swete,
> I am beset with enemyes great;
> And, lady, but ye wyll aryse,
> I shall be dead with myne enemyes.
> *Undo thy dore*, my frely floure,
> For ye are myne, and I am your.'
> That lady with those wordes awoke,
> A mantell of golde to her she toke;
> She sayde: 'Go away, thou wicked wyght,

---

3   There is, however, a necrophiliac moment that takes the fetishisation of courtly love to an extreme, when the princess, mistaking the corpse of the envious steward for her beloved, embalms it to kiss and keep; but this is a singular exception for this text.

Thou shalt not come here this nyght;
For *I wyll not my dore undo*
For no man that cometh therto.
There is but one in Christenté
That ever made that forwarde with me.' (533–54)

The princess, understanding the stakes of allowing access to her bedchamber – especially if the Squire is not who he claims to be – is sensibly wary of complying with his repeated plea to 'undo your doore'. Indeed, recognizing the crux of the text, both Wynkyn de Worde and William Copeland entitled their editions of the *Squire of Low Degree* as 'vndo your Dore', with Copeland adding '*otherwise* called the squyer of lowe degré'.[4] When we attune ourselves to the 'architecture' of the erotic in Middle English romances, we see that the texts and their characters are often strongly attuned to these spaces. This essay focuses on moments of conflict concerning fulfilment or frustration of desire wherein spaces receive more attention than bodies, or compete with bodies for textual attention. A consideration of romances such as *King Horn*, *Sir Gawain and the Green Knight*, Malory's *Morte Darthur* and *Melusine*, as well as the *Squire of Low Degree*, demonstrates how the deployment and contingencies of spaces inflect the medieval English cultural imagination regarding the erotic. This essay, in other words, maps the makeshift, the shifting, the fractured and forbidden bowers of Middle English romance in order to explore how these texts and their characters 'manage' sexual encounters. Inevitably, power and pleasure are not easily disentangled. In tracing the spatial practice of the erotic manifested in some romances, this essay argues that manipulations of space constitute both a powerful language for pursuing and preventing amatory situations, and a way of arousing or articulating sexual desire.

Criticism has productively attended to the ways in which, in medieval texts, power and desire are negotiated between subjects and bodies.[5] However, the currencies of the medieval erotic economy – the commodities that circulate, that are desired and regulated – include not just bodies, but also spaces. The ways in which (private) spaces are themselves deployed as part of these negotiations have been comparatively understudied.[6] Siting the exercise or regulation of power and desire within or beyond social conventions, space is not merely a passive presence. Medieval England offered its own obstacles for those in search of privacy for sexual encounters, difficulties that are unlikely to trouble today's lovers, clandestine or otherwise. In England, separate

---

[4] *Sentimental and Humorous Romances*, pp. 134 and 159.
[5] See, for instance, *Constructing Medieval Sexuality*, ed. Karma Lochrie, Peggy McCracken and James A. Schultz (Minneapolis, 1997), and *The Erotic in the Literature of Medieval Britain*, ed. Amanda Hopkins and Cory James Rushton (Cambridge, 2007).
[6] See, however, Diane Wolfthal, *In and Out of the Marital Bed: Seeing Sex in Renaissance Europe* (New Haven, CT, 2010), which focuses on late medieval and especially early modern visual culture to consider the 'ways in which people learned to transform space [such as the bed and the bath] to suit their sexual desires' (p. 8).

bedrooms – 'bowers' (from Old English), or 'chambers' (a word first appearing in English c. 1300) – only become more common in the early thirteenth century, and even then pertained primarily to the elite and established.[7] Thus, Middle English romances flourished in, and were to an extent co-extensive with, a society in which private domestic spaces were comparatively scarce and protected. Moreover, the 'privacy' offered by these bedrooms was, of course, rather relative, since they often held multiple occupants and saw much traffic. Thus, to obtain complete privacy, one had to do more than simply close (and lock) the door, as is suggested by Neptanibus's attempts to seduce Olympia in the metrical *King Alisaunder*. Neptanibus sends Olympia's retinue away, so that in her chamber 'hym-self was kniȝth, and swayn, / And bouremayde, and chaumberlayn'.[8] Bedrooms and beds were designed to be seen, and often occupied, by many people; indoor privacy for a transgressive lovers' tryst required the transformation of a normally public space into an exclusive one. Would-be romance lovers worry about how to obtain such privacy, while their fathers, husbands, hosts or guardians worry about how to prevent it. For each of these conflicting aims, space is more than a platform or a symbol; it is manipulated, it is made to speak, to ask or grasp or forbid.

The first extant Middle English romance, produced in the early thirteenth century when aristocratic bedrooms were becoming more common, presents some of the ways in which the economic and political possibilities and limitations of the bower reflect upon erotic opportunities and their representation. In *King Horn*, when the exiled Prince Horn travels to the land of Westernesse, King Aylmar invites him to stay and Princess Rymenhild invites him to enter into both her bedroom and a betrothal. Rymenhild's invitations are not unappealing to Horn; complying with her request, 'Horn ferde into bure / To sen aventure'.[9] For the male romance protagonist, the bedchamber is, of course, like the forest, a space of adventure, of opportunities for knightly prowess and advancement – or ruin. Horn's envious subordinate Fikenhild fulfils the revelatory role of the *Squire of Low Degree*'s steward, telling the king of Horn's whereabouts and claiming that Horn's intentions are less than honourable. When he finds Horn embracing Rymenhild in her bedroom, Aylmar is enraged:

> 'Awey ut,' he sede, 'fule theof,
> Ne wurstu me nevremore leof!
> Wend ut of *my* bure

---

[7] Diana Webb, *Privacy and Solitude in the Middle Ages* (London, 2007), p. 98; Michael Thompson, *The Medieval Hall: The Basis of Secular Domestic Life, 600–1600 AD* (Aldershot, 1995), p. 117; John Blair, 'Hall and Chamber: English Domestic Planning 1000–1250', in *Manorial Domestic Buildings in England and Northern France*, ed. Gwyn Meirion-Jones and Michael Jones (London, 1991), pp. 1–21 (p. 15).
[8] *Kyng Alisaunder*, ed. G. V. Smithers, EETS 227 (London, 1952), lines 377–8.
[9] *King Horn*, in *Four Romances of England*, ed. Ronald B. Herzman, Graham Drake and Eve Salisbury (Kalamazoo, MI, 1999), lines 653–4.

With muchel messaventure.
Wel sone bute thu flitte,
With swerde ich thee anhitte.
Wend ut of *my* londe,
Other thu schalt have schonde.' (711–18)

In his doubled imperative ejection, 'wend ut of *my* bure ... wend ut of *my* londe' – not paralleled in the Anglo-Norman version[10] – Aylmar articulates possession not only of his kingdom but also of what *Rymenhild* elsewhere refers to as 'my bur' (329). Here, the patriarchal domain and its feudal interests subsume and incorporate the marginal space and personal desires of the princess and the young protagonist. Private space is not concrete, but rather produced, delimited or forestalled by negotiations of power: 'a space is not a thing but rather a set of relations between things (objects and products).' Here, alongside the spatial theorist Henri Lefebvre, we can ask, 'if space embodies social relationships, how and why does it do so? And what relationships are they?'[11] In romances such as *King Horn*, it is not only bodies, but also spaces such as bowers, that are the battlefields of competing jurisdictions. We can understand the relationship and interactions between kingdom and (royal daughter's) bower, between the patriarchal and the personal, as that between a dominant and a peripheral space respectively:

> The dominant form of space, that of the centres of wealth and power, endeavours to mould the spaces it dominates (i.e. peripheral spaces), and it seeks, often by violent means, to reduce the obstacles and resistance it encounters there.[12]

Certain conduct is expected in certain spaces; according to the dominant interests of the kingdom, ruled by the king from the hall, the bedchamber ought to contribute to the goals of this wider sociopolitical sphere by producing and nurturing legitimate heirs and fostering chivalric alliances.[13] Thus, Aylmar's assertion of ownership of the bower registers his anger at the perceived threat that a sexual encounter transgressing these interests would make to social order – that is, to the normative relationship between dominant and peripheral spaces. Barring the couple from any further 'pleie / Bitwex you selve tweie' (349–50), Aylmar's authoritative rhetoric testifies to the importance of space in how the erotic was conceived, conducted and controlled.

In the fourteenth-century English version of the Horn narrative, *Horn Childe and Maiden Rimnild*, breach of social boundaries is again figured

---

10 Compare the king's more moderate statement to Horn in *The Romance of Horn*, ed. Mildred K. Pope, rev. T. B. W. Reid, 2 vols (Oxford, 1964), I, 1920–6.
11 Henri Lefebvre, *The Production of Space*, trans. Donald Nicholson-Smith (Oxford, 1991), pp. 83 and 27.
12 Lefebvre, *The Production of Space*, p. 49.
13 Ruth Mazo Karras, *Sexuality in Medieval Europe: Doing unto Others* (New York, 2005), pp. 123–4.

through breach of spatial barriers, but seemingly with more strategic awareness on Rimnild's part. This princess invites both Horn and a chaperone into her bower, and:

> Þe mirie maiden hir biþouʒt
> In what maner þat sche mouʒt
> Trewe loue for to ginne.
> Sche sett hir hem bitvene;
> Þe maiden was briʒt & schene
> & comen of kinges kinne.
> Anon hirselue hadde hem ledde
> To sitten opon her owhen bedde:
> Arlaund & Horn wiþ him.[14]

Here, Rimnild manipulates her space both to declare erotic intent and to seek to elicit a similar response. It is worth noting that while Rimnild's counterpart Rigmel in the Anglo-Norman analogue does lead Horn to her bed and sit with him there, Rigmel does not strategize inwardly about what she will do.[15] It is the English Rimnild who asks herself in what manner she will encourage love between herself and Horn. She determines that she will speak her intentions and further her chances of fulfiling them alike by availing herself of the bedroom and then – more intimately – of the bed. Here, that is, space receives the text's and characters' attention as the operative language of articulating and pursuing the sensual. In romances, enclosure is, and suggests, the erotic;[16] this is the case, for instance, here in *Horn Childe*, in the *Squire of Low Degree* and, as discussed below, in *Sir Gawain and the Green Knight*. The contingencies of this enclosure are brought to the fore in *Horn Childe*. Rimnild's bower, and any other bower in her father's court, is shown to belong to the king with particular violence. Firstly,

> Houlac king ʒaf Horn leue
> *In his bour* forto chese
> Þe maidens þat were fre. (433–5)

This 'bour', populated by available females but possessed by the king, sounds almost synonymous with 'harem'; the Emir in *Floris and Blancheflour* describes those from among whom he selects his brides similarly, as 'his maidens in his

---

[14] *Horn Childe and Maiden Rimnild*, ed. Maldwyn Mills (Heidelberg, 1988), lines 364–72. I have reproduced these lines in the order in which they occur in the Auchinleck manuscript, rather than as they appear in Mills's edition. Mills relocates the final three lines of this passage to the beginning of it because he believes it 'makes better sense' (p. 113); however, in respecting the authority of the sole extant version, we see, as discussed below, the emergence of another 'sense'.

[15] Compare *Romance of Horn*, lines 1094–101.

[16] On erotic enclosure (though without a consideration of the romance genre), see Cary Howie, *Claustrophilia: The Erotics of Enclosure in Medieval Literature* (New York, 2007). Howie glosses 'the erotics of enclosure' as a spatial manifestation of a 'desire to hold and be held' (p. 139).

bour'.[17] However, it becomes clear that the king in *Horn Childe* did not mean to include his daughter in his generous offer of the ladies of his court. When he is treacherously deceived into thinking that Horn has slept with Rimnild, the king:

> as he were wode,
> *Into boure* anon he ȝode
> & Maiden Rimnild he souȝt;
> He bete hir so þat sche gan blede;
> ...
> Þei þat Horn was sore adrad,
> *Into boure* he was ladde
> Þe maiden forto se.
> He fond hir liggeand on hir bedde,
> Mouþe & nose al forbled. (496–521)

The king's bloody beating of his daughter reclaims her as his own in a way that is redolent of rape. Both the beating and Horn's witnessing of the effects are explicitly anchored to the bower; neither bower confrontation is in the Anglo-Norman analogue.[18] Although Rimnild has proceeded less far with her desires, the consequences for the desiring woman are more severe in *Horn Childe* than in the earlier *King Horn*; however, in both English versions, the chamber is instrumental for both sensual pleasure and the patriarchal power that does not condone it.

In *Sir Gawain and the Green Knight*, neither fulfilment nor retribution takes place in the bedchamber at Hautdesert, but both are mediated there, largely through Gawain's and the Lady's physical and rhetorical spatial manoeuvres. As has been observed, 'Gawain's secluded bedchamber is [a] necessary element in the story', not least in having 'a door which can be locked or bolted'.[19] The bedchamber is a space that also has internal demarcations, in addition to the boundaries of walls and doors. Aristocratic chambers sometimes had a low partition delineating a more intimate or privileged portion of the room, and Gawain's curtained bed, offering another layer of privacy and intimacy,[20] is a further means of communication and complication: the poet specifies that Gawain 'in gay bed lygez, / ... Vnder couertour ful clere, cortyned aboute'.[21] Gawain's and the Lady's manipulations of the bedchamber space (door, curtains, bed) articulate their desires and intentions, as does their speech about space and movement. Their communication about potentially erotic space is initially non-verbal: as Gawain is drowsing,

---

[17] *Middle English Verse Romances*, ed. Donald B. Sands (New York, 1966), p. 199.
[18] Maldwyn Mills, 'Introduction', in *Horn Childe*, p. 51.
[19] Webb, *Privacy and Solitude*, p. 99.
[20] Karras, *Sexuality in Medieval Europe*, p. 81.
[21] *Sir Gawain and the Green Knight*, ed. J. R. R. Tolkien and E. V. Gordon, rev. Norman Davis (1925; Oxford, 1967), lines 1178–80.

> sle3ly he herde
> *A littel dyn at his dor and derfly vpon*;
> And he heuez vp his hed out of þe cloþes,
> *A corner of þe cortyn he ca3t vp a lyttel*,
> And waytez warly þiderwarde quat hit be my3t.
> Hit watz þe ladi, loflyest to beholde,
> þat *dro3 þe dor after hir ful dernly and stylle*
> And bo3ed towarde þe bed; and þe burne schamed
> And *layde hym doun lystyly and let as he slepte.*
> And *ho stepped stilly and stel to his bedde,*
> *Kest vp þe cortyn and creped withinne*
> And *set hir ful softly on þe bed-syde*
> And *lenged þere* selly longe to loke quen he wakened. (1182–94)

The Lady penetrates the bedroom, and makes it exclusive by shutting the door before she approaches the bed, lifts the curtains and slips inside – each movement a breach of another layer of the decorous distance that ought to exist between a bachelor knight and a married lady. Gawain, meanwhile, by initially choosing sleep-like inactivity, pretending a lack of awareness seemingly in hope of lowering the stakes of having his host's wife in his bedchamber, in fact allows the ensuing sexually charged situation to occur and communicates a spatial and behavioural precedent for the subsequent mornings.[22] In this voiceless yet lucid interchange, Gawain and the Lady speak *through* their relationship to and deployment of space; they also speak *about* space, to pursue or prevent the same potentially sexual ends. Here, space provides a language of innuendo, a currency with which to communicate and press one's desires:

> 'God moroun, Sir Gawayn,' sayde þat gay lady,
> '3e ar a sleper vnsly3e, þat mon may slyde hider.
> Now ar 3e tan astyt! Bot true vus may schape,
> *I schal bynde yow in your bedde* – þat be 3e trayst.' (1208–11)

Gawain's reply includes the same parameters; he responds to the lady in kind, if with different intent:

> 'Bot wolde 3e, lady louely, þen, leue me grante
> And *deprece your prysoun* and *pray hym to ryse*,
> *I wolde bo3e of þis bed* and *busk me better*;
> I schulde keuer þe more comfort to karp yow wyth.'
> 'Nay forsoþe, beau sir,' sayd þat swete,
> '*3e schal not rise of your bedde*.' (1218–23)

While the Lady seeks to bind Gawain to his bed, Gawain seeks to escape it; we understand that in so doing, in engaging in this rhetorical dance, each

---

[22] As on the third morning of this testing, when, with Gawain once again still in bed, the Lady similarly 'comez withinne þe chambre dore, and closes hit hir after' (1742).

of them seeks to configure the space they inhabit in order to influence the expectations of their encounter. This chamber and its curtained bed are ambiguous spaces – in one sense a sexually charged bedchamber, in another sense a prison; and underlying both, of course, the political and moral testing-ground of Gawain by Bertilak, who has sent his wife to try to 'move' Gawain on his behalf. Gawain cannot fulfil, or even acknowledge, such desires as those the Lady seeks to attribute to and provoke in him, without inviting Bertilak's revenge.

Thus, in the bedroom encounters in *Sir Gawain*, as in *King Horn* and *Horn Childe*, the homosocial prevails over the heterosexual – but not, in this case, because Bertilak physically enforces his interests. In the episodes in the Horn romances, the bedroom – like the woman's body – can be seen as the meeting place not only between a dominant and a peripheral interest, but also between two dominant ones, that of the father and that of the lover.[23] The bedroom, in this sense, is a borderland, a space of cultural contact where two chivalric or feudal agendas rub against each other. Perhaps there is less friction between these in *Sir Gawain* than in the Horn romances partly because Gawain is aware that he is not acting only on his own behalf – for his sexual union with Bertilak's wife would not advance Arthur's kingdom in the same way that Horn's union with Rymenhild would advance Horn's own regal interests. Alternatively, if, as Sheila Fisher suggests, it is not Bertilak, but Morgan, who is the prime mover in the poem – who sends Bertilak to Arthur's court to frighten Guinevere and who is also in charge of Gawain's testing[24] – then the female use of sexual temptation in the bedroom manoeuvres would be an attempt to use pleasure to subvert not one, but two, 'dominant' spaces – that of Arthur/Gawain and that of Bertilak.

In Malory's *Morte Darthur*, Launcelot's nocturnal encounters with Elaine, and Gareth's with Lyonnesse, offer further insight into the ways in which manipulations of bower space serve to convene sexual events or intentions in romance. Acting on King Pelles's behalf, the enchantress Dame Brusen dupes Launcelot into thinking that a messenger brings a ring from his beloved Guenevere to requisition him for a rendezvous at a castle, whereas in reality the lady in question is Pelles's daughter Elaine. When transported to the unfamiliar castle, spatial contrivances – magical and yet also thoroughly mundane – enable the situationally dependent sexual encounter in which Launcelot otherwise would never have participated:

> sir Launcelot ayenst nyght rode unto the castell, and there anone he was receyved worshypfully wyth suche people, to his semynge, as were aboute

---

[23] The suitor in the *Squire of Low Degree*, however, unlike the protagonists of most romances, is not a scion of any domain or noble house, but only the king of Hungary's servant (except in the much later and shorter Percy Folio version, where the Squire is given an English identity).

[24] Sheila Fisher, 'Taken Men and Token Women in *Sir Gawain and the Green Knight*', in *Seeking the Woman in Late Medieval and Renaissance Writings: Essays in Feminist Contextual Criticism*, ed. Sheila Fisher and Janet E. Halley (Knoxville, TN, 1989), pp. 71–105 (pp. 78–9).

quene Gwenyver secrete. So whan sir Launcelot was alyght he asked where the quene was. So dame Brusen seyde she was in her bed.

And than people were avoyded and *sir Launcelot was lad into her chaumbir*. And than dame Brusen brought sir Launcelot a kuppe of wyne, and anone as he had drunken that wyne he was so asoted and madde that he myght make no delay but wythoute ony let he wente to bedde. And so he wente that mayden Elayne had bene quene Gwenyver. And wyte you well that sir Launcelot was glad, and so was that lady Eleyne ...

And so they lay togydir untyll underne of the morne; and *all the wyndowys and holys of that chambir were stopped, that no maner of day myght be seyne*. And anone sir Launcelot remembryd hym and arose up and wente to the wyndow, and *anone as he had unshutte the wyndow the enchauntemente was paste*. Than he knew hymselff that he had done amysse.[25]

The 'kuppe of wyne' receives attention as the device altering Launcelot's perceptions and desires, as though this magical potion motivates him to mistake the identity of the lady in the bed ('And *so* he wente that mayden Elayne had bene quene Gwenyver') and accordingly sleep with her. However, the ways in which Launcelot's perceptions of the space he occupies are manipulated, without any magic but rather through discursive misdirection and darkness, seem much more functionally significant: the enchantment cannot work without the availability and construction of a familiar-seeming bower space. Launcelot expects to find Guenevere in the bedchamber because he has been told to expect her there. His desire, while perhaps aroused by the potion, can be acted upon because of the darkened bedchamber, and is dissipated as soon as Launcelot opens a window, breaching the hermeneutically sealed space to which he has been brought and thus breaking the 'spell' of his dis-placed desire.

Launcelot's second inadvertent bedchamber meeting with Elaine likewise relies upon a process of manipulating perceptions of space in order to arouse the desire that is connected to certain spaces – that is, for Launcelot, spaces which he associates with Guenevere:

And than hit was ordayned that *dame Elayne shulde slepe in a chambir nygh by the quene, and all undir one rooff*. And so hit was done as the kynge commaunded. Than the quene sente for sir Launcelot and *bade hym com to her chambir* that nyght, 'other ellys,' seyde the quene, 'I am sure that ye woll go to youre ladyes bedde, dame Elayne, by whome ye gate Galahad.'

'A, madame!' seyde sir Launcelot, 'never say ye so, for that I ded was ayenste my wylle.'

'Than,' seyde the quene, 'loke that ye com to me whan I sende for you.'

'Madame,' seyde sir Launcelot, 'I shall nat fayle you.' (804.1–13)

[25] Sir Thomas Malory, *The Works of Sir Thomas Malory*, ed. Eugène Vinaver, 3rd edn, rev. P. J. C. Field, 3 vols (Oxford, 1990), II, 795.1–23. The darkened chamber and the morning revelation are paralleled in Malory's source, *Lancelot: Roman en prose du XIIIe siècle*, ed. Alexandre Micha, 9 vols (Geneva, 1978–83), IV, p. 211.

Here, Launcelot has a potent warning not available to his counterpart in Malory's French source, which does not contain anything comparable to the queen's 'other ellys' reminder that Launcelot is not to repeat his previous misdemeanour. However, Launcelot fails his promise to Guenevere nonetheless, showing again that his desire is conditioned by space, or by his conceptions of what space he is inhabiting, and why. Dame Brusen again acts as a false messenger, promising to take Launcelot to Guenevere (804.18–28). In both Malory's source and his own version, there is an unstable, proximate relationship between Elaine's and Guenevere's bowers that helps to explain why Launcelot mistakes the former for the latter: in the French version, Elaine is in a corner of Guenevere's bedroom,[26] while in the *Morte*, Elaine's room is so close to Guenevere's that Launcelot's voice carries from one to the other:

> in his slepe he [Launcelot] talked and claterde as a jay of the love that had bene betwyxte quene Gwenyver and hym, and so as he talked so lowde the quene harde hym thereas she lay in her chambir. And whan she harde hym so clattir she was wrothe oute of mesure, and for anger and payne wist not what to do, and than she cowghed so lowde that sir Launcelot awaked. And anone he knew her hemynge, and than he knew welle that he lay by the quene Elayne, and therewyth he lepte oute of hys bedde as he had bene a wood man. (805.15–24)

Here, spatial manipulations and confusions, and the resulting cognitive confusions, again enable sexual desire. Regardless of Dame Brusen's enchantress powers, on both occasions in which Launcelot's desire for Guenevere is channelled toward Elaine, the operative factor lies in space, and particularly in the shifting relationships between spaces. If there is an enchantment, it is one that operates through the management and 'duplicity' of spaces. After suffering Guenevere's recriminations, Launcelot:

> toke suche an hartely sorow at her wordys that he felle downe to the floure in a sowne ... And whan sir Launcelot awooke oute of hys swoghe, he lepte oute at a bay-wyndow into a gardyne, ... and so he ranne furth he knew nat whothir, and was as wylde woode as ever was man. (805.31–806.7)

Here, Launcelot's transformation and the after-effects of his (doubly) transgressive sex are spatially legible: he goes from inner bower to floor, flees to the garden and then beyond such a benign environment to the forest itself. From one space of adventure, his madness catapults him to another, its opposite. And yet, the bedrooms and forests of medieval romance are in other ways so much alike – dark, obscure, unknowable places where danger and desire lurk, where the knight can be made or unmade.

As in the Launcelot and Elaine episodes, when Gareth meets Lyonesse, manipulations and confusions of space effect sexual intentions and events;

---

26 Vinaver, 'Commentary', p. 1527.

here, however, there are additional spatial complications. Moreover, for Gareth, spatial shifts are not only the *cause* of arousal, but also at times its demonstrable symptom, or its mode of diagnosis. After reclaiming his stolen dwarf at Gryngamoure's gates, Gareth is (like Launcelot in the prelude to his first night with Elaine) brought into new surroundings:

> And so sir Gryngamoure toke hym by the honde and ledde hym into the halle where his owne wyff was. And than com forth dame Lyones arayde lyke a prynces, and there she made hym passyng good chere and he hir agayne, and they had goodly langage and lovely countenaunce … and evermore sir Gareth behelde that lady. And the more he loked on her, the more he brenned in love, that he passed hymself far in his reson. And forth towardys nyght they yode unto souper, and sir Gareth myght nat ete, for *his love was so hoote that he wyst nat were he was*. (331.14–26)

This last phrase, 'his love was so hoote that he wyst nat were he was', reads on a figurative level, and yet also on a very physical level. In romances such as this one – as we have seen in Launcelot's meetings with Elaine – language about spatial shifts or confusions is not an unrealistic metaphor for the erotic, but an effective component of a character's affect. When Gareth looks upon Lyonnesse, the way in which he is affected by her is rhetorically and cognitively expressed through his sense, or confusion, of space. For one thing, Gareth is unaware that his new lady-love is the same lady he has attempted to woo elsewhere, at her own castle; perhaps (if we are to read charitably) we can view the comment that 'he wyst nat were he was' as a hint of Gareth remembering that he ought not to be feeling love except when he is somewhere else. In other respects Malory's narrator does not find it at all remarkable, or even worth remarking upon, that Gareth is, at least in intent, unfaithful in love. However we are supposed to evaluate Gareth's sudden feelings for this putatively unfamiliar lady, the use of the trope of unstable spaces shows that we are not supposed to be in any doubt about their existence. This is only the first of several erotic-induced and/or erotic-inducing spatial confusions in Gryngamoure's castle.

When Gareth and Lyonnesse seek to consummate their love, they do so not in a bedchamber, but in the middle of the hall:

> they brente bothe in hoote love that they were acorded to abate their lustys secretly. And there *dame Lyonesse counceyled sir Gareth to slepe in none other place but in the hall*, and there she promysed hym to com to his bed a lytyll afore mydnyght. (332.35–333.3)

Given this surprising manoeuvre, it is again understandable that Gareth 'wyst nat were he was', since his 'hoote' love is something that he and his society associate with a bedchamber rather than with the overtly public space of the hall. However, Lyonesse's plan sees the creation of a bower space in the middle of the hall:

aftir souper was made a clene avoydaunce, that every lorde and lady sholde
go unto his reste. But sir Gareth seyde playnly he wolde go no farther than
the halle, for in suche placis, he seyde, was convenyaunte for an arraunte
knyght to take his reste in. And *so there was ordayned grete cowchis and thereon
fethir beddis*, and there he leyde hym downe to slepe. And within a whyle
came dame Lyonesse wrapped in a mantell furred with ermyne, and leyde
hir downe by the sydys of sir Gareth. And therewithall he began to clyppe
hir and to kysse hir. (333.14–23)

Here, Lyonesse's and Gareth's attempts to sleep with each other involve appropriating or invading the hall space for the activities of the boudoir. Although the would-be lovers are twice prevented from fulfilling their desires by the appearance of a magical knight set upon them by Lyonesse's sister Lynet, nonetheless Lyonesse's transmogrification of the hall into a bower produces a very different relationship of dominant to peripheral spaces than in the Horn romances, as she (almost) appropriates the former for the pleasures of the latter. Here, for the romance reader as for its characters, spatial confusions and shifts indicate, or render legible, the trace of the erotic. Since a bower carries both expectations and possibilities, Lyonesse and Gareth, who do not have access to a ready-made bower, seek to construct such a space for their ends; we might presume that Lyonnesse would not have to go to such lengths if she were in her own castle rather than her brother's. For those who lacked independence or wealth, bowers could be jury-rigged or loaned; they were shifting commodities subject to intercession.[27]

Usually, such intercessory functions – constructing, offering, denying, withdrawing private space – were controlled by men. However, the pleasure sought or prevented through bowers is not solely that of one gender; both partake. In romances – particularly ones such as *Sir Gawain and the Green Knight* and *The Tale of Sir Gareth* – women are sometimes able to exert power and express their desires through manipulations of bowers. In *The Tale of Sir Gareth*, not only is a woman the author of erotic desires, but another woman (Lynet) is the one seeking to prevent these desires. Moreover, in the Melusine romances, a woman forbids access to her *own* bower: a woman who has made her own marriage, and whose power (unlike Triamour's in *Sir Launfal*) is not

---

[27] Jean Verdon, *Night in the Middle Ages*, trans. George Holoch (1994; Notre Dame, IN, 2002), pp. 140–1. Another example of a makeshift bower occurs in the thirteenth-century *Havelok the Dane*, where Ubbe offers the hero and his wife a bedroom that is not really bedroom, a private space without any privacy: 'I shal lene thee a bowr / That is up in the heye tour, / ... / It ne shal nothing ben bitwene / Thi bowr and min, al so I wene, / But a fayr firrene wowe – / Speke I loude or spek I lowe, / Thou shalt ful wel heren me, / And than thu wilt thou shalt me se. / A rof shal hile us bothe o nith' (in *Four Romances of England*, ed. Ronald B. Herzman, Graham Drake and Eve Salisbury (Kalamazoo, MI, 1999), lines 2072–82). It is easy to see how such a makeshift bower – like Gareth and Lyonesse's, or like the space in which Launcelot sleeps with Elaine and from which Guenevere can hear his voice – would not be conducive to an uninterrupted sexual encounter.

derived from her father.[28] Both Jean d'Arras's prose *Mélusine* (late fourteenth century) and Couldrette's abbreviated versification of it, *Le Roman de Parthenay* (produced a few years later), were translated into English in the late fifteenth century. In the prose *Melusine*, the eponymous fairy, cursed by her mother to turn into a serpent from the waist down on Saturdays and to remain mortal only if her husband does not see her in that state, requires Raymond to promise her 'vpon all the sacrements & othes', that 'neuer ... ye shal not peyne ne force your self for to see me on the Satirday'.[29] After some years of happy marriage, Raymond's brother visits Raymond on a Saturday and tells him 'wete it that the commyn talking of the peple is, that Melusyne your wyf euery satirday in the yere is with another man in auoultyre' (296.1–3). Raymond, provoked into jealous suspicion even more easily than Othello, punctures his wife's door with his sword and, peering through, sees his wife bathing: with a serpent's tail, but entirely chaste. Realizing his error, Raymond stops up the hole with wax and says 'My swete loue, now haue I betrayed you, & haue falsed my couenaunt' (297.10–11). In the *Romans of Partenay*, as in the prose version, Raymond breaks his oath to Melusine when his brother tells him that 'Men sain ouerall' that on Saturdays 'hir body Anothir man shall haue, / To you trayteresse, other so to craue'.[30] Raymond, finding Melusine (and her serpentine tail) chastely bathing, reviles his falsely accusing brother:

> 'ye lye vntrewly,
> ...
> Off my lady no more speke ye for shame,
> Sche is pure And clene Als without diffame.' (2830–5)

This visual breach of the bedchamber is precisely what Melusine forbade her husband. Melusine used her erstwhile 'private' bedchamber for a *non*-erotic purpose; however, the way in which the male characters around her seem only able to imagine a woman wanting private space if it is for sexual transgression is a revealing sign of the importance of encloseable, possessable bower space for the erotic in medieval romance.

Middle English romances were produced within a society whose expectations, perceptions, and opportunities were shaped by particularly contingent private space due to the scarcity and control of bedrooms and beds. This essay has focused on moments when these contingencies, the instabilities of these spaces, are especially manifest, in order to address a distinctive deployment of space in a number of Middle English romances. In these texts' sexual economy, space can be played with, circulated, controlled. It is a form of expression,

---

[28] Triamour's pavilion and its fancy bed offer a private space, but both Triamour and her privacy are framed by her father's power (if at a remove), as revealed when Launfal 'fond yn the pavyloun / The kynges doughter of Olyroun': Thomas Chestre, *Sir Launfal*, in *The Middle English Breton Lays*, ed. Anne Laskaya and Eve Salisbury (Kalamazoo, MI, 1995), lines 277–8.

[29] *Melusine*, ed. A. K. Donald, EETS e.s 68 (London, 1895), p. 32 (lines 10–15).

[30] *The Romans of Partenay*, ed. Walter W. Skeat, EETS e.s. 22 (London, 1899), lines 2767–70.

negotiation and pursuit of pleasure as well as of power, capable of generating meaning by adhering to and/or manipulating the cultural legibilities of the central-to-late medieval spatial economy. This mode is not unique to popular romance or even to romance more broadly, as is demonstrated, for instance, by the physical tricks and spatial manipulations in fabliaux such as the *Miller's Tale* and especially the *Reeve's Tale*, and by Pandarus's engineering of bedroom encounters in Chaucer's more courtly *Troilus and Criseyde*.[31] Nor is this mode unique to English literature, as shown, not least, by the scenes in the French *Lancelot* on which Malory drew, and Lancelot's breach of bedchamber window bars in order to sleep with Guinevere in Chrétien de Troyes's *Le Chevalier de la charrette*.[32] However, a number of the English romances discussed here – *Sir Gawain and the Green Knight*, Malory's Tale of Sir Gareth, and the *Squire of Low Degree* – have no (extant) sources,[33] and others – *King Horn* and *Horn Childe* – focus on spatial manipulations concerning the erotic more than their French sources or analogues do. Thus, romances, and particularly English ones, do dwell upon this spatial mode of representing the erotic with some independence and frequency, suggesting its importance to the contemporary (English) cultural imagination.

---

[31] Geoffrey Chaucer, *Troilus and Criseyde*, in *The Riverside Chaucer*, ed. Larry D. Benson, 3rd edn (Boston, 1987), II. 1710–50 and III. 946–1316; see further Webb, *Privacy and Solitude*, pp. 114–16.

[32] Chrétien de Troyes, *Lancelot, ou le chevalier de la charrette*, ed. Jean-Claude Aubailly (Paris, 1991), lines 4597–700; also in Malory's *Morte*, pp. 1131–2.

[33] Vinaver's supposition of a French source for the Gareth section ('Commentary', pp. 1427–34) has been superseded by arguments for an English source based on vocabulary and syntax: P. J. C. Field, 'The Source of Malory's *Tale of Gareth*', in *Aspects of Malory*, ed. Toshiyuki Takamiya and Derek Brewer, Arthurian Studies I (Cambridge, 1981), pp. 57–70; Ralph Norris, *Malory's Library: The Sources of the 'Morte Darthur'*, Arthurian Studies 71 (Cambridge, 2008). However, since there is no extant source but there are partial analogues in both insular and continental romances, Malory may have synthesized his own tale.

4
'Naked as a nedyll': The Eroticism of Malory's Elaine[1]

YVETTE KISOR

IN her 2007 essay '"Wordy vnthur wede": Clothing, Nakedness and the Erotic in some Romances of Medieval Britain', Amanda Hopkins examines the interplay of clothing and nudity in creating erotic moments, noting the connection of eroticism with female aggression on the one hand, and the erotic link between female nudity and passivity on the other.[2] Lancelot's encounter with Elaine at Corbyn in Malory's *Morte Darthur* is marked by erotic moments featuring female nudity that appear emblematic of the latter. The eroticism of the moment when Lancelot rescues the 'dolerous lady' (2.791)[3] from the boiling water by taking her by the hand, 'naked as a nedyll' (2.792), depends both on her total nudity and her status as victim – that is to say that the moment is erotic not just because she is naked, but because that nudity is not of her own making. Later, when Elaine 'skypped oute of her bedde all naked' (2.795) and kneels at Lancelot's feet to beg for her life, both her nudity and her vulnerability work to produce an erotic effect. Certainly Lancelot quickly changes his mind and turns from threatening her to embracing her. Yet to view Elaine as completely passive is a mistake – at the least her passivity is manipulated and Lancelot's presence in her bed is the result of machinations in which Elaine plays a willing part. A comparison with the same scenes in the *Lancelot-Grail* cycle[4] confirms that Malory creates and emphasizes female

[1] A preliminary version of this essay was given as a conference paper at the Forty-fifth International Medieval Congress at Western Michigan University in Kalamazoo, Michigan, in May 2010 as part of the session 'The Erotic in Early England'. Initial work on this essay was supported by an SBR summer stipend from Ramapo College of New Jersey in 2009.
[2] Amanda Hopkins, '"Worthy vnthur wede": Clothing, Nakedness and the Erotic in some Romances of Medieval Britain', in *The Erotic in the Literature of Medieval Britain*, ed. Amanda Hopkins and Cory James Rushton (Cambridge, 2007), pp. 53–70.
[3] Citations are from the three-volume *The Works of Sir Thomas Malory*, ed. Eugène Vinaver, 2nd edn (Oxford, 1967); citations are given by volume and page number.
[4] The *Lancelot-Grail* is clearly the ultimate source, but the *Prose Tristan* is likely Malory's immediate source; as Vinaver states concerning the story of Launcelot and Elaine, 'The

nudity in these two key passages, perhaps in order to further excuse Lancelot and, to return to the connection of eroticism with female aggression as well as passivity, allow us to view the naked Elaine and the nude 'dolerous lady' as erotic figures wielded by women (Morgan le Fay, the queen of North Galys, Dame Brusen) specifically in order to accomplish the seduction of Lancelot.

My discussion includes the possibility that the woman in the boiling water is in fact Elaine, the daughter of King Pelles and the mother of Galahad. This is not a necessary assumption – the woman in the water is never specifically identified as Elaine, and the possibility exists that she is not. Other scholars discussing these scenes treat them as separate characters, though later authors often do not; T. H. White, for example, portrays them as one and the same.[5] My comparison of the corresponding scenes in Malory and the *Lancelot-Grail* does not depend on this identification, as I am examining the two versions of this episode for their erotic content, but a consideration of the morning-after scene between Lancelot and Elaine is deepened if the woman in the boiling water is that same Elaine.

Lancelot's arrival at Corbyn is marked by the episode wherein he saves the maiden from the scalding water. Compared to the corresponding scene in the *Lancelot-Grail* cycle, Malory's version is noteworthy for the woman's passivity and objectification, and Lancelot's fascination with her. The woman has no real existence in the scene except as the beautiful, naked object Lancelot gazes upon and takes by the hand. In Malory's account the people of Corbyn greet Lancelot, beg for his assistance and inform him of Gawain's earlier failure, to which Lancelot responds with his customary humility. Their description of the situation emphasizes the woman's suffering; she is 'a dolerous lady that hath bene there in paynes many wyntyrs and dayes, for ever she boyleth in scaldynge watir' (2.791) and Gawain's failure has 'lefte her in payne stylle' (2.792). Lancelot is taken to the tower, the doors unlock and 'there sir Launcelot toke the fayryst lady by the honde that ever he sawe, and she was as naked as a nedyll' (2.792). The narrative of the scene is then interrupted so we can be told the reason for the enchantment, the jealousy of Morgan le Fay and the queen of North Galys 'bycause she was called the fayryst lady of that contrey' (2.792), the duration of the woman's suffering (five years), and the fact that she could only be released when 'the beste knyght of the worlde had takyn her by the honde' (2.792). The narrative resumes as the people dress her, and

---

relevant section of the French Prose *Tristan* is a borrowing from the Prose *Lancelot*' (3: 1524). For a more detailed discussion, see Elizabeth S. Sklar, 'Malory's "Lancelot and Elaine": Prelude to a Quest', *Arthurian Yearbook* 3 (1993): 127–40 (139, n. 4) and Elizabeth S. Berthelot, 'Malory's Other(ed) Elaine', in *On Arthurian Women: Essays in Memory of Maureen Fries*, ed. Bonnie Wheeler and Fiona Tolhurst (Dallas, 2001), pp. 59–70 (pp. 68–9, n. 2).

5 See Chapter 11 of *The Ill-Made Knight*. T. H. White, *The Once and Future King* (New York, 1987), p. 372. Christopher Bruce makes the same assumption in his entry on Lancelot: 'Lancelot visits Corbenic, the Grail Castle, and rescues Amite, King Pelles's daughter, from an enchanted boiling bath' (Christopher W. Bruce, *The Arthurian Name Dictionary* (New York and London, 1999), p. 308).

'whan sche was arrayed sir Launcelot thought she was the fayryst lady that ever he saw but yf hit were quene Gwenyver' (2.792). Only then does the woman speak, to invite Lancelot to join her in giving thanks to God, to which Lancelot willingly acquiesces.

In the account in the *Lancelot-Grail* cycle, the woman is much more vocal, and arguably more active, and Lancelot significantly less taken with her. Lancelot is brought to Corbenic by a lady who has promised to show him 'la plus bele riens del siècle' (4.201; 'the most beautiful creature in the world' [3.162]);[6] significantly this is not the woman in the scalding water but the Grail-maiden, whom Lancelot will later acknowledge to be the most beautiful woman he has ever seen 'se ne fu en sa dame la roine' (4.205; 'unless it was ... his lady the queen' [3.163]).[7] As he is admiring the castle of Corbenic, 'Il resgarde sor desire et o tune voiz de fame assez pres de lui, ce le ert avis' (4.201; 'He looked to the right and heard a woman's voice that sounded very close' [3.162]). He heads in the direction of the voice and discovers that it is the woman whom Gawain had failed to free earlier. Unlike the woman in Malory's version, this one does not suffer in silence; she cries out through her pain, 'ele crioit: "sainte Marie, qui me getera de ci?"' (4.202; 'shouting, "Holy Mary, who'll get me out of here?"' [3.162]) and when she catches sight of Lancelot she calls out to him, 'Ha, sire, getez moi de caste eve qui m'art!' (4.202; 'Ah, my lord, get me out of this burning water!' [3.162]). This Lancelot does not merely take her by the hand but must pull her out of the water, and she falls to his feet in gratitude, thanking him: 'Ha, sire, beneoite soit l'eure que vos fustes nez, car vos m'avez gité de la greingnor dolor ou fame fust onques' (4.202; 'Oh, my lord, blessed be the hour you were born, for you've saved me from the greatest pain a woman ever endured' [3.162]). Then the room fills with people who escort the lady to a chapel to thank God and Lancelot to the cemetery.

We are not told about the enchantment, or given any explanation for why she is in the boiling water.[8] We simply move on to the next part of the adventure, the lifting of the tombstone and the battle with the dragon. Missing is any reference to her beauty or to Lancelot's noticing her beauty or her nudity.

---

[6] The French text is the edition of Alexandre Micha, *Lancelot*, vol. 4, Textes littéraires français (Geneva and Paris, 1979). Citations are given by volume and page number. The English translation is that of William W. Kibler in *Lancelot-Grail: The Old French Arthurian Vulgate and Post-Vulgate in Translation*, vol. 3, ed. Norris J. Lacy (New York and London, 1995). Citations are given by volume and page number.

[7] It becomes clear in later passages that the Grail maiden is the daughter of King Pelles, but nothing in the narration of this scene here suggests this, nor is there any indication that Lancelot understands that the beautiful maiden bearing the Grail and the woman he inadvertently beds are one and the same. The text only makes this clear when Bors visits Corbenic in LXXXI: 11–12 (4: 270–1; 3: 179) and we are told that she is no longer the Grail maiden because she is no longer a virgin.

[8] This is in part because Gawain's failure to rescue her has been narrated, in terms almost identical to the account of Lancelot's success. In the earlier account, the woman tells Gawain that her presence in the water is due to 'a great sin I committed', and says nothing of enchantment by Morgan le Fay or anyone else, but rather divine punishment (2: 374; 3: 99).

In fact, Lancelot has more to say in praise of the sight of the tower than he does of the woman, finding the tower to be 'la plus bele et la plus fort qu'il onques veist a son esciant' (4.201; 'the most beautiful and strongest he had ever seen' [3.162]); he has no comment nor thought regarding the woman's appearance. It is the townspeople who gather 'por veoir la damoisele' (4.202; 'to see the maiden' [3.162]). Neither do Lancelot and she appear to visit the chapel together.[9] This woman is also more aggressive, crying out for help and seizing verbally on an opportunity to escape when one presents itself. In fact, her verbalization is key to her rescue, because it is in response to the sound of her voice that Lancelot moves towards her. She is in the subject position for a significant portion of the scene; from the moment Lancelot becomes aware of her voice she is the subject of three sentences, equaling Lancelot's three, and she is the only speaker in the scene, speaking three separate times.

Compare the scene in Malory, where the woman's beauty, and Lancelot's response to it, are paramount. We are told three times that she is the fairest lady, twice through Lancelot's gaze, emphasis on his sight, and only in the final line are we given the possible exception of Guenevere. She is more passive than her counterpart in the *Lancelot-Grail* cycle, apparently not verbalizing at all through her suffering, not speaking until the end of the episode, when she requests that Lancelot accompany her to prayer. She exists only to be taken by the hand by the best knight in the world and to be acknowledged by him 'the fayryst lady ... that ever he sawe' (2.792). Her nudity is part of that, a detail all Malory's own. She is 'naked as a nedyll' (2.792), a phrase that refers to total nudity – stark naked, in other words, or in modern American parlance, 'naked as a jaybird'. The phrase 'naked as a needle' is not in and of itself necessarily erotic. The *Middle English Dictionary* lists four other occurrences of this idiom, none of which is remotely erotic and none of which appears in romance.[10] The *OED* gives more recent examples from the nineteenth and twentieth centuries in addition to the medieval ones, which appear similarly non-titillating.[11] The phrase helps qualify the more ambiguous range of meanings 'naked' could hold in the Middle Ages, when it could mean poorly dressed or destitute, rather than totally nude. Thus, the term 'naked' can be seen as having less to do with eroticism and more to do with the vulnerability of the person so designated.

---

9   Possibly. The text is ambiguous here and it does not rule out the possibility that Lancelot also goes to the chapel to give thanks and *then* is taken to the cemetery.
10 Two in *Piers Plowman* and one each in *The Siege of Jerusalem* and *The Wars of Alexander*. See 'nedle, n.', *Middle English Dictionary*, December 2001, University of Michigan, http://quod.lib.umich.edu/cgi/m/mec/med-idx?type=byte&byte=122177041&egdisplay=open&egs=122202789 (accessed 7 January 2012).
11 Specifically, J. H. Ingraham's 1845 American romance *Forrestal* 'The rock looks inaccessible and as naked as a needle' (x. 129), H. Trench's 1919 biographical play *Napoleon* 'We're naked as in the day of judgement! God's eyes! – Naked as a needle!' (II. i. 35), and a 1939 *Notes and Queries* 'As naked as a needle' (15 July 42/1). See 'naked, adj. and n.'', *OED* Online, December 2011, Oxford University Press, http://www.oed.com/view/Entry/124890?rskey=CORNr8&result=2 (accessed 7 January 2012).

Other uses of the idiom 'naked as a needle' bear this out, as only Malory's has any potentially erotic resonance. In *The Siege of Jerusalem*, Vespasian's messengers are taken by the Jews, bound, their hair ripped out, and stripped 'naked as a nedel' (361). Clearly their total nudity is part of their humiliation in the most violent image associated with this phrase. Other uses also emphasize the vulnerable state of the naked one. In *Piers Plowman* (B-text), a description of the robbed man in the story of the Good Samaritan underscores the victim's defencelessness in a series of phrases culminating in his nakedness, for he was

> wounded, and with theves taken.
> He myghte neither steppe ne stande, ne stere foot ne handes,
> Ne helpe hymself soothly, for semyvif he semed,
> And as naked as a nedle, and noon help abouten. (17.53–6)

The phrase is used again in *Piers Plowman* (B-text) in an analogy of taking two men and throwing them into the Thames, 'bothe naked as a needle' (12.162), in order to see which will succeed, the one who can swim or the one who never learned; again the emphasis is on the helplessness of the men. A final example, from *The Wars of Alexander*, describes the Gymnosophists who live in caves and go 'naked [as] a nedill as natour þam schapis' (4026); the emphasis here is on their poverty and their withdrawal from civilization.

Malory's use of the phrase is in line with these in some ways, but ultimately stands out. Like the examples given, Malory's includes an emphasis on vulnerability. Clearly the woman is a victim here, and her nudity underscores that. But Malory's description is the only example where the phrase 'naked as a needle' is applied to a woman. All the others, from non-romance texts less than a hundred years earlier than Malory, apply the phrase to men. Further, Malory couples the phrase with a reference to her surpassing beauty in Lancelot's eyes: 'there sir Launcelot toke the fayryst lady by the honde that ever he sawe, and she was as naked as a nedyll' (2.792). The reference to her total nudity may indeed suggest primarily her vulnerability, but the emphasis on Lancelot's gaze suggests that both her vulnerability and her nakedness are part and parcel of her appeal to Lancelot.

In her thoroughgoing survey of nakedness in medieval British romance, Amanda Hopkins has noted that erotic scenes featuring total nudity of either party are rare, observing that 'complete nakedness seems to be of minimal erotic interest to romance authors'.[12] Instead, elaborate descriptions of sumptuous clothing are much more frequent in sensual scenes, often including bared body parts, suggesting that 'Partial nudity can be more erotic than complete nakedness';[13] in particular women in a seductress role are often described this way – consider the Lady in *Sir Gawain and the Green Knight* who dresses in rich and sumptuous clothing that calls attention to her throat

---

[12] Hopkins, '"Worthy vnthur wede"', p. 60.
[13] Hopkins, '"Worthy vnthur wede"', p. 63.

'al naked' and 'hir brest bare bifore and bihinde eke' (1740–1)[14] or the Lady in *Landavale* who is 'Almost nakyd' (98),[15] her clothes beside her, partially covered in luxurious bedclothes, but uncovered to her waist; her counterpart in *Sir Launfal* is also only partially dressed, her clothes undone 'Almest to her gerdylstede / Than lay sche uncovert' (290–1).[16] Unlike these ladies, however, the woman in Malory's story is no seductress, which may be why she appears not 'almost nakyd', certain areas of the body strategically uncovered, but either 'naked as a nedyll' (2.792) or dressed. Whether she is stark naked or fully clothed, Lancelot finds her appealing. Almost the same phrase is repeated to indicate Lancelot's appreciation of her beauty, the first time juxtaposed to her nudity and the second to her clothed state. She is 'the fayryst lady that ever he saw' both 'naked as a nedyll' and 'whan sche was arrayed' (2.792). Naked, she is silent; once clothed she requests in humble terms that he accompany her to chapel.

This woman invites identification as Elaine, the daughter of King Pelles, because in their initial encounter Malory's Elaine is not the aggressor, nor the seductress, in spite of the fact that Lancelot is tricked into her bed. Like the passive victim of Morgan's sorcery, suffering silently in the scalding water until rescued by Lancelot, she is obedient to her father's will, and it is he, not Elaine, who appears eager for her and Lancelot to conceive. Elaine plays no role in the machinations that bring Lancelot into her bed and all but disappears from the narrative until she goes to bed with Lancelot, at which point we are told that she is glad 'that she had gotyn sir Launcelot in her armys, for well she knew that that same nyght sholde be bygotyn sir Galahad uppon her' (2.795). Compare her counterpart in the *Lancelot-Grail*, who also vanishes from the narrative as the arrangements for the assignation are made, but once she has Lancelot in her bed, her pleasure is not based on the child she is conceiving, for 'cele qui riens ne desirroit for savoir celui de cui terrienne chevalerie estoit enluminee le reçoit liee et joieuse' (4.209; 'she, who wanted nothing so much as to possess the man who was the light of earthly chivalry, welcomed him happily and joyfully' [3.164]). Here too the daughter of King Pelles in the *Lancelot-Grail* seems more active than Malory's version, capable of desire and shown as actively welcoming her lover, where Malory's Elaine is simply 'glad' and thinks of the child prophesied. Though the *Lancelot-Grail* goes on to assure us that her desire was 'ne ... mie tant por la biauté de celui ne por luxure ne por eschaufement de char come ele fait por le fruit recevoir' (4.210; 'not so much for his beauty or from lust or bodily desire, but so as to receive the fruit' [3.164]), the impression still stands.[17]

---

[14] *Sir Gawain and the Green Knight*, ed. J. R. R. Tolkien and E. V. Gordon, 2nd edn, rev. Norman Davis (Oxford, 1967).
[15] *Landavale*, in *Thomas Chestre: Sir Launfal*, ed. A. J. Bliss (London, 1960).
[16] *Sir Launfal*, in *Thomas Chestre: Sir Launfal*, ed. Bliss; Hopkins discusses each of these scenes more fully than I do here.
[17] Elizabeth Sklar reads this scene quite differently than I do, finding Malory's Elaine more active

Lancelot's desire is for the more passive, obedient Elaine present in Malory's version of this scene. The morning after, when Lancelot opens the windows, he is freed from Dame Brusen's enchantment and realizes that he has 'done amysse' (2.795). Taking his sword he threatens Elaine, whom he does not yet recognize, asking 'Thou traytoures! What art thou that I have layne bye all this nyght? Thou shalt dye ryght here of myne hondys!' (2.795). In response, 'this fayre lady Elayne skypped oute of her bedde all naked' (2.795) and kneels before him, telling him of the child in her womb and asking for mercy. Rather than granting her mercy, he again calls her 'false traytoures' and demands to know 'what thou arte' (2.796); when she identifies herself by name, however, he forgives her at once and 'therewyth he toke her up in his armys and kyssed her, for she was a fayre lady and thereto lusty and yonge, and wyse as ony was that tyme lyvynge' (2.796),[18] and after further talk in which she emphasizes that she has obeyed the prophecy of Galahad's birth and her father and urges him to 'owghe me youre good wyll', he takes 'hys leve myldely at that yonge lady Eleyne' (2.796). Lancelot's change from threatening murderous vengeance to embracing her is dizzyingly sudden, and it follows immediately upon her self-identification. If the woman he rescued from the boiling water is in fact Elaine, then that sudden turnaround makes more sense: once he can connect the naked woman kneeling at his feet with the naked maiden he rescued the day before, his anger evaporates and he is affectionate towards her. Even if she is not the same person, the similarity of the two images of passive female nudity may be present in Lancelot's mind; certainly they are connected in the reader's.

The corresponding episode in the *Lancelot-Grail* cycle works rather differently. Here the enchantment is not broken by the letting of light into the room, but begins to weaken as soon as Lancelot 'connut la damoisele charnelment' (4.212; 'knew the maiden carnally' [3.165]). He asks who she is out of confusion rather than anger, and she identifies herself immediately. Only then does Lancelot realize the deception and become upset, but he dresses and arms himself before he returns to the girl intent on revenge and draws his sword. She begs for mercy, but says nothing at any point about the child in her womb or the reasons for the deception. At this point in the episode we are told Lancelot stops and notices that 'la plus bele riens qu'il onques mais veist' (4.212; 'she was the most beautiful creature he had ever laid eyes on' [3.165]) and he is torn; she continues pleading 'devant lui a genouz toute nue en chemise' (4.212; 'on her knees in front of him in nothing but her shift' [3.165]); he

and vocal than her counterpart in the *Lancelot-Grail*; this is partly because she looks at the entirety of Elaine's story arc rather than just this scene. See 'Malory's Other(ed) Elaine', esp. pp. 66–7.

[18] As Jerome Mandel notes, 'The rules of courtesy may have required him to kiss her as a sign of pardon, but Malory's additional comments on her beauty, lustiness, youth, and discretion suggest that Lancelot is motivated by more than mere courtesy and that his action arises "of the harte self."' (Jerome Mandel, 'Constraint and Motivation in Malory's "Lancelot and Elaine"', *Papers on Language and Literature* 20:3 (1984): 243–58 (248)).

gazes on her face and is amazed at her beauty. Swayed by that beauty he lets her live and apologizes for having drawn his sword on her because 'trop seroie cruex et desloiax, se si grant biauté destruioie com il a en vos' (4.213; 'I would be far too cruel and false were I to destroy such great beauty as you possess' [3.165]).[19] She forgives him in exchange for his ceasing his anger, and Lancelot leaves. His departure, though, is abrupt and without the affection Malory shows us, and this Lancelot buries his anger with difficulty and through compulsion. His observation of her beauty brings him neither joy nor desire, but grief; the narrator describes him as 'tant dolanz que nus plus' (4.212; 'more grieved than words can express' [3.165]) and he identifies himself as 'si vaincuz et si recreanz' (4.213 'overwhelmed and defeated' [3.165]). This Lancelot never desires Elaine.[20] Even his appreciation of her beauty is belated and wholly unconnected to desire.

Malory's Lancelot does desire Elaine, and that desire is connected to a nudity that gains its erotic character from its association with vulnerability. Lancelot's appreciative gaze on the naked body of the woman he rescues from the boiling water connects to the naked figure kneeling at his feet in the later scene.[21] In that scene too, female passivity is emphasized, as Elaine is never portrayed as actively desiring Lancelot but conforming to her father's will. Her counterpart in the *Lancelot-Grail* cycle never mentions the prophecy or her father's and Brisane's responsibility for setting up Lancelot, but she is able to manipulate the circumstances to her advantage. The moment Lancelot asks forgiveness for drawing his sword against her, she elicits a bargain, making her forgiveness conditional on his surrendering his anger with her. Even under the threat of his sword she is able to enact some agency over her own rescue. Further, she does it through a state of undress both less and more than that of Malory's

---

[19] Anne Berthelot also emphasizes Lancelot's consideration of the lady's beauty, observing that 'upon awakening next to the daughter of the Fisher King, his murderous impulses are replaced *in extremis* by the ecstatic contemplation of the young lady's beauty – and that is perhaps the true treason in regard to Guenevere, the recognition of a certain willingness to fall into the trap that has been set for him.' Anne Berthelot, 'From the Lake to the Fountain: Lancelot and the Fairy Lover', in *Arthurian Women: A Casebook*, Arthurian Characters and Themes 3, Garland Reference Library of the Humanities 1499, ed. Thelma S. Fenster (New York and London, 1996), pp. 153–69 (p. 164). Translated by Thelma S. Fenster, with Anne Berthelot from 'Du lac à la fontaine: Lancelot et la fée-amante', *Médiévales: Langue, Textes, Histoire*, special issue, 'Au pays d'Arthur', 6 (1984): 5–17.

[20] The daughter of King Pelles is rarely referred to by name in the *Lancelot-Grail*; she is named only once very early in the cycle as Amite, described as one of only two women who could compare with Guenevere for beauty (the other is Elaine the Peerless). The passage states that her beauty was incomparable and gives her 'true name' as Helizabel. However, she is generally known as Elaine, and for convenience's sake I refer to her by the name she is best known by (Micha, *Lancelot*, VII–VIII; Lacy, *Lancelot-Grail*, p. 16).

[21] Mandel has noted Lancelot's response to these women, identifying the source of his later madness to be not Guenevere's harsh rebuke but his own sense of guilt, finding that 'the alternate source for Lancelot's madness lies in his own response to the "dolorous lady" and to Elaine. This is the only tale in the *Morte Darthur* in which Malory shows Lancelot more attracted to other women than he is to the Queen' (Mandel, 'Constraint and Motivation in Malory's "Lancelot and Elaine"', 251).

Elaine, for her nudity is only partial – whereas Malory's Elaine 'skypped oute of her bedde all naked' (2.795), this one, like the seductresses discussed earlier who bare strategic parts of the body, is described not as nude but as 'toute nue en chemise' (4.212; 'in nothing but her shift [3.165]), and Lancelot's noticing her beauty for the first time is connected to that description. She is identified as well as a continually speaking figure who 'cele li crie toutes voies merci' (4.212; 'kept pleading with him for mercy' [3.165]). That image results not in desire, but in amazement and grief at the obligation it places on him not to seek revenge. It has little erotic power for Lancelot. Malory's Elaine is erotic to Lancelot because her nudity is total and associated with her vulnerability, her passivity and her silence.

For these reasons, Malory's version is the more erotic and the more intimate of the two. Malory's version exists as the beginning of an extended episode 'Launcelot and Elaine' within the *Book of Sir Tristram de Lyones*, XIV in Vinaver and Books XI and XII in Caxton. The section begins by announcing 'now leve we Sir Trystram de Lyones' and introducing the new subject matter, the conception of Galahad, and after quickly narrating the mysterious hermit's announcement that he who will sit in the Siege Perilous will be begotten that year, Malory moves immediately to Lancelot's visit to Corbyn.[22] After the account of their night together and Lancelot's departure, Malory intersperses related events after the birth of Galahad (the anger of Elaine's suitor, Sir Bromel, Bors's visit to Corbyn and subsequent adventures) and then moves directly to the rumour of Lancelot's affair with Elaine and the resulting child, Guenevere's anger and subsequent forgiveness, Elaine's arrival at Camelot, their second enchanted night together, Guenevere's discovery and resulting anger and Lancelot's madness. Thus Malory's version is organized and focused around the conception and birth of Galahad, the Grail knight, whereas the version in the *Lancelot-Grail* cycle, though it includes the destiny of Galahad as a digression during the account of Lancelot's night with Elaine, is placed very differently and therefore achieves a very different emphasis.

Rather than being embedded in the *Book of Sir Tristram de Lyonesse*, the corresponding episode in the *Lancelot-Grail* cycle is part of a series of adventures Lancelot has, entwined with the sorcery of Morgan le Fay and her compatriots.[23] It follows the capture of Lancelot by Morgan and two other sorceresses who imprison him at Cart Castle until he will name one of them to

---

[22] Elizabeth Sklar argues that the account of Lancelot and Elaine serves as a bridge between the more secular values of the previous sections of *The Book of Sir Tristram* and the more spiritual values of the next section, 'The Quest for the Holy Grail' (Elizabeth S. Sklar, 'Malory's "Lancelot and Elaine": Prelude to a Quest'). In a similar vein, Larry Benson discusses the place of the Lancelot and Elaine story as the last section of *Sir Tristram*, like Sklar finding it to function as a segue to the Grail story that follows, but also seeing it as embedded in Sir Tristram's adventures (Larry D. Benson, *Malory's Morte Darthur* (Cambridge, MA, and London, 1976). See esp. pp. 128–33.)

[23] It comes towards the end of the long *Prose Lancelot*; as Norris Lacy has divided the text in his translation it comes in the fifth of six parts, Chapter 149 of 179 chapters.

be his mistress; he is freed by a maiden, fights for Bademagu against the king of North Wales, and encounters the lady who takes him to Corbenic. After leaving Corbenic, he has a number of adventures culminating in his capture once again by Morgan; this is interlaced with various adventures of Gawain, Yvain and Bors. Set in this sequence, the encounter at Corbenic becomes one of a series of encounters in which Lancelot is manipulated by women through deception and magic. In this context the increased agency of the women at Corbenic and Lancelot's corresponding lack of interest make sense.

Anne Berthelot has discussed the structure of this section of the *Lancelot*, arguing that the episodes of the poisoned spring (4.133–59; 3.146–52) and the poisoned well (4.300–39; 3.186–93) serve to highlight the encounter that produces Galahad (4.201–13; 3.162–5). They do this by position, 'framing' Lancelot's adventures at Corbenic, and by content, as each includes a potential transgression on Lancelot's part and forces him to contemplate unfaithfulness to Guenevere.[24] Berthelot is surely correct to emphasize these episodes and see them as linked to the episode at Corbenic, but her analysis could be extended. There are a number of women manipulating Lancelot in the episodes surrounding his trip to Corbenic, and a number of potential failures of faithfulness on Lancelot's part. When the narrative picks up Lancelot's adventures again, he has spent six weeks out of action recovering from wounds and the kingdom believes him to be dead due to mistakes arising from exchanged armour (4.126; 3.144; this picks up the narration from 2: LVI; 3.82–3). He is being led by an old woman whose motives are suspect, and while she does not use magic to manipulate him as Brisane later does at Corbenic, she does lie to him in a manner quite similar to Brisane. While Brisane pretends that the queen is waiting for him, the old woman brings him to fight against Duke Calles as well as Gawain's brothers Gaheriet, Guerrehet and Agravain by telling him 'les greingnors mençonges del monde' (4.159; 'the biggest lies in the world' [3.152]); Lancelot's devastation upon discovering that he has fought against his friends foreshadows his grief upon discovering that he has been unfaithful to the queen. In both cases he has believed lies and therefore done something he never would have done if he had all the facts.

If the old woman captures the lies of Brisane, then Morgan embodies her use of magic. Upon departing the battle in which he unknowingly fought against Gawain's brothers and in a wrong cause, Lancelot is captured by Morgan and two other sorceresses while sleeping. They accomplish this capture through an enchantment that keeps him asleep while they move him, and offer him a choice either to choose one of them as lover or to remain in prison. He escapes from that prison, but Morgan captures him again following the adventures at Corbenic, this time utilizing both magic and the lying of women, for she has sent out twelve maidens in search of him with instructions to lie to him and bring him to her castle under false pretences; once there she administers two

---

[24] Berthelot, 'Malory's Other(ed) Elaine', see esp. pp. 162–6.

magic enchantments and imprisons him. Similar to the way the episodes of poisoning frame the encounter at Corbenic and establish a triad, as Berthelot has discussed,[25] the two imprisonments by Morgan accomplished through enchantment frame the episode of Lancelot's being manipulated into bed with King Pelles's daughter through magic. In putting together his sequence of adventures, Malory removes these imprisonments by Morgan, instead placing a reference to her in Corbyn itself, for in his version the woman in the boiling water whom Lancelot saves has been placed there through Morgan's enchantment.

As if two imprisonments by Morgan were not enough, after leaving Corbenic and his encounter with King Pelles's daughter Lancelot again becomes a victim of magic, being trapped in a magic dance such that 'si oublie sa dame' (4.235; 'he totally forgot his lady' [3.170]). It is a remarkable episode where at least temporarily Lancelot violates his faith to his lady, for though the spectre of infidelity with another woman is not raised, he is faithless indeed, having forgotten Guenevere completely, though ironically he dances to a song in praise of her. He eventually achieves that adventure, and proceeds to others, including his rescue from the poisoned well by a maiden. Like his faithfulness to his lady, his faithfulness to the knightly code to protect women is tested, for as he and his rescuer journey from the well, he responds to a feminine cry for help and encounters a knight abusing a woman; however, his intervention is rejected by the knight who cuts off the woman's head and throws it at Lancelot to spite him. Lancelot's shock and devastation at this episode are marked:

> Quant Lanceloz voit ce, si a grant duel, qu'il en est touz esbahiz de couroux, car or dist il bien que la damoisele est occise en son conduit, si n'i ot onques si grant honte de chose qui li avenist com il a de ceste; mais, si com il dist, il n'avra jamais honor ne joie devant qu'il l'ait vanchié del chevalier qui tel desloiauté en a faite. (4.319)

> When Lancelot saw this, he was grief-stricken and overwhelmed with anger, because he considered that the woman had been slain under his protection, and he felt no greater dishonor about anything that had ever happened to him than he did about this. He told himself that he would never again have honor or happiness until he had avenged her on the knight who had wronged her so. (3.189)

Lancelot's distress here is a result of his failure to save a woman under his protection, and his potential to fail in this regard continues to be stressed. He chases and eventually defeats the knight, but in the interim finds his original travelling companion, the maiden who rescued him from the well, has been abducted. He does manage to save her from the fire, but the series of events shows Lancelot failing or almost failing in his obligations to women. He fails to save the lady being abused by the knight whom he considers to be under

[25] Berthelot, 'Malory's Other(ed) Elaine', see esp. pp. 159–67.

his protection; in fact, arguably he causes her death, for the knight's actions in beheading her are motivated by anger at Lancelot's intervention and scorn for his attempted rescue. Lancelot's obligation to respond to a feminine cry for help has gone horribly wrong, and he not only fails, his attempts to fulfill his duty to help women place at risk his original female companion, the woman who saved him from the well. His obligation to respond to a feminine cry for help, acknowledged and supported by the woman he is travelling with, results in her near-death.

Lancelot and the maiden who saved him from the well travel on to Cart Castle where Lancelot fulfils another obligation to a female helper, arriving just in time to rescue the maiden who helped him escape from Morgan's prison prior to his adventures at Corbenic. Yet here too his attempt to obey his duties to protect women leads to a potential conflict of faith for Lancelot, for Morgan presses him to reveal his identity, which he is most unwilling to do, 'et ce estoit la fame el monde que il plus redoutoit' (4.336; 'for she was the woman he most feared in all the world' [3.192]). Guessing it is Lancelot, she calls on him 'por la riens que vos plus amez en cest monde' (4.336; 'in the name of whomever you love most in this world' [3.193]) to remove his helmet; backed into a corner like this, Lancelot must reveal himself or break faith with Guenevere. The ensuing trading of insults between the two cements Morgan's hatred of Lancelot and leads to her second imprisonment of him. The possibility of faithlessness raised here is not realized, and Lancelot fulfils his knightly obligations, but the encounter comes at the end of a series of failures and near-misses, and leads to Lancelot's further suffering at the hands of the magical, deceitful Morgan.

Thus we see Lancelot, in the episodes surrounding the adventure at Corbenic, manipulated by magic, deceived by women and failing to live up to his obligation of faithfulness to Guenevere and to his knightly code to protect women. He is both manipulated by women and stumbles in his obligations to them. In the *Lancelot-Grail* cycle, Lancelot's adventure at Corbenic is part of a series of adventures in which Lancelot's attempts to keep faith with Guenevere and women in general are continually thwarted, leaving him in anguish. As Berthelot has noted,

> The episode of the Fisher King's daughter ought not take a preponderant place in the interpretation of the text: whatever the Grail's function elsewhere in the Arthurian romance in general, here it has a different value, and what happens backstage at Corbenic belongs to the area of amorous experimentation more than to mystical experience. (166)

Placed among several encounters with women in which Lancelot is manipulated, enchanted and lied to, and where he finds himself forced to betray his obligations to the queen and to women in general, the encounter at Corbenic resonates with all of these qualities. The Fisher King's daughter is less prominent as a result, and Lancelot's desire for her reduced. Malory removes all of these episodes from the material surrounding Lancelot's encounter with Elaine at Corbyn, emphasizing instead the conception of Galahad. By so doing, Malory emphasizes as well the figure of Elaine, and allows her to become a figure of desire for Lancelot. Her total nudity, her vulnerability and her passivity become part of that desire, contrasting her with her counterpart in the *Lancelot-Grail* cycle, for both the daughter of King Pelles and the woman Lancelot saves from the boiling water in that text can be seen as more vocal, more active and enacting more agency than Malory's versions. Once Galahad is born, Malory's Elaine becomes more active, and less silent and obedient, but Malory eroticizes their initial meeting by silencing the women of his source, emphasizing their vulnerability and taking their clothes all the way off.

5
'How love and I togedre met': Gower, Amans and the Lessons of Venus in the Confessio Amantis

SAMANTHA J. RAYNER

GOWER'S poetry has more often been associated with the moral than the erotic, courtesy of Chaucer's provocative description in *Troilus and Criseyde*. Studies such as Diane Watt's *Amoral Gower* have gone some way to counteract this, and open up the range of Gower's discourses on the political, ethical and erotic issues of his time.[1] The *Confessio Amantis* connects directly and frankly through the persona of Amans with the tensions age brings to lust and love. Venus may tell Amans that 'Loves lust and lockes hore / In chamber acorden neveremore', but the *Confessio* shows us Gower understood the complexities of impulse and behaviour that age and love created. In this essay I shall concentrate on how these complexities are brought out through the exchanges between Amans and Genius, as well as Amans and Venus, showing how the *Confessio* exploits conventions of courtly and classical literature to examine an essentially human experience with humour, wit and perspicacity.[2]

All of Gower's three largest works look at sexual behaviours, but the *Mirour de l'Omme* (1376–79) and the *Vox Clamantis* (begun in 1377) focus on the sinful nature of lechery, rather than looking at love and the more erotic complications that this can bring. The *Confessio*, written around 1390, chooses to explore this more elusively challenging context, and to do so in English, through the diegetic alter ego of Amans. According to John Fisher, Gower had, since about 1377, already been living in semi-retirement at the priory of St Mary Overeys in London, where it is thought that he had an apartment and access to the library and the scriptorium.[3] There are no records to prove whether he was married before he resided there, but in 1398 he married one

---

[1] Diane Watt, *Amoral Gower* (Minneapolis, 2003).
[2] All references to the *Confessio Amantis* are taken from Russell Peck's critical edition for TEAMS: *Confessio Amantis*, 3 vols, ed. Russell Peck (Kalamazoo, MI, 1999–2004).
[3] John Fisher, *John Gower: Moral Philosopher and Friend of Chaucer* (London, 1965), pp. 59–60.

Agnes Groundolf. Eve Salisbury suggests a link between Gower's wife and his work on the *Confessio* (he was revising it during the time the marriage took place): she looks at the epitaph composed for Agnes by Gower, and notes that he calls her 'uxor Amans' – 'loving wife', a tag that constructs a linguistic bond between this particular wife and the poet's persona, Gower's fictional lover – Amans. In a clever verbal manoeuvre Gower has inextricably bound this *uxor* not only to himself, but to his poetic persona.[4]

Gower's *Confessio* ends with Gower, old, alone and commanded by Venus not even to write about love any more. It is, however, entirely fitting with the optimistic tone that characterizes what could so easily have been a very bleak conclusion that not many years later he would find himself married and to someone he could call his 'uxor Amans'.

Beyond this we know very little of Gower's own relationships, but the *Confessio*, with its direct placement of self (even if a fictionally constructed self) shows a poet, and a man, still very aware of the feelings evoked by erotic love, and still able to describe them convincingly. Donald Schueler, however, says, 'no proper lover in all the pages of courtly literature had ever so explicitly borne his love as though it were a sickness of which he would gladly be cured. Nor had the capacity for passion in a courtly hero ever been so accompanied by the faculty of reason.'[5] It has also been confidently argued that passion is entirely absent – 'deep, earnest passion, to be sure, it does not express'[6] – but this ignores the evidence of passages in the *Confessio* that describe this emotion very explicitly, and it denies the skill in Gower's depiction of a 'full and sympathetic view of his passion'.[7]

In about 1400, in a letter to Thomas of Arundel, archbishop of Canterbury, Gower describes himself as 'senex et cecus … corpus et egrotum, vetus et miserabili totum' ('old and blind, infirm of body, decrepit and totally miserable'),[8] showing him to have been very much aware of his physicality, of the lack of control age gave him over his faculties, and the misery he felt as a consequence. He was aged by now about seventy, and it is tempting to agree with Fisher's speculation that Agnes would have been more of a nurse than a wife, but it is worth remembering that there are examples, like T. S. Eliot's marriage to Valerie Fletcher, thirty-eight years younger than him, that prove how wrong such generalizations can be: though Valerie did nurse Eliot through his illnesses, their relationship was obviously a very passionate one. His poem to her declares:

---

4 Eve Salisbury, 'Promiscuous Contexts', in *John Gower: Manuscripts, Readers, Contexts*, ed. Malte Urban (Turnhout, 2010), pp. 228–9.
5 Donald Schueler, 'The Age of the Lover in Gower's *Confessio Amantis*', *Medium Aevum* 36 (1967): 152–8 (155).
6 William George Dodds, *Courtly Love in Gower and Chaucer* (Gloucester, MA, 1959), p. 80.
7 J. A. Burrow, 'The Portrayal of Amans in *Confessio Amantis*', in *Gower's* Confessio Amantis: *Responses and Reassessments*, ed. A. J. Minnis (Cambridge, 1983), pp. 5–24 (p. 16).
8 Quoted in Fisher, *John Gower*, p. 65.

> No peevish winter wind shall chill
> No sullen tropic sun shall wither
> The roses in the rose-garden which is ours and ours only.

Like Gower, Eliot plays with conventional imagery but underlines the depth beyond this in the final lines: 'But this dedication is for others to read: / These are private words addressed to you in public.'[9] The *Confessio* fits this description too, and so could Gower's epitaph for Agnes. It would be prurient to assume more: but the *Confessio* provides plenty of additional evidence that Gower was more than capable of describing passionate feelings convincingly, and Book 6 contains clear proof of this.

Here Amans describes his lady: a paragon of all the conventional virtues, looks and accomplishments (see 6.744–950). However, this courtly picture is then contrasted with the very red-blooded responses she inspires from Gower/Amans, so the shock of finding his virility so completely demolished in Book 8 is all the greater. When Genius is teaching Amans about the sin of gluttony, there is a section about Delicacy, or sensuality. Genius says that the rich and powerful gorge themselves on rich foods, and then turns the imagery into a metaphor for men who seek sexual pleasure with as many partners as they can get. Amans is quick to deny that he is this sort of a lover, and defends himself by continuing the food and cooking tropes in his confession of the extent of his own appetites. But there is an inherent ironic subversion here, as Gower's poetry eroticizes the language, mixing food and sex imagery in an extended exploration of Amans's sensory experience of his lady's charms: each of the three 'foods' that he describes is personified, so that the actions' voyeuristic detail is intensified by this distancing. His eye sees her face, her forehead, her eyes, her nose and her lips, neck, chin and her hands: all these naked parts he can at least view without blame, he says (6.771–81). His eye roves over her body, and he is so struck by her beauty that he says his eye is like a goshawk's piercing gaze. This phallic imagery of the eye as an invasive element is then reversed as it is also described as the 'gate / Thurgh which the deyntes of my thought / Of lust ben to myn herte broght' (6.824–6). Such ocular conturbations cannot satisfy him, however. His ear also feeds him, as he listens to her speaking, singing and reading. His lady's mouth is the source of many delicacies, but, like a 'cherie feste' (8.891) her words are sweet and soon gone. These two foods are but hors d'oeuvres to the third: Hot Thought keeps him sustained when he is alone,

> namelich on nyhtes,
> Whan that me lacketh alle sihtes,
> And that myn heringe is awaie.
> Thanne is he redy in the weie
> Mi rere souper for to make,

---

9   T. S. Eliot, 'Dedication to my Wife', in *Complete Poems and Plays* (Faber, 2004), p. 206.

> Of which myn hertes fode I take.
> This lusti cokes name is hote
> Thoght, which hath evere hise pottes hote
> Of love buillende on the fyr
> With fantasie and with desir. (8.907–16)

Here, the condensed use of heat and fire imagery reveals the banked up desire Amans feels. These lines are erotic, much more so than the passage they are drawn from in the *Romance of the Rose*:[10] in this work the three attributes are described as gifts, not foods, and Douz Pensers (Pleasant Thoughts) is like saccharine compared to the spicy energy that Hot Thought radiates. Alone at night, Amans's imagination, the 'lusti coke' creates his 'rere souper', or late supper. In the online *Middle English Dictionary*, a search of quotations containing this term shows that it always seems to appear with connotations of dangerous illicit behaviour.[11] In the description of the personified Hot Thought as a cook with many dishes bubbling on the fire, a kinetic activity that reflects a masturbatory atmosphere of frustrated fulfilment in the night-time, solitary setting, Gower creates an anti-climactic climactic conclusion to Amans's description of his ability to keep his sensuality in check:

> Bot as of fielinge and of tast,
> Yit mihte I nevere have o repast
> And thus, as I have seid aforn,
> I licke honey on the thorn. (6.925–8)

Far from creating a convincing picture for Genius of a restrained and 'delicat' diet of love, Amans only manages to reveal his deep physical frustrations, and the success of this whole section in building the imagery of food, cooking, flavours and heat into a sensual, voyeuristic experience for the reader means that even the proverb he chooses to illustrate his dilemma becomes an erotic image. Licking the honey on the thorn becomes suggestive because of the sensory overload of the previous 200 lines, and empathizing with Amans's almost resentful self-pity is not difficult, even though it comes dangerously close to bathos.

If, then, Amans is an old man, as is revealed in Book 8, rather than the hot-blooded vigorous lover portrayed here, how can passages like this be reconciled with this 'reality'? The clues are there, I would suggest, in the way that Gower plays with truth and books and his own poetic voice: before Amans speaks, Genius says

> who that loketh on the bokes,
> It seith, confeccion of cokes,

---

[10] See Peter Nicholson, *Love and Ethics in Gower's* Confessio Amantis (Ann Arbor, MI, 2005), p. 435.
[11] *Middle English Dictionary* online, http://quod.lib.umich.edu/cgi/m/mec/med-idx?type=byte&byte=160652506&egdisplay=open&egs=160657970 (accessed 14 November 2012).

> A man him sholde wel avise
> Hou he it toke and in what wise. (6.653–6)

Readers should challenge what books say: 'confeccion' was a noun that could be used to describe a made-up creative output, or a collection of sources, or, even, in another of its meanings, medicine. For the *Confessio*, any of these meanings operates successfully. The Prologue begins with a focus on books, books from the past which instruct people in the present. Gower says he is going to write 'somewhat of lust, somewhat of lore' (Prol. 19) and take the 'middle weie' (Prol. 17) between the two in his book: a book he declares, in the first recension of the poem, will be 'wisdom to the wise / And pleye to hem that lust to pleye' (Prol. 84–5). In the Prologue Gower also reveals that he is sick, but stresses that this will not stop him from carrying out his promise to his king:

> Though I seknesse have upon honed
> And long have had, yit wol I fonde,
> So as I made my byheste,
> To make a book after his heste. (Prol. 79–82)

This sickness is also revealed in the third recension, revised in 1392. The sickness may be a sign of Gower's old age, or it may be a reference to his love-sickness: again, the motif of health and sickness is so well worked in the *Confessio* that it can operate on both levels successfully. In Book 8 Gower ends the poem by saying that he has now finished the book, 'So as siknesse it soffre wolde' (8.3125), and that his muse now tells him that

> it schal be for my beste
> Fro this day forth to take reste,
> That y no more of love make,
> Which many an herte hath overtake. (8.3141–4)

These lines provoke the metaphor further: Gower may be old and 'feble and impotent' (8.3127) physically, but the achievement of the poem undermines any claim that he is either adjective in his poetic creativity. This is the genius, figuratively and literally, both a personified integral part of the poem and of the author of it, which inspires the revelation of Amans as Gower. Gower disrupts the fictional 'bookish' contexts, creating new 'confeccions' in a way that points to an irony in the lack of virility Venus taunts him with.

So, on the question of age, and Amans/Gower's ability to experience love, the expectation should be that the conventions he employs are not the most reliable sources to look at for evidence of this. Indeed, in Book 1 Gower goes to great lengths to emphasize the ungovernable nature of love, and the universality of its part in human life: he will, he says,

> Speke of thing is not so strange,
> Which every kinde hath upon honde,

> And whereupon the world mot stonde,
> And hath don sithen it began,
> And schal whil ther is any man;
> And that is love, of which I mene
> To trete, as after schal be sene,
> In which ther can no man him reule,
> For loves lawe is out of reule (1.10–18)

Amans will, he says, tell of his own blindness as far as love is concerned, revealing his foolhardiness in trusting in the wheel of fortune, 'noght long' (1.64) ago. Love and Fortune, it will be remembered, are both described in the incipit to this first book as being equal in the contest, both turning their blind wheels to entrap people. Even before this, in the Prologue, when Gower sets out his vision, it is important to note that here, through the vision of Nebuchadnezzar, the Apocalypse and the fall of Rome, he links man's inner harmony with the outward workings of the world: following Gregory the Great's ideas of man as a microcosm, he warns 'whan this litel world mistorneth / The grete world al overtorneth' (Prol. 957–8). If the Prologue's arguments are absorbed by the reader, when Amans begins his personal narrative at the start of Book 1, the concepts of division – body and soul, complexion (via the four humours), and hate and love, are understood to underpin all that will follow. All are on a wheel, and Gower will use that verb, 'torneth' again in the final book to emphasize his own exemplification of this earlier warning: Venus will tell him that 'the thing is torned into was' (8.2435) and once the dart of love has been removed from his heart he stands amazed, 'whan al was turnyd into nought' (8.2956).

In common medieval schemes for the ages of Man, old age was said to come at forty-five, and it was seen, in courtly literature, as a barrier to love: specifically passionate sexual love.[12] Andreas Capellanus says that men over the age of sixty cannot feel it,[13] and Guillaume de Lorris describes Old Age as ravaged by time, without reason and wrapped warmly 'for as you know, it is the nature of all old people to be cold'.[14] Perhaps equally relevant, looking at the debt the poem also owes to Ovid's *Amores*, is Ovid's judgement that 'turpe senex miles, turpe senilis amor' ('a shameful thing is an old warrior and an old man in love'):[15] Cicero's *De Officis*, as Burrow points out, also illustrates this point, and Gower used it in the *Mirour de l'Omme*, saying that the philosopher teaches 'Lechery is vile in every case, but in no case is it so vile as in old people'.[16] Nearly three hundred years later, Rochester was to use this still prevailing general view to shock, subverting it by writing 'A Song of a Young Lady to Her

---

[12] See J. A. Burrow, *The Ages of Man: A Study in Medieval Writing and Thought* (Oxford, 1986), pp. 69–70.
[13] Andreas Capellanus, *De Amore*, 'What Persons are Suited for Love'.
[14] Guillaume de Lorris, *The Romance of the Rose*, trans. Frances Horgan (Oxford, 1994), p. 8.
[15] Ovid, *Amores*, I ix 4.
[16] Quoted from Burrow, 'The Portrayal of Amans', p. 15.

Ancient Lover', where the young lady describes how she will 'All the flattering youth defy' to love her elderly amour, 'without art'. Rochester takes the lyrical conventions and pushes them, content-wise, to the limit: this is no passive courtly romance, but a physical, passionate one. The Lady talks of how

> Thy nobler part, which but to name
> In our sex would be counted shame,
> By age's frozen grasp possessed,
> From his ice shall be released,
> And, soothed by my reviving hand,
> In former warmth and vigour stand.[17]

Like Gower, Rochester plays on expectations: the poem is highly artful in form, but does this mean the contents should be doubted? Can a young woman love such an old man 'without art'? The tone is by turns provocative, tender and forcefully seductive. It is also undeniably erotic, and deliberately so. Though Gower may be less overt, he can still portray the heat of love effectively. The difference between their approaches is perhaps what Terry Pratchett described in *Eric*: Gower is 'just erotic. Nothing kinky. It's the difference between using a feather and using a chicken.'[18]

In an essay in the companion volume to this one, Robert Rouse looks at the eroticism of heat:[19] just as he argues for a connection between the heat of summer and sexual desire, there is also a connection between the heat associated with youth and sexuality, and this connection works in its negative pairing of age and loss of sexual capability, too. According to Shulamith Shahar, 'the accepted theory was that with the diminution of natural heat and the radical moisture an old man's desires cool, including the sexual desire'.[20] The 'firy dart' (1.144) that the King of Love throws at Amans (whether for mischief or for anger) compounds his love-sick state: he is full of a vigour that belies his years. As readers encounter Amans for the first time, there are no obvious clues to his age[21] (all except one known manuscript depict a young Amans kneeling before Genius in illuminations at the beginning of the work[22]), so that the deception plays on the readers' own pre-suppositions about lovers and their ages. It is not until Book 8, when, still 'fulfilt of loves fantasie' (8.2211),

---

[17] 'A Young Lady to her Ancient Lover', in *John Wilmot, Earl of Rochester: The Complete Works*, ed. Frank H. Ellis (London, 1994) p. 71.
[18] Terry Pratchett, *Eric* (London, 2000), p. 8.
[19] Robert Allen Rouse, '"Some Like it Hot": The Medieval Eroticism of Heat', in *The Erotic in the Literature of Medieval Britain*, ed. Amanda Hopkins and Cory Rushton (Cambridge, 2007), pp. 71–81.
[20] Shulamith Shakar, *Growing Old in the Middle Ages: Winter Clothes Us in Shadow and Pain* (London, 1997), p. 77.
[21] Although some critics have argued that clues are there: see, for instance, Schueler, 'The Age of the Lover', 152–8.
[22] This is Bodley 902, fol. 8r. For a discussion of the illuminations in manuscripts of the *Confessio*, see Derek Pearsall, 'The Manuscripts and Illustrations of Gower's Works', in *A Companion to Gower*, ed. Siân Echard (Cambridge, 2004), pp. 73–97.

Amans writes his letter to Venus, that the reality is made clear, and the lack of fundamental heat, or youth, exposed:

> Non estatis opus gelidis hirsute capillis,
> Cum calor abcessit, equiperabit hiems;
> Sicut habet Mayus non dat natura Decembri,
> Nec poterit compar floribus esse lutum;
> Sic neque decrita senium iuvenile voluptas
> Floret in obsequium quod Venus ipsa petit.
> Conveniens igitur foret, vt quos cana senectus
> Attigit, vlterius corpora casta colant. (8.iii)[23]

Here the ice/heat, winter/summer, age/youth oppositions are unequivocally blunt: the authoritative tone in this Latin insertion is preparation for Venus's equally brutal pronouncement that 'Loves lust and lockes hore / In chamber acorden nevermore' (8.2403–4). The descriptions here focus on the body – and on the implicit sexual activities that Amans/Gower is no longer capable of. Venus is not pulling any punches:

> 'Min herte wolde and I ne may'
> Is noght beloved nou adayes;
> Er thou make eny suche assaies
> To love, and faile upon the fet,
> Betre is to make a beau retret; (8.2412–16)

This section of the *Confessio* compares uncomfortably with the erotic good fortunes of the lover at the end of the *Romance of the Rose*, as Venus continues to underline Gower's impotence, that inability 'to holde love his covenant' (8.2420). His will may be strong, but 'mor behoveth to the plowh, / Whereof thee lacketh, as I trowe' (8.2426–7), she says, and 'What bargain sholde a man assaie, / Whan that him lacketh for to paie?' (8.2431–2).

However, there are other French poems that include discussions of love and old age which Ardis Butterfield has argued have close affinities with Gower. Machaut's *Voir Dit*, a collection of letters and lyrics between the elderly poet and a young girl, also includes elements of a possible autobiographical truth in the narrator's role: this poem 'ends in hope rather than fact – the kind of hope that contains within it a powerfully suppressed sense of incipient failure'.[24] Froissart's *Le Joli Buisson de Jonece*, which also ends in a failed romance, shows an aging poet unable to compose because it is so long since he was in love. He is rejuvenated by a dream showing him his lady as she was ten years ago. He

---

[23] 'Winter, hairy with icy locks, is not equal to summer's work, when its heat has receded. Nature does not give to December just as May has, nor can clay compare to flowers; and thus old men's lust does not flower in youthful compliance, as Venus herself demands. It would be appropriate therefore, for those whom white old age touches henceforth to cultivate chaste bodies.'

[24] Ardis Butterfield, '*Confessio Amantis* and the French Tradition', in *A Companion to Gower*, ed. Echard, pp. 165–80 (p. 179).

is, however, awakened from this dream to realize that this past is just that, and any more such thoughts are not suitable for someone of his age. The end is a *lai* to the Virgin Mary. Gower's debt to these two poems can be easily seen, but Gower's use of the confession as a frame, and the exempla that form the vehicle for Amans's progress, make his portrayal of the elderly lover/poet far more complicated: likewise, J. A. Burrow has drawn attention to Froissart's *Espinette Amoreuse*, which, he argues, gives the tradition from which the self-portrait of Gower as Amans is drawn.[25] More recently, Ad Putter has written about old age in the poems of Charles d'Orléans and Langland, and shows how these two poets give sharply differing approaches to it: Langland's more explicit descriptions are 'less tidy, less cerebral, and embarrassingly physical'[26] than the later poet's, but Charles writes very much more in the courtly vein, and with material in one particular instance that is very similar to that of the *Confessio*.[27] Gower's portrayal of age is clearly something more complex that either of these approaches, but contains elements of both attitudes, as well as those of Froissart, Machaut and classical authors. The *Confessio* shows age as both messy and natural, comic and poignant, and, in its portrayal of Amans, who is fictional and oddly real as Amans-as-Gower, the Lover is shown to be a puzzle of nature. He should, by all conventions, be past the age of loving, and yet, clearly, he is not.

Book 8 confronts these conventions: by naming himself as Amans, Gower deliberately disrupts the narrative conventions he has used to this point. By withholding Amans's true age and persona from the reader, Gower exposes and plays with the reader's own prejudices about love: while Genius is retelling stories as exempla for Amans (and the reader) to reflect on and learn from, Gower-as-writer is skilfully building a kaleidoscopic context of experiences and attitudes that shift so often it is difficult to navigate through with confidence. Divisions run deep in this poem, and divisiveness is at the core of the themes of both love and good governance right from the beginning: Book 1 begins with an incipit that stresses the restless paradoxes of love, 'Est amor egra salus, vexata quies, pius error, / Bellica pax, vulnus dulce, suaue malum' ('Love is a sharp salvation, a troubled quiet, a pious error, a warring peace, a sweet wound, a soothing ill'), and the gloss to the side of this first section underlines the strength of this feeling: 'nonnulli amantes ultra quam expedit desiderii passionibus crebro stimulantur' ('some lovers are often goaded by the passions of desire beyond what is appropriate').

Love is dangerous, then: it destabilizes reason, and being 'oute of reule'(1.18) is beyond any human capability to control or predict. 'Ther is no man / In al

---

[25] Burrow, 'The Portrayal of Amans', p. 8.
[26] Ad Putter, 'Personifications of Old Age in Medieval Poetry: Charles D'Orléans and William Langland', *Review of English Studies* 63 (2011): 388–409 (409).
[27] See Putter, 'Personifications', pp. 400–1. The ballade sequence (entitled the *Songe en complainte* in the French) has no title in English; its incipit is 'Aftir the day, that made is for travayle', line 2540 in *Fortunes Stablines: Charles of Orleans's English Book of Love*, ed. Mary Jo Arn (Binghamton, NY, 1994).

this world so wys, that can / Of love tempre the mesure' (1.21–3), yet God, who keeps all of Nature in balance, has set this 'thing' (1.31) and Gower says that his poem will try and tell people about his own 'unsely jolif wo' (1.88) so that they might learn from his experiences. Already, like tectonic plates moving beneath the surface, the opposing forces of love and reason are causing ripples of tension: the poem is a huge mass of words, but peculiarly and poignantly specific in the placing of key terms or phrases. The 'thing' will return in Book 8, and sits in this first book like a carefully cloaked time-bomb: which, in the scheme of the whole poem, it figuratively is.

There are 469 uses of the word 'thing' in the *Confessio*, and a further ninety-seven uses of 'thinges',[28] a high enough dose to justify closer examination. Ad Putter has written about Gower's use of 'thing', beginning by looking at the line in Book 8 that has just been referred to, when Venus, concluding her lecture on Gower's impotence, tells him not to forget that 'The thing is torned into was' (8.2435). This wonderful line, as Putter says, 'shows Gower at his most inventive', as the verb turns into a noun, intensifying the underlying sense of an active sexual state turning into an inert one. The 'thing' here is a euphemism for sexual virility in a general sense, as well as the particular love affair Amans/Gower has been pursuing during the poem. It can also be seen as referring specifically to the penis: just as the Wife of Bath refers to male and female sexual organs as 'bothe thynges smale' (III.121) Venus is clearly, in the context of the passage, talking about impotence, as has already been explored. It is also provocative, for the way that Gower has used 'thing' in the rest of the *Confessio* means that it resonates with much more than just a comment on the poet's personal condition. Putter explains:

> The most obvious connection is that 'thing' is typically anaphoric, referring back to something that has already been mentioned, and to that extent presupposes a prior discourse, a pre-text. The word thus lies, interestingly, somewhere in between the category of noun and pronoun. Syntactically, it behaves like a noun, but semantically and pragmatically it has all the characteristics of a pronoun. Like a pronoun, it has little or no inherent meaning. If it is not anaphoric it refers to something that is about to be introduced or points exophorically to something that is accessible to both speakers from their communicative situation or from common knowledge.[29]

What Putter does not expand upon, though, is the *amount* of pre-texts that exist in the *Confessio* leading up to this line in Book 8. There are enough for a rewarding separate study of these to be undertaken, but for the purposes of this essay it is important to note how the erotic connotations 'thing' can hold

---

[28] See *A Concordance to John Gower's* Confessio Amantis, ed. J. D. Pickles and J. L. Dawson (Cambridge, 1987).
[29] Ad Putter, 'The Poetry of "Things" in Gower, *The Great Gatsby*, and Chaucer', in *The Construction of Textual Identity in Medieval and Early Modern Literature*, ed. Indira Ghose and Denis Renevey (Tübingen, 2009), pp. 63–82 (p. 64).

are connected to wider political, spiritual and legal 'things'. Putter looks at the rape of Helen in Book 5, where Paris's men are told to be ready and armed 'For certein thing which was to done' (5.7530): this shows how 'the dramatic power of the passage depends on the stirring of a secret'.[30] This is not the only place such a dangerous secret sexual 'thing' appears. Look, for instance, in Book 8 at the start of the tale of Apollonius, when Antiochus rapes his own daughter and she 'lay stille, and of this thing / Withinne hirself such sorghe made, / Ther was no wight that mihte hir glade' (8.314–16). Her nurse cannot see a solution to stopping it happening again, and Genius comments 'Whan thing is do, ther is no bote, / So suffren thei that suffre mote' (8.339-40). The link between sexual 'things' and secrets, or mysteries in the wider sense is unavoidable in the *Confessio*: in the first ten lines of the Prologue it is used three times:

> It stant noght in my sufficance
> So grete *thinges* to compasse,
> Bot I mot lete it overpasse
> And treten upon other *thinges*,
> Forthi the stile of my writings
> From this day forth I thenke change
> And speke of *thing* is noght so strange,
> Which every kinde hath on honed. (Prol. 4–11)

The shift Gower makes here, from the huge mysteries, or things, which he cannot grasp, to the more earth-bound ones that he can (and will, pulling in themes of governance and rule), to the very specific 'thing', love, which every individual can experience and understand, is a masterly summary of what his *Confessio* will do.

According to C. S. Lewis, who considered Andreas Capellanus's *De Amore* to hold the key to appreciating Gower's *Confessio*, the way that this earlier work extended the erotic code so that 'it almost coincided with the ethical code'[31] gave Gower the scope to enlarge this into the framework of his own book. Andreas 'proposes both to teach and repudiate passionate love',[32] and Gower, too, manages to merge these two seeming opposites into a poem that is didactic and entertaining, sober and yet full of joy. The use of 'thing' to contain all these conflicting ideas is one of the key linguistic tools Gower uses to achieve this. As Putter concludes, '"thing" may not look like a poetic word but modern writers and medieval writers appreciated its versatility and its usefulness. As John Gower and F. Scott Fitzgerald understood, the word is great at keeping secrets.'[33]

---

[30] Putter, 'The Poetry of "Things"', p. 66.
[31] C. S. Lewis, *The Allegory of Love* (Oxford, 1936), p. 199.
[32] Robert R. Edwards, *The Flight from Desire: Augustine and Ovid to Chaucer* (Basingstoke, 2006), p. 5.
[33] Putter, 'The Poetry of "Things"', pp. 79–80.

The paradoxical nature of love, stated right at the start of the poem, binds the narratives, both exemplary stories and the frame of the confession between Amans and Genius: while the priest and his pupil pull in opposing directions, the exempla-driven journey through the seven deadly sins builds links and destroys obstacles between them. Love is the thematic vehicle that Genius emphasizes holds all this together: 'I with love am al witholde' (1.263). Amans must listen, and he must learn, so that his confession can be honestly made. The *Confessio* is 'a dialogue between a profoundly divided pupil and a profoundly divided teacher. The end result is a profoundly and insurmountably divided text.'[34] These divisions are not flaws in the poetic construction, however, but reflections of the struggles going on as Amans tries to learn and eventually accept the lessons Genius is showing him. They are also completely in accord with the Prologue's emphasis on the divisions in the world: 'Division aboven alle / Is thing which makth the world to falle' (Prol. 971–2). 'Thing' here becomes a massive, critical fault-line, compared with the use of it at line 930, where Gower emphasizes the importance of harmony, with 'every thyng in his degree' reflecting the order of the regulated universe.

The Prologue also glorifies the past as a time of ideal life: 'If I shal drawe into my mynde / The tyme passed, thanne I fynde / The world stod thanne in al his welthe' (Prol. 93–5). The past, like Amans's youth, is a golden age: an age of opportunity, of lawfulness, and a time when there was 'unenvied love' (Prol. 115). In expanding this depiction of the past into a commentary on the present, Gower stresses that love's absence from the world now is the cause of all the unrest and upset. Just as Amans is disturbed by his amorous feelings, so too is the wider world out of kilter with what is right, in loving terms. Love is, in Gower, all around: the *Confessio* 'employs the language of courtesy or erotic petition in order to explore the much more dangerous subject of power – individual, communal, and regal'.[35]

At the end of the tale of Apollonius, discord seems everywhere, as Amans and the priest argue with each other, Amans refusing to accept what the priest tells him, angrily accusing him of not understanding – 'Mi wo to you is bot a game, / That fielen noght of that I fiele' (8.2152–3) – while Genius, rather tetchily, becomes more forceful: 'Yit is time to withdrawe' (8.2133) and finally, exasperated, 'Now ches if thou wolt live or deie' (8.2148). As Ardis Butterfield has pointed out, this quarrel provokes a narrative break, as the poem's form shifts from couplets to the twelve rhyme-royal stanzas of Amans's letter to Venus. This literal transformation of the poem breaks itself in a succeeding series of revelations, the first and most dramatic being the disclosure of Amans as Gower himself. This is not going to be an easy ending: acceptance of old age, and putting romantic, erotic love aside, in both literal senses of physically and creatively, mean that 'the process of knitting things together is itself painful

---

34 Alice Spencer, *Dialogues of Love and Government: A Study of the Erotic Dialogue Form in Some Texts from the Courtly Love Tradition* (Cambridge, 2007), p. 186.
35 Lynn Staley, *The Languages of Power in the Age of Richard II* (University Park, PA, 2005), p. 2.

and discordant'.³⁶ Amans has listened to over a hundred stories, the majority of which do not have love as their major theme,³⁷ and he cannot yet appreciate their relevance to his plight, or see the future that awaits him.

When Venus tells him to remember that he is old (8.2439), Gower is hit with a cold feeling so strongly that he faints, and has a dream where young lovers come and appear before him, 'with here loves glade and blithe' (8.2539). He sees happy lovers, unhappy lovers, a 'grete compaignie' (8.2659) who reference many of the stories mentioned earlier in the *Confessio*. Gower then sees Elde coming towards the field, and he also has 'gret compaignie / Bot noght so manye as Youthe hadde' (8.2669–70). Elde comes 'a softe pas' (8.2667), a phrase that also crops up several times in the *Confessio*,³⁸ culminating in the end lines of the poem, where Gower says 'homward a softe pas y wente' (8.2967). Literally meaning coming slowly, or softly, 'softe' can also be used to describe the feebleness of age, and the slowness of a medicine's efficiency, or to describe a slow and prolonged death.³⁹ Yet again Gower shows how word choice can reflect a Russian doll-like series of meanings, for the 'softe pas' is his own slow journey towards peace, even as it is also a gradual healing learning process which shows the death of one key part of the human experience of love.

The elderly lovers depicted in his dream (King David, Solomon, Aristotle, Virgil, Socrates, Plato and Ovid) allow Gower to feel 'lasse aschamed' (8.2722) of his own feelings, and to hope for grace from Venus. These lovers pray to Venus for Gower, and soon their voices are joined by the younger ones, and the noise presses in on Gower from all sides. Some say that 'for no riote / An old man scholde noght assote' (8.2765–6), but others dispute this, saying 'that the wylde love rage / In mannes lif forberth non age' (8.2773–4). This passage is an important one: Gower brings in examples of elderly lovers to support his case that love can exist at an advanced age, and that no one is immune from love's impact. When Cupid takes pity on him, and withdraws the 'fyri lancegay' (8.2798) from his heart, all these lovers, and Cupid himself, vanish, and Gower is left alone with Venus and Genius. Venus anoints him with a cream which soothes his damaged heart and allows him to see himself as Venus sees him. This 'wonder mirour' (8.2821) reflects, finally, Gower's physical appearance, and like the portrayal of the ugly old woman in the Tale of Florent, it is not a pretty sight:

> Myn yhen dymme and al unglade,
> Mi chiekes thinne, and al my face

---

36 Ardis Butterfield, 'French Culture and the Ricardian Court', in *Essays on Ricardian Poetry in Honour of J. A. Burrow*, ed. A. J. Minnis, Charlotte C. Morse, and Thorlac Turville-Petre (Oxford, 1997).
37 For a breakdown of the stories into main themes, see Fisher, *John Gower*, p. 188.
38 See for example, 2.1509, 3.1386, 7.4970.
39 See *Middle English Dictionary* online: http://quod.lib.umich.edu/cgi/m/mec/med-idx?type =byte&byte=185152995&egdisplay=open&egs=185229523&egs=185232913 (accessed 19 November 2012).

> With elde I myhte se deface,
> So riveled and so wo besein,
> That ther was nothing full ne plein,
> I syh also myn heres hore. (8.2826–31)

This ruthless self-observation could be seen as part of a defeat of some sort, but Gower does not make himself into an object of pity. Venus gives him some black beads which have the words 'por reposer' – 'for rest' – on them. She urges him to take reason as his guide from now on, and to reject love, 'which takth litel hiede / Of olde men upon the nede, / Whan that the lustes ben awaie' (8.2915–17). Moreover, she says she will never speak to or see him again, because it is outside the law of her community. As we have seen before, this is harsh treatment, but Gower, after standing 'amasid' for a while, begins to smile as he thinks about the black beads (8.2957–8), and what they mean. He finds joy in the comfort that prayer will bring, and is able to go home with a 'softe pas' because he is shriven and healed and content.

Critics have seen the end of the *Confessio* as full of a sense of defeat: Diane Watt concludes 'even at its closure, *Confessio Amantis* is characterized not by success but by failure, not by reconciliation but by division'[40] and Peter Nicholson suggests that 'Gower speaks fully in his own voice now, and when he refers to love, it as one who has written about love rather than as one who has experienced it.'[41] Winthrop Wetherbee is more forthright: 'the questions of Gower's priest-confessor Genius gradually unveil the futility and self-delusion of Amans, his inability to engage the sexual and social realities of love directly.'[42] I cannot agree with any of these judgements: Gower ends the poem successfully at peace with love, shriven by Genius, and by the confession the poem relates. Confession brings release and, importantly, it does bring reconciliation: reconciliation with reason and with God. The Christian context of this poem, emphatically brought in here, as it was at the start of the poem, underlines the Christian message that love, as charity, will bring access to heaven, where 'oure joie mai ben endeles' (8.3172). As Robert Edwards explains: 'for Christian writers, the objects of erotic investment are, at least from the retrospective of grace, signs of a divine providence that subsumes all desire.'[43] There is acceptance of a new view of life, of new priorities and new explorations, not a portrait of a man defeated, or even of a man saying that love has been an illusion. Unlike many of the sources, Amans is not part of an elaborate dream sequence: the fact that he is revealed to be Gower emphasizes the attempt to make his experiences more real, more relevant to the audience receiving them. Amans becomes Gower so that the poem becomes

---

[40] Watt, *Amoral Gower*, p. 160.
[41] Nicholson, *Love and Ethics*, p. 392.
[42] Winthrop Wetherbee, 'Latin Structure and Vernacular Space: Gower, Chaucer and the Boethian Tradition', in *Chaucer and Gower: Difference, Mutuality, Exchange*, ed. R. F. Yeager (Victoria, BC, 1999), p. 8.
[43] Edwards, *The Flight from Desire*, p. 7.

a very potent and ultimately optimistic experience. Age will come to all, just as love will, but there are positives. There is no delusion: love happens to old people – to all people. It is part of 'all thinges' (8.2981) that God makes, and Gower repeatedly reminds the reader of this. And the confession itself shows that although Amans is frustrated in his ambitions for love, he is certainly not unengaged from the realities of the situation he finds himself in. 'By elevating love as a topic for serious literary treatment, medieval writers provided the necessary condition – a structure of established conventions, generic codes, and readerly expectations – for expressing desire, even if such expression is oblique or only partially acknowledged or even disavowed.'[44] Desire is deeply embedded in the *Confessio*, and Amans is shown as a passionate lover, aroused by the sight, sound and thought of his lady. Gower uses literature as a means to portray the mundane and the sublime, the pain and the relief from that pain, the macrocosmic view and the microcosmic, too. In this he achieves, simultaneously, a constantly mirroring set of exempla and narratives and a bigger reflective surface that makes the poem itself an experience 'por reposer' for the reader: 'Texts not only convey movements of the soul toward objects invested with beauty and value; they can also constitute such objects themselves in the pleasures of reading and imagination.'[45]

In Southwark Cathedral, Gower's tomb still stands today, but his bones have long since disappeared. There is, as Rosamund Allen argues, a 'double paradox' in this tomb, commissioned by the poet himself, for here his effigy, 'attired like a courtier-lover, like Amans in fact' stands witness to the 'eternally pristine quality of poetic fame in the face of worldly dissolution'. This seems ironic, when all of Gower's major works stress the transience of life: but they also stress the immortality of the Christian spiritual life, too. Gower constantly revised his poems when he was alive, and indeed, they survived and have been revived in the centuries since: his tomb, too, has seen several refurbishments and redecoration, so that today it looks astonishingly bright with colour, and Gower 'wearing a chaplet of roses, still gazes at a rose-strewn vault more emblematic of eternal youth than of the mysteries of heaven'.[46] The roses symbolize youth – and love. Ultimately Gower shows that the lessons of love, whether taught by Venus or by God, to young or to old, are timeless. Or, as J. A. Burrow admits:

> More than any other medieval poem known to me, accordingly, *Confessio Amantis* conveys what it must feel like to be a *senex amans* – which is much the same as what it feels like to be any other sort of lover.[47]

---

44 Edwards, *The Flight from Desire*, p. 165.
45 Edwards, *The Flight from Desire*, p. 9.
46 Rosamund S. Allen, 'John Gower and Southwark: The Paradox of the Social Self', in *London and Europe in the Later Middle Ages*, ed. Julia Boffey and Pamela King (Exeter, 1995), pp. 111–47 (147).
47 J. A. Burrow, *The Ages of Man: A Study in Medieval Writing and Thought* (Oxford, 1986), pp. 160–1.

6
'Bogeysliche as a boye': Performing Sexuality in William of Palerne

HANNAH PRIEST

THE Middle English alliterative verse *William of Palerne* (sometimes known by its early title, *William and the Werewolf*) is a fourteenth-century translation of the Old French *Guillaume de Palerne*. Both the English and French narratives tell the interlinked stories of William, a prince of Palerne, who escapes from the plotting of his murderous uncle with the help of a benevolent werewolf, and of Alphons, the Spanish prince who is forced into lycanthropic form by his necromantic stepmother. There are, however, some striking differences between the insular and continental versions of the story (which also appears in later English and French prose versions, as well as an Irish adaptation), and this essay will go some way to examining what we might note as a particular thematic concern of the Middle English verse narrative. In his 1985 edition of the poem, G. H. V. Bunt argues that the English poet 'has written a very different poem from his French source', and I would like to offer some exploration of themes of sexual and gender performance which I believe characterize the English poem particularly.[1] The first half of the English *William* reveals a preoccupation with disguise and role-playing, which is not found in the French source text. This is especially apparent in the presentation of the relationship between William and Melior, the emperor of Rome's daughter, and in their meeting, attraction and elopement. As I will show, the disguises employed to facilitate this relationship, provided by Melior's handmaiden Alisaundrine, offer opportunities for 'bending' gender positions, without rejecting 'essential' gendered identities. Melior performs a conventionally 'male' mode of sexuality when she first meets and woos William; Alisaundrine dresses as a boy in order to help the lovers elope. This gender-bending then extends further, and the text provides instances of 'species-bending', perhaps as the next logical step. These superficial

---

[1] *William of Palerne: An Alliterative Romance*, ed. G. H. V. Bunt (Groningen, 1985), p. 36.

metamorphoses are characteristic of the English text, and might be read alongside other instances of transformation and love in insular romance. I will conclude by exploring the implications of the narrative's early concern with 'fancy dress' and disguise for the way in which we read the figure of the werewolf. In order to understand the presentation of the English Alphons, it is necessary to examine the way ambiguities of gender and species identity are constructed within the poem.

Melior first falls in love with the eponymous hero William after he has been discovered living as the foster son of a cowherd by the emperor of Rome. Taken to court, William is entrusted into the care of Melior, who soon falls in love with the boy. What follows (after a missing folio) is a lengthy speech by Melior, who describes and bemoans the 'sickness' into which she has fallen. It becomes clear from this monologue that Melior's love for William is decidedly 'courtly'. She begins by debating what is to blame for her suffering, pathologizing her love by cursing in turn her 'wicked eyiȝen' (458) and her 'wicked hert' (482).[2] Although Melior has known William for several years at this point, her love for him has not grown gradually over time, but rather has attacked her suddenly and without warning. Indeed, the woman herself describes it as having 'pierced' her heart (612), following the courtly love topos of love-as-wounding. Her description of the 'attack' reminds us of James Schultz's formulation of courtly lovers as going about their daily business 'until some particular attribute of a particular individual impinges upon them, penetrates to the core of their being and causes them to be captivated by love'.[3] Once struck by love, Melior dwells on the beauty of her beloved, with a repeated emphasis on sight and eyes:

> I have him portreide an paynted in mi hert wiþinne,
> þat he sittus in mi siȝt, me þinkes, evermore;
> and faire so his figure is festened in mi ȝout,
> þat wiþ no coyntise ne craft ne can y it out scrape. (445–8)

Melior goes on to refer to her love as a sickness and an 'evele' (558), wishing for a 'leche' (576) who might cure her, and worrying that one might not be found. There follows a brief summary of the standard symptoms of love-sickness that afflict Melior: she does not sleep; she does not eat; her physical health begins to fail; she pines; her complexion loses its colour (571–9). She feels love as a 'suffering' and attributes its cause to her sight of William: 'what sorwes and sikingges I suffer for his sake!' (566). In this respect, the princess's love for the young man appears to meets the criteria for Andreas Capellanus's definition of 'Love': 'an inborn suffering which results from the sight of, and uncontrolled thinking about, the beauty of the opposite sex'.[4]

---

[2] All line references are to Bunt's edition.
[3] James Schultz, *Courtly Love, the Love of Courtliness, and the History of Sexuality* (Chicago and London, 2006), p. 75.
[4] *Andreas Capellanus on Love*, ed. and trans. P. G. Walsh (London, 1982), p. 33.

However, in one very important respect, Melior is not the typical courtly lover. She is, of course, a woman. It should be remembered here that Capellanus – and, indeed, Schultz at that particular point in his study – refers to *male* lovers and *female* beloveds. If she adopts the typically masculine position of afflicted lover, rather than objectified beloved, to what extent can we say that Melior appropriates a masculine mode of sexuality? Melior's love-sickness is not gender-bending in itself. Other women in Middle English romance also suffer forms of the condition, and unrequited love can sometimes cause a woman to pine and sicken. However, though Melior's physical health is affected by her emotional state, she does not waste away or die as a result of her love for William. Instead, she ends the second part of her speech by swearing an oath to God, declaring that she will freely give her love to William for the rest of his life (569–70). The active agency of this oath – and her actions that follow it – sets Melior apart from women such as Malory's Elaine of Astolat, for example, who 'cryed and wepte as she had bene wood' and eventually dies because she 'had no myght to withstonde the fervent love' she feels for Lancelot.[5] Carolyn Hares-Stryker describes Malory's Elaine as 'a provincial and poignantly naïve' woman, who is 'ignorant' of the conventions of courtly romance.[6] Though she might claim that her love will leave her 'ded as dorenail' (628), Melior performs a very different mode of sexuality to that of a passive lover such as Elaine of Astolat. She is neither 'provincial' nor 'naïve', as the daughter of the emperor of Rome; moreover, the *gendering* of her complaint problematizes her relationship to the conventions of romance without merely implying ignorance.

William of Palerne's love-sick heroine repeatedly blames her eyes and her heart for the pain she feels. What is striking is that these organs are gendered male, and are presented in an almost feudal relationship to one another, and to the rest of her identity:

> Min ei3en sorly aren sogettes to serve min hert,
> and buxom ben to his bidding, as boie to his master. (463–4)

Melior's eyes, then, behave like a 'boie', while her heart is the 'master'. This gendering of the heart and eyes continues throughout the monologue, and yet Melior seeks to distance her own identity (the 'I' of the speech) from the wickedness of these 'male' treacheries. She sets her reason against her eyes and heart, declaring:

> What? fy! Schold I a fundeling for his fairenesse tak?
> Nay, my wille wol nou3t asent to my wicked hert. (481–2)

---

5 Thomas Malory, 'The Book of Sir Launcelot and Queen Guinevere', in *Works*, ed. Eugène Vinaver, 2nd edn (Oxford and New York, 1971), pp. 609 70, p. 636, 640 (Book XVIII, Chapters 17–19).
6 Carolyn Hares-Stryker, 'The Elaine of Astolat and Lancelot Dialogues: A Confusion of Intent', *Texas Studies in Literature and Language* 39:3 (1997): 205–30 (221).

She goes on to state that to lay her love 'so lowe' (484) – i.e. on the foundling William – would be a disgusting and monstrous thing, and if she found herself doing so she would 'blame [her] hert' (486). Thus, for a moment, the masculine mask of 'courtly lover' slips, and we see the cool, rational (if somewhat imperious) princess beneath. Melior's eyes might behave like a 'boie', but her 'wille' is that of an emperor's daughter. Her 'What? fy!' interjection represents both a change in tone and a change in the identity position being expressed. Melior moves, though only momentarily, from the love-sick knight to the haughty (unattainable) lady, from a normative male sexuality to a normative female sexuality. This reveals a fluidity of gender categories, which will continue throughout Melior and William's early relationship.

Her potentially masculinized performance of love notwithstanding, Melior does not continue to behave like a lovesick knight. She does not, for example, swear herself symbolically into William's service. Rather, she draws on a typically feminine romance relationship to seek a cure: she asks for help from her resourceful handmaiden Alisaundrine. The initial presentation of Melior's kinswoman and confidante here follows a familiar pattern which can be found elsewhere in romance: for example, Lunete in *Ywain and Gawain*, sits in 'gude cownsayl' with the suffering Alundyne, just as Alisaundrine offers 'cunsail' (595) to Melior.[7] Like Lunete, Alisaundrine's lady comes to her for help and advice, and the handmaiden uses her cunning and wisdom to alleviate her lady's suffering. Continuing the image of sickness and healing, Alisaundrine offers a 'grece' to cure Melior and 'vanisch [her] soris' (639). As it transpires, the 'grece' will not be used on Melior, but on William: the medicine the woman needs is a love potion. Alisaundrine's 'grece' is not found in the French source. In the continental verse, though the handmaiden offers assistance to the lovers, she does not effect any love magic. The hero falls in love with heroine as the result of an unexplained erotic dream, and not in consequence of affirmative action on the part of the women.[8]

Judith Weiss argues that, although they appear in some Anglo-Norman and Middle English romances, 'wooing women are not the heroines of French romances; they are not presented with sympathy or admiration'.[9] The shift, then, from the French handmaiden's suggestions of an interview with Guillaume to the English women's decisive (and bodily) 'assault' on William is perhaps in keeping with narrative tropes found in some insular romance, as opposed to its continental counterpart. However, while Melior does take action in order to acquire her beloved, she does not fully fit with Weiss's

---

7   *Ywain and Gawain* in *Middle English Romances*, ed. Stephen Shepherd (New York and London, 1995), pp. 75–173, line 939.
8   *Guillaume de Palerne*, ed. Alexandre Micha (Geneva, 1990), lines 1082–108. All subsequent references to *Guillaume de Palerne* will be taken from this edition.
9   Judith Weiss, 'The Wooing Woman in Anglo-Norman Romance', in *Romance in Medieval England*, ed. Maldwyn Mills, Jennifer Fellows and Carol M. Meale (Cambridge, 1991), pp. 149–62 (p. 149).

formulation of the insular 'wooing woman'. While Melior does help to 'chart' the 'development' of William into 'an active and positive figure', the episode with the 'grece' is not 'used humorously, to burlesque ... or simply to make us laugh at a reluctant lover'.[10] In truth, it is hard to argue that Melior (or Alisaundrine as her proxy) 'woo' William at all, as in actuality they drug him to ensure compliance. What follows might be read 'humorously', but the happy resolution of the William/Melior plot demonstrates that the outcome, far from being a 'burlesque', is the best result for both participants. Moreover, Melior's performance of love-sickness, more usually associated with chivalric male sexuality, further distances her from this particular romance characterization of femininity.

The love-sick woman and her cunning maid show a considerable amount of agency in their plan to make William fall in love: Melior is not a passive sufferer. But the decisive action of the women is thrown into sharper relief by the presentation of William's passivity and youthfulness – and by the immediate (and comic) consequences of the love potion. During her declaration of love, Melior repeatedly refers to William as a 'child' and a 'barne', and insists that he has no knowledge of the 'kraft' of love (540–66). When Alisaundrine sneaks into the sleeping boy's room to administer her potion, he is again referred to as a 'child' (656). The young man here is presented as innocent and inexperienced, and completely at the mercy of the 'conyng' women who act around him. If, as Ruth Mazo Karras suggests, '[l]ate medieval knightly masculinity was defined by sexual object choice', what happens to the man if he himself is the 'object' or the 'choice'?[11] The construction of the child William through the gaze of the apparently more (socially) experienced Melior results in the objectification of the young man. This is heightened by the addition of the love potion plot by the English redactor.

As a result of the potion, William begins to dream of Melior, clasping his pillow and greeting it as though it was the princess. The scene continues:

> Þat pulvere clept he curteisly and kust it ful ofte,
> and made þerwiþ þe most merþe þat any man schold. (675–6)

Although the reader is not explicitly told what the 'most merþe' a man can have is, the implication here is that William has sex with his pillow while he dreams of Melior. This reading is supported by reference to other uses of the word 'mirth' to connote sexual activity in romance.[12] When William later agonizes over the events of the previous night, he claims that he and his lady had been 'lakyng togaderes' (699) and that he had enjoyed 'his layk wiþ þe ladi

---

[10] Weiss, 'The Wooing Woman in Anglo-Norman Romance', pp. 156 and 160.
[11] Ruth Mazo Karras, *From Boys to Men: Formations of Masculinity in Late Medieval Europe* (Philadelphia, 2003), p. 50.
[12] See, for example, the repetition of the word 'myrthe' to describe Gawain's nightly activities with his new wife in *The Wedding of Sir Gawain and Dame Ragnelle* and the night of 'play' the same knight enjoys with his host's daughter in *Sir Gawain and the Carl of Carlisle*.

to pleie' (678). This use of the word 'pleie' links to the earlier word 'merþe', suggesting love-play. The humour here lies in the fact that, while William believed he was engaged in play with his 'ladi', in truth he has 'clept' and 'kust' his 'pulvere'.

The pillow-dream is not found in the French *Guillaume*. The earlier text offers an expanded (and eroticized) description of Guillaume's vision of Melior, without drawing attention to the practical reality of what the knight's body is doing as he dreams (1118–68). The Middle English addition of the pillow directs the audience's attention to the discrepancy between William's mental and physical performances, entailing that the young knight's body becomes a (potentially comic) focus. The man is understandably confused when he wakes and looks around his chamber for the woman with whom he believes he has spent the night. Eventually, he realizes it was a 'fanteme' (703) and falls into despondency.

William's response to his dream is curious. It could be argued that the 'child' William, on the course to becoming a knight, has befouled himself with a strange sinful mixture of nocturnal emission, masturbation and the dishonouring of his lord's property (both in the actual despoiling of his furniture and the imagined defloration of his daughter). And yet William's despondency does not result from a realization of shame, but rather from his regret that, when he woke up, the woman of his dreams was no longer present. We might contrast this with another (somewhat different) example of a man having sex with household objects drawn from medieval literature. In the *vita* of St Anastasia found in Jacobus de Voragine's *Legenda Aurea*, the would-be rapist of Anastasia's handmaidens is tricked into having sex with a pile of pots and pans. Jocelyn Wogan-Browne has described this as 'divine intervention … of a comic and ingenious sort'.[13] However, while the assailant in the *Legenda Aurea* is humiliated by his encounter with the kitchen utensils and 'unrecognised by his men, and beaten up as a demon', William, conversely, benefits from his accidental paraphilia.[14] It marks an important stage in his transition from 'child' to 'knight', and he emerges from his pillow-dream apparently more knowledgeable of the 'kraft' of love than when he went to bed.

Although William does benefit as a result of this experience, he nevertheless does not enter into it willingly. Prior to the application of the 'grece', William has shown no interest in, or desire for, Melior – other than to serve her correctly as a man of his rank should. Unlike the attacker in the *Life of St Anastasia*, William is not being punished by 'divine intervention', but instead undergoes a kind of sexual coercion brought about by magical, rather than divine, means. This is further exacerbated by the fact that what William 'consents' to under enchantment is not actually what happens. The young

---

[13] Jocelyn Wogan-Browne, 'Saints' Lives and the Female Reader', *Forum for Modern Language Studies* 28:4 (1991): 314–32 (321).
[14] Wogan-Browne, 'Saints' Lives and the Female Reader', 321.

man agrees to sexual relations with a woman; in reality, he has intercourse with the soft furnishings. It is this slightly absurd element that, in part, distinguishes this episode from other romance tales of love potions. There is no parity in the relationship between Melior and William here: she (with Alisaundrine) has complete power to make the young man do things that no knight should really be caught doing. And yet the women's 'trick' is never criticized or censured. Though their actions might be read as undermining William's masculinity, this is presented as an integral first step to securing a happy ending for the lovers. This is not the same sort of magical coercion that Lancelot endures with Elaine of Corbenic, for instance. In Malory's tale, Elaine's handmaiden Dame Brusen, who was 'one of the grettyst enchaunters that was that tyme in the worlde', uses a potion to make Lancelot believe he is sleeping with Guinevere, when in fact he is sleeping with Elaine.[15] Despite the fact that Alisaundrine is also presented as an enchantress, who is '[f]ul conyng' of 'charmes and of chantemens' (653–4), she never receives the level of approbation accorded to Brusen in Malory's narrative.[16] On discovering the nature of Brusen and Elaine's deceit, Lancelot exclaims 'that same lady dame Brusen shall lose her hede for her wycchecrauftys, for there was never knyght disceyved as I am this nyght'.[17] Though Alisaundrine's actions transform a pillow into Melior in the same way as Brusen transforms Elaine into Guinevere (at least, as far as the knights are concerned), William is able to let this go in a way that Lancelot is not. Part of the reason for this lies in the fact that Brusen's enchantment causes Lancelot to break his oath to another, thus undermining his identity as a 'lover', whereas Alisaundrine's 'grece' opens William's eyes to the possible (and, in narrative terms, appropriate) relationship he might enjoy with Melior, thus awakening his identity as 'lover'.

However, I would suggest that, placed within the context of Melior's gendered complaint, and her adoption and rejection of masculine and feminine 'masks', we might also read William's lack of anger and humiliation as characteristic of the poem's overall treatment of gender and sexual transformation. There is a sense in this early part of the narrative that William and Melior are 'playing' various roles, and this is underscored by William's own references to 'mirth' and 'play' as he remembers his dream. This is heightened by the continued focus on dress and disguise when the young man awakens and eventually confesses his new feelings to Melior. Once the two lovers are aware

---

[15] Malory, 'The Book of Sir Tristam de Lyones', in *Works*, pp. 227–512, pp. 479–80 (Book XI, Chapter 2).
[16] It should also be noted that Alisaundrine is described in near identical terms as Alphons's necromantic stepmother, whose knowledge of witchcraft is explicitly described as shameful. I have discussed the figure of the stepmother in *William of Palerne* in detail elsewhere. See Hannah Priest, 'The Witch and the Werewolf: Rebirth and Subjectivity in Medieval Verse', in *Hosting the Monster*, ed. Holly Lynn Baumgartner and Roger Davis (Amsterdam and New York, 2008), pp. 81–100.
[17] Malory, 'Tristram', p. 48 (Book XI, Chapter 3).

of one another's feelings, Alisaundrine is, once again, called upon to act as a facilitator of their relationship. And this facilitation is, once again, effected by the employment of gender-bending.

William and Melior love one another secretly for three years, but the woman's father eventually promises her in marriage to the son of the Greek emperor. The lovers decide to flee Rome in disguise, and Alisaundrine suggests that they disguise themselves as bears. To procure the requisite bearskins, the maid dresses herself as a boy, so she can join the men who are skinning animals in the kitchens:

> Wi3tly, boute mo wordes, sche went fo[r]þ stille,
> and blive in a bourde borwed boi3es cloþes,
> and talliche hire atyred ti3tli þerinne;
> and bogeysliche as a boye busked to þe kychene,
> þer as burnes were busy bestes to hulde,
> and manly sche melled hire þo men forto help,
> til sche say tidi time hire prey for to take. (1704–10)

This episode, again, is not found in the French source. In *Guillaume de Palerne*, it simply states that Alisaundrine dresses '[c]omme serjans [as a domestic servant]' (3056); the English poem expands a half-line statement to a seven-line description, describing not only the woman's attire, but also her imitation of male speech and mannerisms. She is 'bogeysliche [saucy or boastful] as a boye', and 'melled [spoke]' in a 'manly' way.[18]

Alisaundrine's brief transvestite moment is, however, not to be taken seriously. She takes the clothes 'in a bourde [as a joke]', and her actions are presented as a comical necessity for the facilitation of the lovers' escape.[19] Randy Schiff suggests that this appropriation of male attire and attitude means that we might read Alisaundrine as 'a trickster figure capable of coordinating class play with gender play'.[20] By highlighting the fact that the woman wears the clothes, not simply of a servant, but of a *male* servant, the English poem develops the identity 'play' of its French source, adding further layers to the handmaiden's disguise.

Alisaundrine is not alone as a romance woman who wears men's clothes. However, while women in texts such as the *Roman de Silence* or *Yde et Olive* cross-dress as part of a systematic adoption of male identity (which, in the

---

[18] The *MED* gives the definition of 'bogeysliche' as 'puffed up, haughty, saucy', and it appears the word is a variation on 'boggish'. In his edition of the poem, Walter Skeat glosses the word as 'in a boasting, boisterous, or bold manner'. See Walter W. Skeat, *The Romance of William of Palerne: Otherwise Known as The Romance of William and the Werewolf; Also a Fragment of the Romance, Alisaunder*, EETS (London, 1867; 1890), p. 258.

[19] The *MED* defines 'in a bourde' as 'as a joke, in a jesting manner, facetiously'; Skeat glosses 'bourde' as 'jest' and Bunt as 'in jest; as a joke'. See Skeat, *The Romance of William of Palerne*, p. 259; Bunt, *William of Palerne*, p. 357.

[20] Randy P. Schiff, 'Cross-Channel Becomings-Animal: Primal Courtliness in *Guillaume de Palerne* and *William of Palerne*', *Exemplaria* 21:4 (Winter 2009): 418–38 (430).

case of Yde, eventually includes anatomical transformation), Alisaundrine's transvestitism is a temporary one. Unlike in the 'transvestite romances' which, as Peggy McCracken argues, 'directly challenge the primacy of the body in determining gender',[21] Alisaundrine's performance as a boy, like Melior's earlier adoption of the language and physical affectations of the knightly lover, offers a presentation of masculine identity positions that can be picked up and put on like a set of clothes, without undermining the essential female identity underneath. That this performance responds to a particular practical necessity links Alisaundrine more to Josian, wife of the eponymous protagonist of *Bevis of Hampton*, who disguises herself first as a palmer and then as a minstrel, in order to search for Bevis.[22] Josian also uses an 'oiniment' (3890) to lighten her skin colour as part of her disguise, suggesting that she is as adept at 'coordinating' race and gender play as Alisaundrine is that of class and gender. Alisaundrine and Josian are both referred to in terms of boldness or bravery, suggesting that their cross-dressing might be seen as an example, not of a challenge to anatomical determination of gender, but rather of the way in which, as Valerie Hotchkiss asserts, 'disguised women combine traditional feminine virtues with stereotypical male qualities of daring, strength and perseverance'.[23] However, Josian's disguise is a response to different circumstances from Alisaundrine's. The former is acting on a direct threat to herself and her husband, whereas Alisaundrine's cross-dressing is referred to in terms of jokes, jests and boasts. Although Melior is in danger of being forced into a marriage against her will, her handmaiden's borrowing of boys' clothes is not a direct response to external pressures, and the narrative undermines any potential danger through its semantic insistence on game and play.

That female-to-male transvestitism should be associated in a fourteenth-century English romance with fun and games is not as subversive as it may seem. Katie Normington posits a number of 'more formal examples of both male to female and female to male cross-dressing practices' in late medieval England, including 'tournaments and civic divertissements ... entertainments and dancing'.[24] She cites one example of a tournament organized by Edward III in 1348, at which fifty women attended dressed as men.[25] Alisaundrine's performance, unlike that of Josian, is 'in a bourde', and might therefore be read as part of the aristocratic gender play found at court. In discussing male-to-female transvestitism in romance narratives, Ad Putter writes that '[b]ehind the transvestite joke thus lies a deep conservatism, for

---

[21] Peggy McCracken, '"The Boy Who Was a Girl": Reading Gender in the "Roman de Silence"', *Romanic Review* 85:4 (1994): 517–36 (517).
[22] *Bevis of Hampton*, in *Four Romances of England*, ed. Ronald B. Herzman, Graham Drake and Eve Salisbury (Kalamazoo, MI, 1999), lines 3893–948.
[23] Valerie Hotchkiss, *Clothes Make the Man: Female Cross Dressing in Medieval Europe* (New York and London, 1996), p. 4.
[24] Katie Normington, *Gender and Medieval Drama* (Cambridge, 2004), p. 58.
[25] Normington, *Gender and Medieval Drama*, p. 58.

getting it requires our acceptance of the incompatibility of the two sexes'.[26] The 'bourde' of Alisaundrine's female-to-male cross-dressing lies in a similar 'conservatism': the joke works because we, as the audience, are aware that Alisaundrine remains unchanged. The 'incompatibility of the two sexes' means that, however well she 'melled', it is not possible for her to truly transform gender.

Alisaundrine's wearing of boys' clothes is an example of a temporary identity performance. Putter suggests that 'transvestitism is funny only when it does not become too convincing'.[27] Though the occupants of the kitchen are apparently convinced by Alisaundrine's performance (as she is able to take the bearskins without getting caught), the audience of the poem is 'in on the joke', and never doubts that the 'boye' they are seeing is, in truth, a girl. We might extend Putter's assertions about transvestitism and use this in a consideration of other ostensibly radical transformations in *William of Palerne*. If the 'gender-bending' in the narrative 'does not become too convincing', what about 'species-bending'? To what extent might we also read the metamorphoses of human to animal as being done 'in a bourde'?

Having disguised herself as a boy, Alisaundrine sneaks into the kitchen and steals two white bearskins. She sews William and Melior into the skins to enable them to escape unseen from the emperor's court. What is significant here is that these skins are not sexed; there is no differentiation between the skin William wears and the one worn by Melior. The narrative uses almost identical phrases to describe the couple: Melior is 'so breme a wilde bere' (1733), and William is 'so breme a bere' (1742). When the two bears are spotted and reported to the emperor, the witness describes them as 'tvo þe bremest white beres' that he has ever seen (2162). These descriptions, unlike the later presentation of the lovers in deerskins, resist sexual differentiation between the animals.

Away from the regulation of the emperor's court, William and Melior can continue their love affair in the forest. Alone – except for the werewolf – the couple (literally) sleep together. This passage is notable for the absence of any difference between the bodies of the lovers. They kissed 'eche oþer' (1833); they slept 'samli togadere' (1835). Hotchkiss argues that 'the epicene ideal of beauty in medieval romance ... illustrates that, in the context of courtly fiction, the body does not always exhibit sexual differences',[28] and William and Melior's escape to the forest implies this through its obscuring of the 'sexual differences' between the lovers' bodies. This is reminiscent of the Middle English *Floris and Blanchefleur*, in which the eponymous couple are discovered asleep in the same bed together 'nebbe to nebbe and mouth to mouth', without any sense

---

[26] Ad Putter, 'Transvestite Knights in Medieval Life and Literature', in *Becoming Male in the Middle Ages*, ed. Jeffrey Jerome Cohen and Bonnie Wheeler (New York and London, 2000), pp. 279–302 (pp. 280–1).

[27] Putter, 'Transvestite Knights', p. 291.

[28] Hotchkiss, *Clothes Make the Man*, p. 122.

of which mouth is which.²⁹ The Old French *Floire et Blanchefleur* develops this trope further, suggesting throughout the text that the lovers are so similar in appearance as to be mistaken for one another. Simon Gaunt suggests that these lovers 'appear to belong to a pre-symbolic, imaginary order of mirror images in which there is no sense of self and other, no individuation, and no sense of sexual difference'.³⁰ In *William of Palerne*, as William and Melior sleep in their bearskins, the narrative erodes the individuation between them. They are no longer 'opposite sexes'; the reader is directed to their sameness, rather than their difference. Gaunt characterizes this sameness as the 'pre-symbolic'; one could also interpret it as a yearning for a prelapsarian lack of sexualization.

However, although Floire and Blanchefleur are consistently depicted as near identical, William and Melior are simply wearing identical disguises. The audience have been told that William has laced the bearskin 'craftly above his cloþes, þat comly were and riche' (1737). If the lovers here 'partake in a mythical wholeness', it is a transitory one. The next disguise they adopt – the deerskins – begins their return to the gender systems of the courtly world. These skins *are* sexed. William wears the skin of a hart, Melior that of a hind, and they leave the forest. The 'wholeness' or prelapsarian lack of gender was just as much a disguise as Alisaundrine's 'bogeysliche' boy. William and Melior clearly enjoy it, but it is taken off and replaced with something else as they 'close ranks around themselves, emerging relatively unscathed from the animalized games'.³¹

Though William and Melior 'emerge unscathed' from their 'animalized games', the narrative's presentation of their potential transformation is somewhat ambiguous. For instance, as William and Melior don the deerskins, the narrative begins to speak of the couple as though they had adopted the animal identity of the skins: 'Of þis hert and þis hinde hende now listenes!' (2713). On the other hand, the bearskins, though ungendered, seem to be more closely connected to the human. Although there is a choice of animal skins available, Alisaundrine suggests those of bears because 'þi be alle maners arn man likkest' (1694). Bunt argues that this assertion possibly follows a medieval belief that bears are closest to humans 'because they are able to walk on their hind legs'.³² Given the potential confusion of human and animal forms, how might we read the implications of William and Melior's cross-species-dressing? A hint is given as to a possible reading of the lovers' metamorphoses in the preceding lines of the poem. Just before Alisaundrine hatches the bearskin-disguise plan, a delegation arrives in Rome to celebrate Melior's intended wedding to the son of the Greek emperor. In a minor, but rather telling, deviation from the French source, the English poem describes the entertainments as including 'daunces

---

29 *Floris and Blanchefleur*, in *Middle English Verse Romances*, ed. Donald Sands (1966; Exeter, 1986), pp. 279–312, line 890.
30 Simon Gaunt, *Gender and Genre in Medieval French Literature* (Cambridge, 1995), p. 89.
31 Schiff, 'Cross-Channel Becomings-Animal', 422.
32 Bunt, *William of Palerne*, p. 302, line 1694 n.

disgisi' (1620); the French poem simply notes that there was '[g]rant joie [great joy]' throughout Rome in response to the announcement. (2653). Bunt glosses 'daunces disgisi' as 'masked dances, fancy-dress dances, mummings'.[33] Though a small detail, these dances do serve to set the tone for an extended sequence of 'fancy dress' disguises that will allow the lovers and their friend to adopt different gender (and species) positions without ever really undermining their 'real' identities.[34]

If the emphasis on fancy dress and costume has implications for how we read William and Melior's cross-species disguise in the English poem, then we might also extend this to a reading of Alphons, the Spanish prince who has been transformed into a werewolf by his stepmother and who serves as both guide and protector to the lovers. I would argue that, although older studies have posited 'lost originals' in which the lovers were actually transformed into animals, as Alphons was 'transformed' into a wolf, what the Middle English poem in fact does is cast doubt on how fully Alphons himself is transformed, by situating him within a textual environment of masks and disguise.[35] Hotchkiss argues that '[g]ender inversion is perhaps the most radical form of disguise because it contravenes not only societal rules but also biological fact'.[36] In Alphons, however, we see a far more 'radical form of disguise' that goes even further to contravene 'biological fact': he is made into a different species.

And yet, the English werewolf seems to retain a lot of his humanity – more so than his French counterpart. This is effected, in part, by the English poet's addition of a werewolf prayer of thanks (103), for which there is no equivalent in the French source and which strengthens a later assertion of the werewolf's relationship with God (1840). Though his body has changed shape, Alphons's relationship to God has remained stable. For Schiff, it is Alphons's aristocracy, rather than his Christianity, that provides continuity between forms: 'The werewolf's furnishing of the lovers with cultural necessities during their woodland stay both furthers the poem's naturalization of aristocratic habits of consumption, and demonstrates Alphonse's status as a human–animal hybrid who has avoided the total metamorphosis into animality threatened by his loss of linguistic skills.'[37] Schiff's assertion here also draws attention to another significant facet of the werewolf's humanity: his consistent association with the pair of lovers at the heart of the poem, which might contrast with, for

---

33 The *MED* defines 'disgisi' as '(a) [o]f a person: disguised, in disguise; (b) of a dance: ?masked', but offers only line 1620 of *William of Palerne* as evidence of this secondary usage. Skeat glosses the word as 'in disguise, masked, mummerwise' (p. 266).
34 The word 'disgisi' and its variants appear a number of times in the poem: at line 2715 in the sense of 'strange, unfamiliar, extraordinary'; 'disgised' in lines 1677, 1693, 2530, 3888 meaning 'disguised'; 'disgisili' in line 485 meaning 'extraordinarily, monstrously'; 'desgeli' in line 5014 meaning 'extraordinarily, exceedingly'. See Skeat, *The Romance of William of Palerne*, p. 266; Bunt, *William of Palerne*, pp. 370, 371.
35 See Kate Watkins Tibbals, 'Elements of Magic in the Romance of *William of Palerne*', *Modern Philology* 1 (1903–4): 355–71.
36 Hotchkiss, *Clothes Make the Man*, p. 10.
37 Schiff, 'Cross-Channel Becomings-Animal', 426.

instance, the feudal allegiance to a king that defines the werewolf's humanity in Marie de France's *Bisclavret*. Thus, Alphons retains connection to Christian performance, aristocratic consumption (and, in the latter part of the poem, violence) and sexuality. He belongs to the world of William and Melior, despite the animal skin that covers him. Nevertheless, I would suggest that the clearest rejection of the idea of 'total metamorphosis' comes from Alphons himself. After being returned to human form by his now contrite stepmother, the formerly lycanthropic prince announces to the assembled company: 'I am he, þe werwolf' (4520).[38] Just as the narrative previously referred to William and Melior as a hart and a hind when they were dressed as such, the end of the Middle English poem slips easily between naming the Spanish prince 'Alphons' and calling him 'the werewolf'. Added to this, the woman who transformed him, who is described in such similar terms to the 'bogeysliche' Alisaundrine, faces no punishment or vengeance for her enchantment. Schiff suggests that the English poet's addition of Alisaundrine's 'magical powers' serves to forge 'a structural link between the stories of actual and virtual animalization'.[39] I would go further and suggest that the link between 'actual and virtual animalization' is both structural *and* conceptual. It is as if Alphons has simply worn the skin of something else for a while, and is now dressed as himself.

This conceptualization of lycanthropic metamorphosis as a process of dressing and undressing is borne out by the text. In both the English and French narratives, clothing is presented as a fundamental part of Alphons's transformation. This reminds us of the presentation of lycanthropy in *Bisclavret*, in which a knight regularly transforms into a werewolf, but is able to return to human form by recovering his clothes. When his wife prevents him from dressing as a human, he must stay as a werewolf.[40] In *Guillaume de Palerne*, Alphons must have a spell worked upon him by his stepmother in order to return to being human again. For the ritual to be completed, he must choose the person he wants to honour by letting them bring his clothes. He chooses Guillaume over his own father (7786–93). The English poem follows the French source in presenting the mechanisms of (re)transformation; however, it also offers a significant rewording. When Alphons makes his choice as to who will bring his clothes, the stepmother relays his decision to William thus: 'þe werwolf þe bisecheþ / þat tow tit com him to to tire him in his wedes' (4477–8). William is not simply presenting Alphons with his clothes as part of a ceremony or ritual; he is helping 'þe werwolf' to dress as a human again.

As in the story of William and Melior's elopement, Alphons's cross-species-dressing is connected, albeit in a less direct way, with his sexuality. After his disenchantment, Alphons makes two requests of William. The first, as

---

38 There is nothing equivalent to this announcement in the French transformation scene (lines 7843–72), resulting in a more radical disjunction between Alphons's two identity positions in the continental text.
39 Schiff, 'Cross-Channel Becomings-Animal', 428.
40 See 'Bisclavret', in *Lais de Marie de France*, ed. Karl Warnke (Paris, 1990), pp. 117–34.

noted above, is that William provide him with his clothes. The second, a few hundred lines later, is that he is granted permission to marry William's sister (4738–41). Both wishes are granted. Thus, William performs both a literal and a symbolic 're-dressing' of Alphons: the clothes allow him to perform as a human; the princess allows him to perform as a man. It is possible to read these 're-dressings' as an inverted reciprocation of the werewolf's earlier provision of deerskins for William and Melior. Alphons supplies animal skins in order for William to further his relationship with his lover; William supplies human clothes in order for Alphons to step into his role as a lover (husband). There is a symmetry here that emphasizes performance and problematizes any sense of permanent or radical transformation.

When Alphons – like William and Melior – is dressed as a human again, the species-performance comes to an end. Significantly, so too does the variable gender-performance. In bringing Alphons his clothes (and taking precedence over the Spanish king in this respect), William performs a chivalric and aristocratic masculinity that finally replaces the last shadows of the vulnerable and inexperienced child who was drugged and coerced into having sex with his pillow. He regains his lands, marries, and fathers children. Concomitantly, Alphons moves from being William's animal companion to being his sworn brother and brother-in-law, thus performing a more 'correct' knightly masculine relationship with William. The women, too, are stabilized within appropriate gender roles. Melior and Alisaundrine cease to be courtly lover and 'boye' and become wives and mothers. The stepmother becomes a more conventional maternal figure.[41] Though various identity positions have been adopted during the course of the narrative, everyone is back in the 'right' place at the end.

I have suggested here that the Middle English *William of Palerne* is far more concerned with disguise and fancy dress than its French source, including some original episodes of gender and sexuality performance that have no analogues in the continental text, and that these transfigurations of identity are treated in a light-hearted and often ironic way. As with a masked dance or a mumming, the world of this poem allows for girls to be boys, ladies to be knights, pillows to be ladies, lovers to be bears, princes to be wolves – but this is pure performance, and none of it is permanent. At the end of the story, everyone can put on their own clothes again, and live happily – and correctly gendered – ever after.

---

[41] See Priest, 'The Witch and the Werewolf', p. 94.

7
Fairy Lovers: Sexuality, Order and Narrative in Medieval Romance

AISLING BYRNE

> Me dremed al this nyght, pardee,
> An elf-queene shal my lemman be
> And slepe under my goore.
>
> 'An elf-queene wol I love, ywis,
> For in this world no womman is
> Worthy to be my make
> In towne;
> Alle othere wommen I forsake,
> And to an elf-queene I me take
> By dale and eek by downe!' (787–96)[1]

Sir Thopas's resolution to forsake human women in order to seek out an elf-queen as his lover satirizes one of the most well-known romance motifs: the fairy mistress who offers herself to the human protagonist of the narrative.[2] It is characteristic of this motif that, with relatively few exceptions, the fairy offers sexual intercourse to the hero without any demand for the commitment of marriage and without stipulating any directly connected negative consequences. The motif's origins are a good deal earlier than those of romance – it features in several early medieval Irish narratives – but it is with romance that the motif is most particularly associated. It is noticeable that this extra-marital sex is generally not explicitly condemned in the romances. Of course, romance authors are not prone to sermonizing digressions, so this might be passed over as merely a reflex of the genre; however, condemnation need not

---

[1] Geoffrey Chaucer, 'Sir Thopas', in *The Riverside Chaucer*, ed. Larry D. Benson, 3rd edn (Oxford, 1987), pp. 212–16.
[2] The motif has been examined in Helen Cooper, *The English Romance in Time: Transforming Motifs from Geoffrey of Monmouth to the Death of Shakespeare* (Oxford, 2004), Chapter 4, and in James Wade, *Fairies in Medieval Romance* (New York, 2010).

be overtly stated to still be clear and, in this respect, romance differs markedly from fabliaux, the other genre which frequently portrays extra-marital sex. Sexual misconduct in fabliaux may be comic, but it is almost always potentially exemplary; after all, it tends to involve consequences, often of an embarrassing or unpleasant kind. The apparent 'free love' offered by this motif in romance seems, on the face of it, to involve nothing of the sort.

We are, perhaps, apt to read a motif like that of the fairy lover rather too readily as the natural outpourings of a (supposedly) sexually repressed society. For instance, Corinne Saunders has observed of the most noted text to deploy this motif, *Lanval*, 'all is couched within the dream-like context of the otherworld, so that the narrative also becomes one of desire and wish-fulfilment'.[3] There can be no doubt that medieval accounts of the fairy lover have this wish-fulfilment dimension, but authors also use the motif to explore other concerns. This becomes particularly apparent when this motif is viewed, not only on its own terms, but in terms of its place within the overall structure of the plots in which it features. Most recently, James Wade has argued that supernatural beings and realms open up 'adoxic' (as distinct from orthodox or heterodox) spaces in narratives allowing certain actions to take place in an environment that neutralizes the social and moral problems that would arise from them in the human world.[4] Considering literary uses of the motif in these terms is a considerable step beyond reading them as merely titillating and also evades the pitfalls of the so-called 'anthropological approach', with its appeal to folklore and half-remembered pagan traditions.[5] This essay builds on this narratological approach to fairy lovers and suggests that, when seen from this perspective, the use of the trope in some of these texts has a pronounced ethical dimension. It argues that certain authors shape nuanced explorations of ideas of order and disorder and the nature of narrative action around this motif. It contends that what some authors are most interested in when they use the fairy lover motif is not sex or sexuality, but the humanizing effects of an ordered approach to both gratification and restraint. It also suggests that the norms of romance writing provided a particularly compelling backdrop to these considerations.

Several Irish narratives, some of a very early date, insist on the possibility of sinless extra-marital sex in an explicitly prelapsarian otherworld. These texts represent the largest body of treatments of the motif of the fairy lover before the era of romance writing. A direct line of transmission has often been posited between Celtic-language material on this theme and romance treatments of it.[6] There are numerous historical and cultural reasons why positing such a line of

---

[3] Corinne Saunders, *Magic and the Supernatural in Medieval English Romance* (Cambridge, 2010), p. 41.
[4] Wade, *Fairies*, p. 15
[5] C. S. Lewis, 'The Anthropological Approach', in *English and Medieval Studies Presented to J. R. R. Tolkien on the Occasion of his Seventieth Birthday*, ed. Norman Davis and C. L. Wrenn (London, 1962), pp. 219–30.
[6] The lengthiest analysis in this vein is John Revell Reinhard, *The Survival of Geis in Mediaeval Romance* (Halle, 1933), pp. 218–99.

transmission is problematic and, even if it could be proven, it would tell us little about the appeal of the motif in the very different cultural milieu for which romance texts were written. Nonetheless, Irish treatments of this motif are worth considering here, not as a means of probing any potential lines of influence on the romance material, but rather as a means of highlighting the fact that genre is an important factor in how this motif is used. Although the motif being deployed is recognizably the same in both Celtic and romance writing, Irish treatments of the fairy lover provide some telling points of contrast with later romances.

Among the most prominent uses of the motif in Irish are *Tochmarc Étaíne* (The Wooing of Étaín) and *Immram Brain* (The Voyage of Bran). Both of these texts are relatively early: *Tochmarc Étaíne* is usually dated to the ninth century and *Immram Brain* to c. 900, both surviving in their earliest copies (albeit as fragments) in the late eleventh-century codex, *Lebor na hUidre* (Dublin, Royal Irish Academy, MS 23 E 25).[7] In both these texts, in contrast to the later romance material, the apparent moral problems inherent in the fairy lover motif are addressed directly and the attempt made to neutralize them is couched in very Christian terms. In *Tochmarc Étaíne*, the fairy Midir tries to convince the married human woman Étaín to accompany him back to his *síd* by means of the sort of detailed lyrical description employed elsewhere by otherworld women. He describes a land where people are eternally youthful and where dwell:

> Stately folk without blemish,
> conception without sin, without lust.
> We see everyone on every side,
> and no one seeth us.
> It is the darkness of Adam's transgression
> that hath prevented us from being counted.[8]

The passage seems to owe something to Augustine's influential notion of lustless sex in a prelapsarian world.[9] *Immram Brain* also rationalizes its fairies' behaviour in Christianized terms. Early in the narrative, the supernatural Mannanán Mac Lir tells Bran that the inhabitants of the otherworld operate according to a different moral law:

> A beautiful game, most delightful,
> They play sitting at the luxurious wine,
> Men and gentle women under a bush,
> Without sin, without crime.[10]

---

7 'Tochmarc Étaíne', ed. Osborn Bergin and R. I. Best, *Ériu* 12 (1938): 137–96; *Immram Brain: Bran's Journey to the Land of Women*, ed. Séamus MacMathúna (Tübingen, 1985).
8 'daine delgnaide cen ón. / combart cen pecadh cen chol. / Atchiam cach for cach leath. / & nícon aice nech. / teimel imorbuis Adaim / dodonarcheil ar araim', 'Tochmarc Étaíne', ed. Bergin and Best, 181.
9 Augustine of Hippo, *Concerning the City of God against the Pagans*, trans Henry Bettenson (Harmondsworth, 1972), 14.26.
10 'Clu(i)che n-aímin n-inmeldag aigdit fri find-immarbáig, fir is mná míni fo doss cen peccad cen immarboss', *Immram Brain*, ed. MacMathúna, p. 40.

Such activity seems to be encouraged by the living arrangements during the time Bran's company spend in the Land of Women. The account notes that 'they went into a large house, in which was a bed for every couple, even thrice nine beds' (62),[11] and leaves the audience to draw their own conclusions. Throughout the text the descriptive depth with which the otherworld is constructed reinforces the impression that the laws of the actual world do not apply here. The point is driven home by another assertion of Mannanán's: he claims that otherworld beings are immortal because 'the sin has not come to us' (44)[12] and it must be assumed that, here too, the prelapsarian nature of the realm obviates any propensity for lust on the part of its inhabitants and so makes their sexual behaviour considerably less problematic.

It is noteworthy that explicitly Christian rationalizations of the sort developed in *Immram Brain* and *Tochmarc Étaíne* do not tend to appear in romance material. This is curious, because there is no obvious reason why romance authors might be less likely to see a moral problem here than the authors of *Immram Brain* and *Tochmarc Étaíne*; nonetheless they make no attempt to articulate a framework that explains or excuses the sexual morality of otherworld beings. This silence is potentially unsettling in a way that the Christianizing rationalizations of the Irish material are not. The unglossed presentation of these behaviours ensures that there is no rationalizing refuge for the audience; it presents human gratification at its most absolute and, therefore, the consequences at their most dramatic.

The question of consequences brings us to the wider function of the fairy lover motif within literary plots. One of the tropes most frequently associated with the fairy lover is the imposition of a taboo on the human protagonist. For instance, in *Immram Brain*, the delights in which Bran's company indulge in the otherworld appear to bind them and exact a price. The company is warned against touching the earth of Ireland on its return there and the only member of the group who does, Nechtán, turns to ashes immediately. Similar injunctions appear in romance material. The conjunction of otherworld sexual gratification and the imposition of a taboo in these narratives is often overlooked, perhaps because the taboo rarely bears any obvious relation to sexuality. An exception is Wade's treatment of the interrelation of gifts and taboos in *Fairies in Medieval Romance*. He argues that

> [i]n a system that combines the machinations of supernatural gifts with the logic of taboos ... fairy mistresses never emerge as simple vehicles for wish-fulfilment. Rather they function as complex narrative devices who can arbitrarily reward, abandon, and forgive, who can provide for that which will lead to a happy ending, but who can also challenge along the way.[13]

---

[11] 'lotar íarom i tegd(a)is máir. Ar-ránic imdai cecha lámamn(a)e and .i. trí noí n-imdæ', *Immram*, ed. MacMathúna, p. 44.
[12] 'nín-táraill int immarbuss', *Immram*, ed. MacMathúna, p. 40.
[13] Wade, *Fairies*, p. 145.

The primary impact of this link between gift (in this case the fairy's gift of sexual access) and taboo is to take the encounter with the fairy out of the realm of anything approaching modern ideas of 'free love'; the taboo ensures that a bond arises and an obligation is articulated, even if it is not (initially or ever) that of marriage. Building on Wade's insight that fairies are 'complex narrative devices', it seems to me that certain romance authors use the motif of the fairy lover to articulate an entirely orthodox ethic. They construct narratives that, far from providing straightforward wish-fulfilment, highlight the potential problems that untrammelled gratification presents in the mortal world and in the world of romance, in particular. These romances tend not to announce their moral interests directly. They do not fall back on Christianizing rationalizations like the Irish narratives discussed above; instead, they articulate their ethic more subtly, but, potentially, more convincingly, through the operations of narrative.

Perhaps, the paradigmatic instance of the fairy lover motif occurs in the various versions of Marie De France's *Lanval*.[14] The supernatural environment of *Lanval* is characterized by the depth and focus of its description in all versions of the text. Because the encounter with the fairy injects a whole set of new expectations into the plot, the audience's belief in the text's supernatural framework is crucial. This narrative devotes considerable attention to describing the pavilion in which the fairy initially meets the knight. In its boundedness and opulence, it suggests a space within the real world where the rules of the otherworld might be expected to operate. The depth of description is particularly marked in the Middle English versions. The author of *Sir Landevale* notes that the pavilion was 'With treysour i-wrought on euery syde' and that each pommel was worth the price of a city.[15] The pavilion is topped with the figure of a heron that holds a light-emitting carbuncle in his mouth. Thomas Chestre's version, *Sir Launfal*, describes the pavilion as the 'werk of Sarsynys' (266), that has 'pomelles of crystal' (266) and is surmounted by an eagle of burnished gold and enamel who has eyes of carbuncle: 'As the mone they schon anyght, / That spreteth out ovyr all' (272–3).[16] The crystal decoration is characteristically otherworldly and the role of the carbuncle in providing twenty-four-hour illumination to a dwelling-place is also a conventional otherworld trope.[17]

Extensive descriptions that encourage the audience to suspend disbelief are particularly important in stories where supernatural encounters produce situations that contravene moral laws observed in the actual world. The potentially

---

[14] Marie de France, *Lanval*, in *Lais*, ed. A. Ewert (Oxford, 1978), pp. 58–74; translated in *The Lays of Marie de France*, trans. Glyn Burgess and Keith Busby (Harmondsworth, 1986).
[15] *Sir Landevale*, in *The Middle English Breton Lays*, ed. Anne Laskaya and Eve Salisbury (Kalamazoo, MI, 1995), pp. 423–37, lines 79–82.
[16] Thomas Chestre, *Sir Launfal*, in *The Middle English Breton Lays*, ed. Laskaya and Salisbury, pp. 201–62.
[17] For the fullest account of conventional otherworld tropes see Howard Rollin Patch, *The Other World According to Descriptions in Medieval Literature* (Cambridge, MA, 1950).

problematic sexual behaviour related in *Lanval* may contribute to the focus on otherworldly description in the various versions of the story. On the face of it, the extra-marital liaison between the fairy and the knight can only be divested of its seeming immorality if the alterity of the fairy, unfettered by the morality of the actual world, is firmly established. In the Middle English versions of *Lanval*, the descriptive richness that, on one level, renders the unfamiliar otherworld landscape more tangible may also be directed at establishing a very clear defamiliarization of the narrative's context. So far, this recalls the Irish material, like *Immram Brain*, which also features lengthy descriptions of otherworld locations; however, *Lanval*'s engagement with the motif is more complex than this and must be situated within the overall structure of the narrative. With his mistress's love and her generosity, Lanval lacks for nothing and this presents a problem: perfect bliss is no catalyst for narrative. The very presentation of the fairy's pavilion has already gestured towards this – it is described at length and in loving detail, but it is static; in contrast to the paradigmatic landscape of romance, there are no opportunities here for onward exploration and, hence, the necessary conditions for further plot development are lacking. This bliss of the fairy's bower is, formally and materially, a narrative dead-end and this problem is particularly acute in romance. Romance typically enacts a process of loss and recovery, or quest and reward. The satisfaction of the happy ending is in proportion to the perils and hardships endured to achieve it. In this respect, Lanval's happiness is not the happiness of the conventional romance ending. Since the fairy's love is freely given and unproblematically achieved (unlike Thopas, Lanval neither expects nor seeks out the fairy's favour), the narrative has had few serious complications before this point. The queen's proposition and Lanval's financial worries are certainly tests, but they do not directly impact on the hero's attainment of the fairy's love; at this stage in the narrative they look like completely unrelated storylines. Lanval's perfect bliss with his fairy lover threatens to short-circuit the narrative, placing the happy ending so close to the opening that it becomes banal.

This is where the taboo comes in. The fairy tells Lanval to keep their liaison secret and never to mention her to others. On the most obvious level, this enjoinder reanimates the narrative and Lanval's eventual violation of the taboo provides the necessary complication for the onward movement of the plot. Yet, the taboo itself is curious, primarily because it bears no relation to the situation at hand. It seems completely gratuitous and appears to have no clear moral or ethical import. It is difficult to escape the feeling that the imposition of the taboo is a piece of poetic expedience, a rather clumsy *deus ex machina* introduced to solve a plot problem of the poet's own making. However, the persistence with which authors engage with these sorts of taboos, and the quality of the texts they produce, argue against such an interpretation. As Wade has stressed, the caprice and arbitrariness of fairies in romance create an ideal space for literary experimentation, a sort of literary laboratory.[18]

---

[18] Wade, *Fairies*, pp. 3–6.

The taboos are defined by their illogic and arbitrariness and, as such, draw attention to themselves in a manner that goes some way to foreground and emphasize the machinery of the plot. Such an exposition can have what might be considered an ethical dimension. It queries unproblematic and unfettered wish-fulfilment, but does so in narratological, rather than ideological, terms. It highlights the fact that completely fulfilled desire imposes a limit on narrative. In this respect, the treatment of the motif in a romance like *Lanval* is distinct from its treatment in texts like *Immram Brain* and *Tochmarc Étaíne*. Though never rationalizing or explaining the fairy's morality in terms of Christian ideas like prelapsarian behaviours, texts like *Lanval* still use the motif to produce plots that highlight distinctly non-transgressive ideas.

The ethical dimension of this literary experimentation is even clearer when we consider how the experience of narrative stasis affects the human protagonist of the romance. The human's peril is not explicitly moral, but, in romance terms, it is real and acute. It might be characterized in terms of a certain diminution on the level of both the plot and the individual, a potential curtailing of the narrative action that mirrors a stunting of the personal growth so fundamental to romance. Complete fulfilment without effort, self-denial or sacrifice, paradoxically, gives rise to a certain loss. Breaching the taboo provides the means, not only to reanimate the plot, but to test the human protagonist. Lanval's sufferings when he realizes that his taboo-breach has lost him his love are described at great length in all versions of the story. The necessity of some sort of personal sacrifice as a prelude to fulfilled desire is articulated particularly emphatically in the very similar narrative of *Graelent*. In this text the fairy only forgives the protagonist for breaking the taboo when he nearly dies in the attempt to follow her across a turbulent river (680–731).[19] This gesture of self-sacrifice leads to fulfilment of a more complete kind than the initial one. Their relationship is healed by the gesture and the fairy takes Graelent definitively into the otherworld (732).

Lanval also ends with the hero's disappearance into the otherworld. The treatment of this final episode in these two texts usually attributed to Marie is worth considering further. On the most obvious level, the removal of the hero to the otherworld is the logical thing to do. As long as he continues to straddle the real world and the supernatural world, the stasis of fulfilled desire is problematic and, in a sense, dehumanizing since it is out-of-kilter with the trajectory of human existence in the temporally bound world. But this ending is also indicative of the rather nuanced position of these two texts with regard to desire and gratification. The narrative shape of both *Lanval* and *Graelent* asserts the value that should be placed on fulfilled desire, while also recognizing the limitations and problems that attend it in the human world. These romances avoid the twin poles of puritanical anxiety and sensual fantasy by stressing that

---

[19] *Graelent*, in *Eleven Old French Narrative Lays*, ed. Glyn S. Burgess and Leslie C. Brook (Cambridge, 2007), pp. 349–412.

this world is not the natural place for unfettered gratification, but that another one might be. The echo of Christian rhetoric is obvious and is most pronounced at the end of *Lanval* and *Graelent* when removal to the otherworld is figured in terms very reminiscent of death. Human life and the progress of narrative are drawn together particularly clearly in Thomas Chestre's version of *Lanval*; definitive abandonment of this world is the point where this narrative breaks down, where the reach of words ends, and silence takes over:

> Thus Launfal, wythouten fable,
> That noble knyght of the Rounde Table,
> Was take ynto Fayrye;
> Seththe saw hym yn thys lond noman,
> Ne no more of hym telle y ne can
> For sothe, wythoute lye. (1033–8)

The association with death is made even more explicit in *Graelent*, where the narrative dubs itself the *Death of Graelant* (755–6),[20] even though a few lines earlier it is noted that the hero lives on in the otherworld (734). Death is the ultimate experience of stasis and definitive removal to the otherworld therefore provides both a natural correlative for it and an arena where complete fulfilment of desire no longer limits the hero, because trial and ensuing personal growth are no longer a condition for happy human existence.

Not all uses of this motif in romance follow the pattern developed by Marie in *Lanval* and *Graelent*. However, the problem of narrative stasis and the difficulty protagonists have in straddling the human world and the otherworld are still key concerns. The Middle English romance *Sir Degaré* sees the gender roles in the motif inverted. A princess becomes separated from her companions in the forest and encounters a fairy king who declares he has loved her for a long time and then proceeds to force sexual intercourse on her.[21] The fact that the human protagonist is female is important. On the most obvious level, the inherent power disparity between fairy and human becomes particularly pronounced when the human involved is female. The fairy's superior supernatural capacity is not balanced by superior physical strength in the human protagonist and the description of the rape makes the lady's powerlessness and distress very clear (107–13). However, the fact that the human protagonist is female in this text also ensures that the plot implications of the encounter are rather different from those in, for instance, *Lanval*. In *Degaré* the princess becomes pregnant and therefore the encounter does not constitute a narrative dead-end – the subsequent birth of her son, the eponymous hero of the romance, propels the plot onwards. Notably no taboo is imposed on the human in this text, primarily because there is no narrative necessity for it.

---

[20] '.I. lai en firent li Breton; Graalant Muer l'apele l'on'. *Graelent*, ed. Burgess and Brook, p. 408.
[21] *Sir Degaré*, in *The Middle English Breton Lays*, ed. Laskaya and Salisbury, pp. 89–144.

The romance of *Melusine* provides another variation on this theme. It begins with the fairy Pressine agreeing to marry Elynas, on the condition that he never sees her in childbed and when he violates the terms of this taboo, she leaves him. Her daughter Melusine imposes a similar taboo on Raymond of Poitiou who comes across her in the forest and proposes marriage to her. She mandates that he must never enter her chamber on a Saturday. When he violates this taboo he discovers that she is, for that day, part-human and part-serpent.[22] There is, perhaps, a distinction to be made between the use of this trope in romances that have a clear investment in the historical world, like *Melusine*, and those that have not, like *Lanval*. *Melusine* concerns the origins of the house of Luisgnan and functions as a supernatural foundation myth for that dynasty. In this context, it is not surprising that both Pressine and Melusine marry their human lovers, producing heirs who are not only privileged with supernatural origins, but are also unambiguously legitimate.[23] The connection of sex with genealogy and, hence, dynastic power is made clear in the terms in which Melusine's taboo is couched: she stresses that, if the hero breaks the compact not only will he lose her as his lover, but he and his heirs will lose their lands:

> Iff thys poyntement hold noght in thys deuise,
> Ye shall me lese, be therof certane,
> Without sight of me any maner wise;
> After that, ye and al your hoires playn
> Shal begin to fall, and thaim-selfe distayn
> Off landes, honoures, and heritages;
> Then doloures shall be in their corage[s]. (505–11)

Thomas of Erceldoune presents a particularly notable instance of the fairy lover motif operating in a text with historical import. The encounter with the fairy mistress in what is usually termed the 'romance' section of the text gives rise to the influential series of prophecies relating to British history with which the figure of Thomas is particularly associated.[24] *Thomas* includes several variations on the typical fairy-lover plot. In this text, the otherworld journey is more of a punishment than a reward and the treatment of taboos is not entirely as one might expect. In fact, the imposition of the journey to the otherworld operates like a taboo, rather than wish-fulfilment:

> Scho sayd, 'Thomas, take leue at sonne & mone
> And als at lefs that grewes on tree;
> This twelmoneth sall ou with me gone,
> And Medill-erthe sall þou none see.' (157–60)

---

[22] Coudrette, *Le Roman de Mélusine ou Histoire de Lusignan*, ed. Eleanor Roach (Paris, 1982). The Middle English translation is edited in *The Romance of Partenay, or of Lusignen: Otherwise Known as The Tale of Melusine*, ed. W. W. Skeat, EETS e.s. 22, rev. edn (London, 1899).
[23] For further consideration of the myth in its historical context, see *Melusine of Lusignan: Founding Fiction in Late Medieval France*, ed. Donald Maddox and Sara Sturm-Maddox (Athens, GA, 1996).
[24] *Thomas of Ereceldoune*, ed. James Murray, EETS o.s. 61 (London, 1875).

In contrast to Lanval and Graelent, Thomas is enjoined to silence in the otherworld, not in the real world, where the prophetic role he takes on ensures that silence about his adventures is neither desirable nor possible. In this romance the treatment of this motif appears to have come full circle. When Thomas, asks for her love, the fairy replies with great anxiety:

> Scho sayde, 'þou mane, þat ware folye,
> I praye þe, Thomas, þou late me bee;
> ffor I save þe full sekirlye,
> þat synne will for-doo all my beaute.' (101–4)

The lady here clearly conceptualizes Thomas's proposition as 'synne', an unusual formulation in the romance tradition. This protestation comes before Thomas forces himself on her, so the fairy's anxiety is certainly about the idea of extra-marital sex (the fairy is already married), rather than Thomas's attempt to coerce her. It is true that other romances, such as *Graelent*, include scenes where the human protagonist appears to force himself on the fairy, but such actions are not usually, as in *Thomas*, explicitly condemned or placed, even tentatively, within a Christian framework of ethics. It might be possible to place *Thomas* alongside romances like *Melusine*, where the narrative's engagement with real-world history limits its capacity to operate in a completely adoxic space and, therefore, requires a slightly different approach to the issue of sexuality. The fairy–human union in *Thomas* does not produce offspring or constitute the origin of a human dynasty, but Thomas's encounter with the fairy produces prophetic material that has on-going relevance in the real world. Indeed, in its emphasis on prophecy, *Thomas* would seem to constitute a particularly strong endorsement of order: knowledge of the future offers control of potential disruption and chaos. The trajectory of the narrative appears to be one where initial disorder in the form of the sexual encounter between Thomas and the fairy is transformed into order in the form of the gift of prophecy, via a process of self-denial articulated through a series of taboos.

In the course of their journey to the otherworld, the fairy imposes a further taboo on Thomas. They come upon a rich feast during their journey through the mountain and the fairy urges him not to take any food. She warns him that the devil will take him if he partakes in this meal:

> He pressede to pulle frowte with his hande,
> Als mane for fude þat was nere faynt;
> Scho sayd, 'Thomas! þou late þame stande,
> Or ells þe fende the will atteynt.
> If þou it plokk, sothely to saye,
> Thi saule gose to þe fyre of helle;
> It commes neuer owte or domesdaye,
> Bot þer in payne ay for to duelle.' (185–92)

The troubling sexual encounter of earlier in the romance may, perhaps, make more sense when placed alongside this episode. The explicitly moral dimension of the fairy's warning recalls the warning against 'synne' that she gives earlier in the narrative. Some degree of personal growth is in evidence here: on this occasion, Thomas heeds the warning and passes the test. Here we have a similar pattern to that of *Lanval*: fulfilled desire transformed into sacrifice or self-denial, only on this occasion sensual desire has been linked to desire for power, in the form of rape. Thomas's enforced sojourn in the otherworld requires a consistent surrender of that power, before his final re-empowerment through the gift of the prophecies. The pattern of self-denial leading to reward that we observed in other texts is also present in *Thomas*, though on different terms.

Rationalizing encounters with fairy lovers in terms of subversion, wish-fulfilment or titillating release seems inadequate, both to the complexity and intricacy of the motif as it is explored and expanded in many texts and to the careful crafting of romance texts generally by their authors. Sex and sexuality are obviously genuine concerns of these authors, but they are not, necessarily, the primary concern of writers deploying this motif. When the sexual encounter with a fairy lover is placed within the context of the overall structure of the plot, the main theme that emerges is not sexuality, but the progress of narrative and its correlative, human growth. The supernatural context in which the encounter takes place allows it to be as complete as possible an experience of wish-fulfilment with the acute problems of narrative stasis that result. A realm of completely unfettered sexual experience is not as interesting as a world where actions have consequences, and a plot needs complications to justify its existence. This is why there is often a clear distinction between instances of the motif where the human is male and where the human is female and why generative sex has rather different plot implications from non-generative sex. In the latter case, the desirability of rules and boundaries is asserted conspicuously through the device of the taboo. These taboos have the obvious function of sustaining narrative interest, but their arbitrariness means that they draw attention to themselves and to their role in reanimating the plot. In this way they expose the machinery of the plot and the problems that absolute gratification poses for narrative. Genre also matters here, because a narrative patterned on self-denial as a prelude to final fulfilment is characteristic of romance.

Romance uses of the fairy-lover motif might often, despite first appearances, be characterized as ethical, only their ethics are articulated in narratological, rather than explicitly didactic, terms. Despite appearances, they do not necessarily celebrate chaos or advocate complete licence in human affairs. What might be termed the 'romance ethic' of self-denial or sacrifice leading to fulfilled desire is preached through narrative action, rather than through words. The point in texts like *Lanval* or *Graelent* or even, in less elevated mode, *Thomas of Erceldoune* is not that restraint or self-sacrifice is an absolute good, but that they are necessary for the growth and development of individuals in a human world where arriving at a point of complete rest and satisfaction is impossible this side of death. In romance, with its insistence on the perfectibility-through-trial of human beings, the emphasis on personal growth as the only means to ultimate gratification is particularly acute.

8
Text as Stone: Desire, Sex, and the Figurative Hermaphrodite in the Ordinal and Compound of Alchemy

CYNTHEA MASSON

GEORGE Ripley, in his apostrophic preface to God in the *Compound of Alchemy*, claims to have 'renounced ... fleshly lust' and asks God to provide him (and, presumably, other worthy alchemists) with His 'secret treasure': 'Shew us thy secrets and to us be bounteous' (21.4).[1] Throughout the *Compound*, Ripley guides readers away from worldly pleasures, urging them instead to focus their desires on God-granted alchemical secrets and 'our stone of great delight' (37.2). Likewise, Thomas Norton, in his prologue to the *Ordinal of Alchemy*, warns of avaricious would-be alchemists who 'in fyre / Of brennyng couetise haue therto desire' (27–8). Norton emphatically shuns 'wordly werkis' in favour of alchemical 'connyng', advising his reader to 'sett fully his trust' in God and 'in connyng be fixid al his lust' (509, 517, 535–6): 'For above all erthlye thynge / I mooste desire & love connynge' (2595–6). Desire or lust, in both the *Compound* and the *Ordinal*, is thus redirected from the physical body and material world toward the divinely inspired knowledge of the alchemical corpus. Moreover, as I will illustrate, Norton and Ripley both direct their reader to focus on the text's rhetorical structures in order to achieve desired alchemical objectives. A novice reader of alchemy may find this easier said than done given what Andrea De Pascalis describes as the classic 'frustrating experience' encountered by 'first-time readers of alchemy': 'enigmas, contradictions, allegories, symbols, interruptions, veiled meanings

---

[1] The editions used for the primary texts in this essay are as follows: George Ripley, *Compound of Alchemy*, ed. Stanton J. Linden (Aldershot, 2001) and Thomas Norton, *Ordinal of Alchemy*, ed. John Reidy, EETS 272 (London, 1975). Citations to the *Compound* appear by page and stanza number; citations to the *Ordinal* appear by line number. The original works of Ripley and Norton are dated 1471 and 1477 respectively. Both works form part of an extensive collection of English alchemical poems compiled by Elias Ashmole in *Theatrum Chemicum Brittanicum* (London, 1652).

and apparent absurdities are enough to make even the most indefatigable neophyte wonder if he is not the victim of some bizarre joke.'[2] Such experiences and subsequent descriptions are based on the assumption that the goal of reading alchemy is to interpret the text metaphorically – that the reader is to decipher what each figurative word or phrase literally means. This process is encouraged by comments such as Ripley's response to the question 'What is our stone' (22.9): 'To this I answere that *Mercurie* it is I wis, / But not the common called quicksilver by name' (23.10). In other words, the Stone is figurative Mercury but not literal Mercury; thus, the reader is left to deduce the text's meaning. I posit an alternative possibility: that both the *Compound* and the *Ordinal of Alchemy* can be read not only for metaphoric content but also for metonymic effect.[3] That is, the alchemical text, metonymically, acts as a substitute for the alchemical goal itself: the creation of the Philosopher's Stone. According to Madhavi Menon, metonymy is 'the mode by which one indirectly approaches desire'.[4] As such, if the alchemical text *is* the Stone, then alchemical desire is fulfilled through reading the text.

A good deal of serious literary scholarship focusing on the subject of alchemy takes as its primary sources not the works of the alchemists but the works of satirists, with the overwhelmingly predominant source of such scholarship in English medieval literary studies being, of course, Chaucer's *Canon's Yeoman's Tale*.[5] Thus alchemy, when discussed as a subject of Middle English poetry, is often limited to the context of Chaucer and a tale that highlights the association between alchemy and fraud. Even scholars such as Jane Hilberry and Mark J. Bruhn, who build thorough and convincing arguments regarding Middle English poetics and alchemical practice, focus primarily on Chaucer. The insightful rhetorical theories of Hilberry (who contends that alchemy's 'primary attraction lies in the language that surrounds the practice'[6]) and Bruhn (who argues that alchemy is 'as much a textual ... discipline ... as a scien-

---

[2] Andrea De Pascalis, *Alchemy: The Golden Art: The Secrets of the Oldest Enigma* (Rome, 1995), p. 77.

[3] For a detailed discussion of metonymy (through definitions and uses), I direct the reader to Madhavi Menon, '*Richard II* and the Taint of Metonymy', *English Literary History* 70 (2003): 653–75. As Menon explains, 'metonymy implies the substitution of one name for another' (657). I use the term here to suggest that an attribute of alchemical practice (the alchemical text) acts as a substitute for the alchemical goal (the Philosopher's Stone).

[4] Menon, '*Richard II* and the Taint of Metonymy', 658. In the immediate lead-up to this quotation, Menon explains, 'Metonymy depends on an affinity rather than an innate link between two things ... One can metonymically substitute a shoe for the person one loves (because it is in contact with his or her body), but one cannot say the person one loves is like a shoe without inviting a certain amount of ridicule, since those two terms are not linked in the mode of necessity.'

[5] For a discussion of Chaucer in relation to hermaphroditic poetics, see Cynthea Masson, 'Of Course There's Something Queer about the Canon: A Reader of Chaucer's *Canon's Yeoman's Tale* in Relation to the Alchemical Hermaphrodite', in *Pataphysica 2: Pataphysica e Alchimia*, ed. Dr Faustroll (Lincoln, NE, 2004), pp. 102–16.

[6] Jane Hilberry, '"And in Oure Madnesse Everemoore We Rave": Technical Language in the *Canon's Yeoman's Tale*', *The Chaucer Review* 21:4 (1987): 435–43 (435).

tific ... one'[7]) could well be applied to the works of both Norton and Ripley, two of late medieval England's most renowned and prolific alchemical poets. Indeed, Norton's *Ordinal* and Ripley's *Compound* each provides an exquisite example of alchemy as a poetic or rhetorical discipline; indeed, each author purposefully and repeatedly draws attention to the written text. Later in this essay, I will explore gendered grammatical play within the rhetorical structure of the *Compound* and the *Ordinal* to illustrate the ways these texts mimic alchemical conjunction through language, thus metonymically substituting the text for the Stone. First, though, I want to further explore the connection between the practice of alchemy and the reading of alchemy. Arguably, in order to substitute the text for the Stone, each author must convince his reader not only to desire alchemical knowledge but also to associate the fulfilment of that desire with the specific alchemical text.

In the *Ordinal*, Norton redirects the reader's desire to attain alchemical secrets away from false alchemical doctrines toward his own text and its alchemical truths. Thus, in his prologue, he promises the reader, 'To shew the trouth in few wordis & playne, / So that ye may fro fals doctrine flee, / If ye geve credence to this boke & to me' (96–8). He warns the reader against 'bokis writen of receytis' (recipes), claiming that 'al such receptis be ful of deceytis' (99–100). Norton later provides a series of examples involving misplaced desire for these false alchemical recipes: he speaks of a monk who found 'a boke of receptis' and then elaborates on the monk's 'desires that were so nyce' (554, 576); thereafter, he writes of a 'persone of a litylle towne' who 'trowid that lampis with light of fyre / Shulde wel performe his nyce desire' (627, 651–2). These men follow false and deceitful alchemical texts; consequently, their desires are 'nyce' or foolish. Norton also warns the reader that

> Euery man shalle grete peyne haue
> when he shalle first þis arte covyte & crave.
> He shalle ofte tymes chaunge his desire
> with new tydyngis whiche he shalle hyre. (725–8)

In contrast, shortly thereafter, Norton speaks of finding a 'trew mastir' whose 'trew love' will teach the prospective alchemist the secrets to 'making of oure delycious stoone' (740, 742, 744). Norton's own master tells him, 'Your stedfast mynde shall your desire a-vaunce' (848). Thus, according to Norton, foolish and fickle desire must be replaced by constant and true love.

---

7 Mark J. Bruhn, 'Art, Anxiety, and Alchemy in the *Canon's Yeoman's Tale*', *The Chaucer Review* 33:3 (1999): 288–315 (292). See also a discussion of the way in which alchemy is 'concerned with interpretations of the written word' in Christine Chism, 'I demed hym som chanoun for to be', in *Chaucer's Pilgrims: An Historical Guide to the Pilgrims in* The Canterbury Tales, ed. Laura C. Lambdin and Robert T. Lambdin (Westport, CT, 1996), pp. 340–56 (p. 354); and note the claim that 'the problem with alchemy is above all linguistic' in Lee Patterson, 'Perpetual Motion: Alchemy and the Technology of the Self', *Studies in the Age of Chaucer* 15 (1993): 25–57 (41).

Throughout the *Ordinal*, Norton links the word 'desire' to specific alchemical practices and elements: 'And seth in this arte your chief desyre / Is to haue colour which shulde a-bide fire'; 'Then must ye conioyne euery element, / As watir and erthe after youre desire / welle compowned with Ayre and fyre'; 'A nother sorte said no liquour was a-bove / The liquour which congirs most desire & love' (1457–8, 1596–8, 2257–8).[8] Desire, then, is directly associated with the methodology of alchemy; however, as Norton emphasizes repeatedly, those desires can be satisfied only through the *Ordinal*. Thus, he instructs his reader, 'Trust to this doctrine, sett herin yowr desyris' (2981). Even more remarkably, Norton asserts an essential function for his book in relation to all other alchemical texts:

> The autours fornamede, with this boke of myne,
> Shewith of alchymye all the doctryne,
> If ye complecte theire sentencis all
> Not bi opinyon, but aftire this ordynall;
> For in this ordynall, I sett yow from all dowte,
> Is no thynge sett wronge, nothir on poynt lafte owte. (3077–82)

The reader *must* read the *Ordinal* in order to understand not only alchemical practice in general but all alchemical books. If the reader sets his desires on the *Ordinal*, he will be set free from all alchemical doubt.[9]

As in the *Ordinal*, the word 'desire' in Ripley's *Compound* is linked directly to alchemical practices and elements: 'Therefore make fire thy glasse within / ... if thou wilt winne / Our secrets according to thy desire'; 'Of water and ayre, with earth and fire, / But that each element into other may be lad, / And so abide fore ever to thy desire'; 'And so continue it till all be fixed, / And well fermented to thy desire, / Then make Projection after thy pleasure' (40.17, 43.5, 70.7).[10] Most notably, according to Ripley, 'our stone' will 'multiply his kinde after thine owne desire', provided that 'God vouchsafe thee to inspire, / To know the truth, and fansies to eschew' (50.20). Ripley suggests here a direct connection between one's desire and the success of creating the Stone. Like Norton, the abstract element of emotional desire is as crucial to alchemical practice as the concrete elements (of fire, water, earth, air). Also like Norton, Ripley emphasizes the need for his specific text to understand true alchemy and thus fulfil the reader's desires: 'But listen to me', he exhorts the reader, 'for truly I will thee teach' (23.11): 'by my writing whoso guided will bee, / Of his intent perfectly speede shall bee' (27.27). In a section near the end of

---

[8] See also the following lines in the *Ordinal*: 884, 1195, 1916, 2434, 2454, 2654, 2712, 2794, 2853, 2985, 3002 and 3085.
[9] Norton also writes, 'Desire not this boke to shew thingis alle, / For this boke is but an Ordynalle' (2495–6). Norton may imply here the necessity to learn from a master or teacher (in addition to reading the *Ordinal*) or, in relation to the passage quoted from lines 3077–82, the necessity to use the *Ordinal* alongside other books.
[10] See also the following lines in the *Compound*: 35.13, 50.20, 58.3, and 71.12.

the *Compound* entitled 'Erronious Experiments', Ripley directly outlines his position on the function and truth of his work:

> I sawe never true worke truly but one,
> Of which in this Treatise the truth I have told:
> Studie only therefore how to make our Stone,
> For thereby maist thou winne both silver and gold,
> Upon my writing therefore, to ground thee be bold:
> So shalt though loose nought if God be thy guide,
> Trust to my doctrine, and thereby abide. (87.12)

Ripley's 'Trust to my doctrine' is virtually echoed by Norton's 'Trust to this doctrine'. Both authors promote the *Compound* and the *Ordinal* respectively as a text that will allow the reader to fulfil his goal. Furthermore, as I will now illustrate, each author rhetorically structures his text as a metonym of alchemical sexual conjunction, the ultimate fulfilment of alchemical desire.

The main goal of alchemy – to create the Philosopher's Stone – is, in effect, a quest for original unity. As the alchemists emphasize, this quest is linked with divine truth or revelation: the alchemical secret is revealed only to worthy recipients by the divinity. But the quest is also linked with human sexual union, figurative or otherwise, in that the male and female alchemical principles must procreate in order to achieve the original unity of human nature before the Fall. Taking the argument one step further, this reading of the alchemical quest can be linked to a medieval understanding of the connection between fallen language and fallen sexual nature. Alexandre Leupin details this intricate relationship between language and sex in *Barbarolexis: Medieval Writing and Sexuality*.[11] As an introduction to his theories, Leupin reminds the reader of Augustinian theory that opposes human language (which is 'mortal and transitory') to divine substance (which is 'simple, unified, and eternal').[12] He then complements Augustine's theories with those of Nicolas of Amiens who, in the twelfth century, claimed that the essential human linguistic copulation of subject with predicate is 'alien' to the ineffable divinity.[13] As Leupin explains, 'as the cause without cause, the principle of difference without difference, God cannot be signified through the copula of predication. Predication supposes difference, a mode of being proper to the created but not the creator.'[14] In other words, created (human) language is flawed (divided) in its reliance on the grammatical copula of subject and predicate, whereas the ineffable divinity is perfect (whole), residing beyond human language.

---

[11] Alexandre Leupin, *Barbarolexis: Medieval Writing and Sexuality*, trans. Kate M. Cooper (Cambridge, MA, 1989). Leupin's argument is complex and can be outlined only briefly in this essay; I refer the reader to his book for a more detailed explanation of the sexual/linguistic connections.
[12] Leupin, *Barbarolexis*, p. 7.
[13] Leupin, *Barbarolexis*, p. 7. (Leupin quotes at length from Nicolas of Amiens' *De arte catholicae fidei*.)
[14] Leupin, *Barbarolexis*, p. 7.

Having explored human reliance on the grammatical copula, Leupin segues into a discussion of sexual copulation in relation to fallen human nature. In particular, he discusses 'the original unity of human nature' and Erigena's theory that the necessity of sexual copulation for procreation was a direct result of the Fall:

> Without original sin, then, man and woman would have had no need of copulative union in order to reproduce themselves; this analogy leads to the metaphorical transfer of sexual relations in linguistic terms and vice versa. The Fall thus marks the intervention of both history (death) and sexual difference. Had it not occurred, man would have multiplied in the mode of angels ... [T]he division of original unity will be overcome when the second coming takes place. Again according to Erigena, gender differences will then give way to an asexual neutrality designating no less than man in his own essence (*homo*, as opposed to *vir/mulier*).[15]

The separation of original unity of human into the fallen binary of man and woman is linked to the human linguistic need for the binary of subject and predicate. Human beings require this binary difference in order to create (another human or a written text):

> Sin, sexual differentiation, and loss of linguistic propriety are thus bound together in a rather curious configuration: metaphorically, the issue of the relation between sexes touches the very heart of the philosophical and linguistic question of predication. In the same way that predication necessitates the copula of the verb 'to be' in order to express attributive difference, so Adam and Eve must temporarily join their divided natures to perpetuate themselves.[16]

Original unity involved the conjunction of difference (that is, a lack of difference) in both linguistic and sexual natures. It should be no surprise, then, that the alchemical quest for origin – the quest for divine substance in the form of the Philosopher's Stone attained through alchemical conjunction – combines elements of the two: language and sex.

Alchemical conjunction, as it has been explored through various examples from medieval texts, is defined in Gareth Robert's *The Mirror of Alchemy* as the 'mixture or union of elements or substances *figured* as marriage, copulation, uniting of male and female or brother and sister or king and queen sometimes to form an androgyne'[17] or, as it is alternatively called within alchemical literature and scholarship, the alchemical hermaphrodite.[18] If the creation of the Stone can be accomplished only through divine revelation, and if, furthermore, the

---

[15] Leupin, *Barbarolexis*, p. 11.
[16] Leupin, *Barbarolexis*, p. 12.
[17] Gareth Roberts, *The Mirror of Alchemy: Alchemical Ideas and Images in Manuscripts and Books from Antiquity to the Seventeenth Century* (Toronto, 1994), p. 105. 'Conjunction', according to the *Middle English Dictionary* [MED] (definition 1.b), is 'sexual union or intercourse'.
[18] The alchemical hermaphrodite is also referred to as the 'Rebis' and is noted to be 'one of the most famous symbols in alchemy' in De Pascalis, *Alchemy: The Golden Art*, p. 56. See also the

Stone is the hermaphrodite (or 'asexual neutrality') representing human nature before the Fall and after the Second Coming, the alchemists are self-proclaimed scribes of God, attempting to put into words that which will return humanity to its divine origin. This theoretical premise is aptly illustrated in both Ripley's *Compound* and Norton's *Ordinal*. Arguably, both authors structure their texts to represent figuratively the sexual conjunction necessary for the creation of the Philosopher's Stone. They regularly interchange active and passive (male and female, subject and predicate) grammatical elements within their instructions for the manipulation of alchemical elements, thereby recreating the alchemical hermaphrodite within the very act of writing and reading. Such gendered grammatical play within the rhetorical structure of the *Compound* and the *Ordinal* demonstrates a means by which late medieval alchemical writers could metonymically mimic alchemical conjunction and transformation through language. In this sense, the mystical goal becomes the literary feat.

Alchemy to Norton is a 'trew science ... blessid & holye', which he has learned 'bi grace fro hevyn' (143–4, 137). Norton claims that the *Ordinal* 'Is a boke of incomperable price, / whose trowth shal nevir be defilede' (134–5). As discussed briefly above, its doctrine will teach readers to 'know fals men fro þe trewe' so that they 'may fro fals doctryne flee' in their pursuit of the Philosopher's Stone (or 'oure stone'[19] as Norton calls it throughout the *Ordinal*) (8, 97). In Chapter 4, he reiterates to his readers, 'To teche yow truth is myn entent' (1207). Norton offers in his book a type of divine knowledge set in direct opposition to that found in other false alchemical books. If the *Ordinal* is 'the boke of incomperable price', it may well be the figurative pearl meant to represent a divine revelation or truth whose secret language is comprehensible, as Norton explains, 'only bi vertue & grace' (3074). Norton, moreover, may well associate the Philosopher's Stone (the *Ordinal*'s intended creation) with Christ. As Mark J. Bruhn has illustrated, 'Through the Middle Ages the elusive Philosopher's Stone came to be seen as a metaphor for Truth, or Christ, the *Logos*'.[20] Alchemy itself is praised as a divine gift in the opening lines of the *Ordinal*'s first chapter:

> A wonderful science, secrete philosophie,
> A singuler grace & gyfte of almyghtie,
> which neuir was fownde bi labour of man,
> But it bi teching or reuelacion bigan. (183–6)

In lines reminiscent of a mystic[21] speaking of her visions, this passage asserts a divine origin for the alchemical secret in a revelation given by the 'almyghtie'

---

definitions of 'Androgyne', 'Hermaphrodite', and 'Rebis' in Diana Fernando, *Alchemy: An Illustrated A to Z* (London, 1998).
[19] For example, see lines 148, 744, 1038, 1080 (and others).
[20] Bruhn, 'Art, Anxiety, and Alchemy in the *Canon's Yeoman's Tale*', 293.
[21] See for example, Julian of Norwich, who describes one of her mystical visions as revealing a 'hey privitye [secret] hid in God, which privity He shall openly make knowen to us in Hevyn, in which knowyng we shal verily see the cause why He suffrid synne to come, in which syte we shall endlesly joyen in our Lord God' (Chapter 27, lines 961–3). *The Shewings of Julian of*

God and, by implication, connects the *Ordinal* to that origin. Likewise, Norton's advice to withdraw from 'wordly werkis' in pursuit of alchemical knowledge is similar to an aspect of medieval mystical tradition in that it echoes advice given to mystics in their pursuit of a union with God (509).[22]

In its quest for the Philosopher's Stone, alchemy presents the alchemist/writer with a linguistic dilemma. On the one hand, if the Stone does *not* exist (as a tangible object), the alchemists cannot explain how to make it. This is the possibility that Lee Patterson suggests in 'Perpetual Motion: Alchemy and the Technology of the Self': 'Because the non-existence of the philosopher's stone lured alchemy into a quest without a goal, it was forced to discover the endlessness of writing, to confront the nonidentity between language and that which it seeks to represent.'[23] On the other hand, if the Stone does exist (as the figurative pearl or the divinity), its divine truth is ineffable, existing beyond language. Thus, as with the mystic who points toward God and the visionary experience in her text, the alchemist can write only of the possibility of the Philosopher's Stone. The Stone, as described in each text, theoretically exists as only a figurative concept representing a union with or unity of the divine.

In numerous alchemical texts, including both the *Ordinal* and the *Compound*, the Stone is figured through its conjunctive, sexual stages. In this way, the sex act is an integral part of one's pursuit of divine truth and union. Erotic language is relatively common in medieval mystical works; Christ is often portrayed as the lover of the mystical bride. In alchemical works, however, the divinity is not the lover but the figurative result (in the form of the Philosopher's Stone) of sexual conjunction between passive and active partners. Sex does not occur *with* the divine but leads *to* the divine, thus subverting proscriptions separating bodily pleasures from spiritual work.[24] Norton and Ripley, writing within medieval alchemical tradition, construct their descriptions of the Stone's creation using not only sexual conjunction but also grammatical patterns that mimic the conjunctive sex act and figure the alchemical hermaphrodite – that is, the union of sexually gendered opposites or asexual neutrality.

This intersection among figurative grammar, sex and the hermaphrodite can be found in Alan of Lille's (twelfth–century) *Plaint of Nature*:

> The active sex shudders in disgrace as it sees itself degenerate into the passive sex. A man turned woman blackens the fair name of his sex. The witchcraft

---

Norwich, ed. Georgia Ronan Crampton, TEAMS: Middle English Text Series (Kalamazoo, MI, 1994).

[22] See, for example, *The Cloud of Unknowing*, in which the anonymous author advises, 'put a cloude of forgetyng bineth thee, bitwix thee and alle the cretures that ever ben maad' (Chapter 5, lines 423–4). *The Cloud of Unknowing*, ed. Patrick J. Gallacher, TEAMS: Middle English Text Series (Kalamazoo, MI, 1997).

[23] Patterson, 'Perpetual Motion', 47–8.

[24] For further exploration of divine conjunction, see Cynthea Masson, 'Queer Copulations and the Pursuit of Divine Conjunction in Two Middle English Alchemical Poems', in *Intersections of Sexuality and the Divine in Medieval Culture: The Word Made Flesh*, ed. Susannah Chewning (Burlington, VT, 2005), pp. 37–47.

of Venus turns him into a hermaphrodite. He is subject and predicate: one and the same term is given double application.[25]

Shortly thereafter, Alan discusses conversion as a sin against nature, which (in grammatical terms) is 'the interchange of the subject and predicate'.[26] (The active man is subject and the passive woman is predicate.) We also find in the *Plaint* reference to the 'defect of inverted order' – that is, a change in regular word order.[27] Alan appears to equate the sodomite, whom he figuratively condemns throughout the *Plaint*, with the hermaphrodite (mentioned in the quotation above).[28] Each term suggests a conjunction of active and passive within the same body. Whereas the hermaphrodite is figured as half man/half woman, the sodomite is understood to exchange the active for passive role in the sexual act and, thus, potentially embody both active and passive within the same (male) body. The key point within an alchemical understanding of this issue, regardless of the terminology, remains the necessity of the active and passive components co-existing in a single body. Whereas Alan emphasizes the negative and sinful outcome of confusing gender (masculine and feminine), of interchanging the subject and predicate (male and female), of inverting the passive and the active, alchemists advocate such union or interchange. Both the union of opposites and the conversion from one form to another are essential stages within the conjunctive creation of the Philosopher's Stone. Thus, unlike the hermaphrodite's negative depiction in the *Plaint*,[29] in alchemy the hermaphrodite's portrayal positively figures the intended goal of alchemical conjunction. Indeed, the hermaphrodite is aptly described by Johannes Fabricius as 'the much-coveted goal of the opus alchymicum'.[30]

At various points in the pursuit of their alchemical goals, both Norton and Ripley advise readers to pay particular attention to their language and writing. The written text will lead, or is intended to lead, to the creation

---

[25] Alan of Lille, *The Plaint of Nature*, trans. James J. Sheridan (Toronto, 1980), pp. 67–8. Both Steven F. Kruger and Carolyn Dinshaw discuss aspects of the relationship between 'sodomy' (or hermaphroditism, as figuratively explored by Alan of Lille) and language in medieval literature; however, neither author discusses this relationship within the context of alchemical literature. Steven F. Kruger, 'Claiming the Pardoner: Toward a Gay Reading of Chaucer's *Pardoner's Tale*', *Exemplaria* 6:1 (1994): 115–39 (especially third section). Carolyn Dinshaw, *Getting Medieval: Sexualities and Communities, Pre- and Postmodern* (Durham, NC, and London, 1999) (especially first chapter).
[26] Sheridan, notes to Alan of Lille's *Plaint*, p. 69, n. 7.
[27] Alan of Lille, *Plaint*, p. 134. In regard to proper word order, see also John of Garland who says, 'A noun precedes a verb, both by nature and by art' in *The Parisiana Poetria of John of Garland*, ed. and trans. Traugott Lawler (New Haven, CT, 1974), p. 111.
[28] Dinshaw refers to the 'late-medieval confusion' between the terms hermaphrodite and sodomite in *Getting Medieval*, pp. 79–80.
[29] For another discussion of a negative, though different, understanding of 'hermaphrodite', see Anne Hudson, 'Hermofodrita or Ambidexter: Wycliffite Views on Clerks in Secular Office', in *Lollardy and the Gentry in the Later Middle Ages*, ed. Margaret Aston and Colin Richmond (New York, 1997), pp. 41–51.
[30] Johannes Fabricius, *Alchemy: The Medieval Alchemists and Their Royal Art* (Copenhagen, 1976), p. 90.

of the Philosopher's Stone. Norton, clearly concerned with the *writing* of alchemical secrets, makes numerous overt references to his language and rhetoric throughout the *Ordinal*. In his prologue, for example, Norton advises the reader to 'wisely consydire þe flowris of thise booke' (16). Although 'flowris' is glossed as 'excellency' in John Reidy's edition, Norton may be referring here to rhetorical flowers or figures in an attempt to draw attention at the outset of his *Ordinal* to the structure of the written text.[31] Further along in the prologue, Norton warns 'that no man for better ne for wors / Change my writyng, for drede of goddis curs' (169–70). Indeed, says Norton, a few lines thereafter, 'changing of som oone sillable / May make this book vnprofitable' (173–4). He is concerned with exact replication. Alchemy emphasizes change, yet in this passage Norton insists upon a lack of change. His writing must remain unchanged in its structure to represent permanently alchemy's 'selcouth priuyte' (marvellous secret) necessary for alchemical transformation (172). It seems reasonable to conclude that Norton suggests here that the secrets of alchemy are hidden within the precise wording rather than in the generalized meaning of his text – that, to extrapolate further, his words *are* the secret of alchemy, or at least figuratively represent it, rather than merely outlining a practical, laboratory-based process. This hypothesis certainly fits an understanding of, if not a general consensus on, alchemical discourse as expressed succinctly by Gareth Roberts: 'The condition of its language and the way that that language expressed its physics and metaphysics may be seen as constituting alchemy.'[32] Norton, moreover, using a type of paronomasia – that is, the repetition of a word in another form[33] – changes the verb 'change' (in the phrase 'no man ... / Change my writyng') to the gerund 'changing' (in the phrase 'And changing of som oone sillable'). In doing this, he changes a predicate to a subject. Notably, Leupin, in his discussion of 'The Hermaphrodite' in Alan of Lille's work, refers to paronomasia as one of the rhetorical figures assigned to 'hermaphroditic performance'[34] – that is, the figurative representation of transgressive sexual relations. *Paronomasia* is often used by Norton and Ripley in passages that ask readers to pay attention to their writing or that emphasize alchemical transformation.

---

[31] The association of 'flowers' with 'rhetorical figures' or 'rhetorical colours' is widespread. An early example would be the eleventh-century work by Alberic of Monte Cassino, *Flowers of Rhetoric* (or *Flores Rhetorici*). This association continued into the Renaissance, as illustrated by Henry Peacham's sixteenth-century *The Garden of Eloquence*. The extended title of Peacham's work refers to 'the figures of Rhetorick' and 'all manners of flowers, colours, ornaments'.

[32] Roberts, *The Mirror of Alchemy*, p. 92.

[33] Paronomasia is defined by pseudo-Cicero as 'the figure in which, by means of a modification of sound, or change of letters, a close resemblance to a given verb or noun is produced, so that similar words express dissimilar things'; *Ad Herennium*, trans. Harry Caplan (Cambridge, MA, 1989), pp. 301–3. One type of paronomasia depends on 'a change of case in one or more proper nouns' (p. 307); this is also referred to as polyptoton. Richard Lanham defines polyptoton as 'Repetition of words from the same root but with different endings' in *A Handlist of Rhetorical Terms* (Berkeley, 1968), p. 78.

[34] Leupin, *Barbarolexis*, p. 69.

As discussed above, Ripley draws attention to the written text both in the preface and in the final section of his *Compound* (see especially 27.27 and 87.12). He summarizes his alchemical doctrine as follows:

> For to bring this Treatise to a finall ende,
> And briefly here to conclude these secrets all,
> Diligently looke thou, and to thy figure attend:
> Which doth in it containe these secrets great & small,
> And if *thou* it *conceive* both theoricall and practicall:
> By figures and colours, by scripture plaine,
> It wittily *conceived, thou* mayst not worke in vaine. (82.1)[35]

Ripley asks his reader to attend to 'thy figure' and to conceive by 'figures', 'colours' and 'scripture'. These terms have various possible meanings within alchemical instruction; however, 'figures', 'colours' and 'scripture' each can be read as a reference to writing – the first two to rhetorical figures, the third to writing itself or written characters.[36] Note again, the use of paronomasia with the repetition of the verb 'conceive' as 'conceived'. Although the repeated word remains a verb, an interchange of subject and predicate nonetheless occurs in that 'thou it conceive' becomes 'conceived thou' within the chiastic structure of this passage. Andrew Cowell describes chiasmus as an 'intertwined copulation' that represents 'the copulation of the literal and the figural'.[37] Furthermore, since 'conceive/conceived' in reference to the Philosopher's Stone often connotes sexual union through conjunction, the choice to use those words here is likely deliberate.

Indeed, as outlined by Åsa Boholm, metaphors of birth and conception in alchemical literature are common.[38] As part of her argument, Boholm discusses intercourse as a metaphor for the alchemical union leading to the conception of the Stone, depicting 'an embrace of Sun and Moon, in the guise of a King and Queen'.[39] The result of that sexual union is 'the Royal Hermaphrodite: the King-as-merged-with-the Queen'.[40] Neither Norton nor Ripley directly name the alchemical hermaphrodite – that is, they do not call the alchemical/sexual union by the word 'hermaphrodite'; however, they both insist that opposites must conjoin as one during the alchemical process in order to create the Philosopher's Stone. In the *Ordinal*, to give one example, Norton

---

35 My emphasis.
36 For a discussion of rhetorical 'colour' in relation to desire, see Andrew Cowell, 'The Dye of Desire: The Colors of Rhetoric in the Middle Ages', *Exemplaria* 11:1 (1999): 115–39. Both Ripley and Norton discuss 'colours' extensively in terms of their importance to alchemical practice. The interchange between literal and rhetorical colours in alchemy is an extensive topic that I will leave for another essay.
37 Cowell, 'The Dye of Desire', 116.
38 Åsa Boholm, 'How to Make a Stone Give Birth to Itself: Reproduction and Auto-reproduction in Medieval and Renaissance Alchemy', in *Coming into Existence: Birth and Metaphors of Birth*, ed. Göran Aijmer (Göteborg, 1992), pp. 115–53.
39 Boholm, 'How to Make a Stone Give Birth to Itself', p. 137.
40 Boholm, 'How to Make a Stone Give Birth to Itself', p. 138.

asserts that 'our stone is oon', though made of diverse materials (1122), and Ripley contends that the two alchemical bodies necessary for the alchemical process are 'One in gender' (33.2).[41] Presumably, both authors would have been aware of the figurative hermaphrodite through their familiarity with the alchemical literary and iconographical tradition.

Like Alan of Lille, Ripley condemns 'Sinfull sodomites' who, in his opinion, 'for ever were shent' (19.10); nonetheless, he plays with interchanging 'active' and 'passive' throughout the *Compound*. In regard to conjoining alchemical elements, Ripley goes as far as to say, 'This poynt also for any thing beare in minde; / That passive natures you turne into active' (92.15).[42] He not only directly advocates the interchange of passive and active, but in the structure of the quotation he inverts regular word order in both clauses. In the first quoted line ('This poynt also for any thing beare in minde'), '[t]his poynt' is the predicate object to be borne 'in minde,' which places the object before both the verb and the subject, the latter of which is not even stated directly.[43] Likewise, in the second quoted line ('That passive natures you turne into active'), 'passive natures' is the predicate object of 'turne'. Thus the subject and predicate are inverted out of regular word order in lines referring to the necessity of turning passive into active.

Ripley discusses alchemical transformation as *conversion* – a concept used in Alan of Lille, as noted earlier, to refer to 'the interchange of the subject and predicate'.[44] In a chapter entitled 'Of Congelation', Ripley describes qualities that are 'contrarious of everie element, / Till after blacke in white be made an union / Of them for ever, congeald without division' (61.16).[45] He speaks of 'this *conversion* / From thing to thing, from one state to another' and then immediately describes the 'sperme and heate' necessary for the conversion as 'sister and brother, / Which be *converted* ... / By action, and passion at last to perfect man' (61.17).[46] Elsewhere, Ripley refers to the alchemical 'sister and brother' as 'agent and patient ... coessentiall to our intent' (33.2) and contends that 'Things into things must therefore be rotate, / Untill diversitie be brought to perfect unitie' (34.8). Both 'action' and 'agent' and 'passion' and 'patient' have similar meanings parallel to active and passive states – one acts, the other is

---

41 See also: 'Of all kyndis contrarie brogth to oon accorde, / Knytt by ye doctrine of god oure blesside lorde' (Norton, 2517–18) and 'Thy waters dividing into partes two, / ... But thou must turne them all into one thing' (Ripley, 38.5). Note that in Ashmole's edition of the *Compound* (in *Theatrum Chemicum Brittanicum*) 'Matter' is used in place of 'waters' in this stanza.
42 This line occurs in a section of Ripley's work known as 'The Epistle' (or, as it is fully titled in Linden's edition, 'The Epistle by the same Author written to King Edward the 4').
43 The grammatical subject of this line (implied through the imperative verb) is *you*, the reader.
44 Sheridan, notes on Lille's *Plaint*, p. 69 n. 7.
45 'Congelation' refers to the knitting together of alchemical elements (58.1). This chapter (and the alchemical process to which it refers) follows chapters on 'Conjunction' and 'Putrefaction'. For another example of Ripley's play with conversion, see 75.8.
46 My emphasis.

acted upon.⁴⁷ The pairing of 'sister and brother' with 'agent and patient' (in the latter example) suggests that the woman (sister) is the active party and that the man (brother) is the passive. Note, as well, in the first quoted passage, that the noun 'conversion' (in 'this *conversion* / From thing to thing') is changed to the verb 'converted' (in 'sister and brother, / Which be *converted*'), emphasizing once again a grammatical conversion to parallel the alchemical conversion of active and passive elements.

Norton likewise plays with the word 'conversion' in a passage describing the 'principal agent' of the alchemical process. This principal agent requires 'grete serch made bi subtile reson' and is only perceived by a few masters since most alchemists 'marke not how colours a-ryse bi rew' (develop in sequence) (1753–6). The principal agent

> hath power Royalle ...
> The remenant qualitees to *conuerte* to his kynde;
> Of which *conuersion* Anaxagoras makiþ mynd
> In his boke of *conuersion* naturalle. (1758–61).⁴⁸

Here the verb 'conuerte' becomes the noun 'conuersion' in a discussion of changes in colour incited by the principal agent. Norton refers literally to physical colours in this passage: the alchemist is to watch for colour changes within the alchemical compounds in the laboratory. However, the passage could also allude to rhetorical 'colours' and the necessity of the reader to understand those colours. In terms of Cowell's theories in 'The Dye of Desire: The Colors of Rhetoric in the Middle Ages', 'the dyed text, by initiating desire, dyes the body of the reader'.⁴⁹ The principal agent of alchemy may figure the author, the writer who controls the 'colours' of the text through composition and, thereby, influences the response of the reader.

Mark J. Bruhn, enumerating the tasks of the alchemical adept, lists 'composition' as the third task.⁵⁰ He refers to the ability of the alchemist to write within and be inspired by the alchemical tradition. 'Composition', along with its meaning (both medieval and modern) as an act or body of writing, is also an alchemical term referring to the composition of elements, as in this passage from the *Ordinal*:

> And so of Alchymy þe trewe fundacion
> Is in composicion bi wise graduacion
> Of hete and colde, of moyste and drye,
> Knowing othir qualitees engendride therbye. (1571–4)

---

47 Definitions in the *MED* include the following: 'accioun' as 'an act, a deed'; 'agent' as 'an active principle'; 'passioun' as 'fact or condition of being acted upon, passivity'; and 'pacient' as 'a passive principle, something that is acted upon by an agent'.
48 My emphasis.
49 Cowell, 'The Dye of Desire', 124.
50 The first two are 'the reception and interpretation of a complex textual tradition' and 'laboratory experimentation, the application or "imitation" of the interpreted tradition' (Bruhn, 292).

In terms of practical alchemy, Norton advises here a balanced composition of various alchemical ingredients or components. '[H]ete and colde' and 'moyste and drye' can represent figurative opposites of masculine and feminine – components by which other qualities are 'engendride' through conjunction, to which Norton refers shortly thereafter. He uses the word 'coniunccion' (1584) and then advises the reader to 'conioyne euery element, / As watir and erthe after youre desire / welle compowned with Ayre and fyre' (1596–8). In both of these passages, which bring together opposites within the process of conjunction, we also find words that can have grammatical meanings: 'composicion' and 'compowned'.[51] The 'trewe fundacion' of alchemy could be its written composition or the way in which parts of speech are compounded to form the alchemical text. The act of writing the text requires the same process as creating the Stone. The poet-alchemist converts two elements (the blank page and the pen's ink) into another form (the text), thereby enacting the alchemical process through writing. Alchemy is not merely 'a metaphor for … poetry' (as Bruhn contends),[52] but rather the poetic alchemical text *is* a figurative representation of the Stone, as Ripley's and Norton's grammatical and rhetorical structures suggest.

In Chapter V, the longest and most technically descriptive chapter of the *Ordinal*, Norton advises his readers,

> Conioyne your elementis *Grammatically*
> with alle theire *concordis* conueniently;
> whiche *concordis* to helpe a clerke
> Be chief Instrumentis of alle this werke;
> …
> Alle the *gramarians* of Inglond & of fraunce
> Can not teche yow those *concordance*. (1637–44)

Granted, Norton hereafter also advises his reader to join elements arithmetically, musically and astrologically; however, here he asserts that his alchemical text can teach the reader something about 'concordance' that the grammarians cannot. Alchemically, 'concorde' or 'concordance' is a state of harmony, but this word also refers to grammatical concord or agreement. Again, textual language is used in the context of alchemical instructions – agreement between both alchemical and grammatical elements is thus the 'chief instrument' of alchemy. Note as well the use once again of paronomasia with 'Grammatically'/'gramarians' and 'concordis'/'concordance'. The word 'concordis' appears twice in successive clauses – first as part of the predicate, then as a subject; 'concordis' then changes to 'concordance' in the final line, where it is again part of the predicate. Similarly, 'Grammatically' is part of the predicate; 'gramarians' is part of the subject.

---

[51] According to *MED*, definition 4, 'compound' had a grammatical sense of a word composed of root and suffix. 'Compound' also refers in general to something (including a word or phrase) that consists of parts.
[52] Bruhn, 'Art, Anxiety, and Alchemy in the *Canon's Yeoman's Tale*', 307.

George Ripley also uses language that has both grammatical and alchemical connotations at the beginning of his chapter on 'Conjunction'. He explains that whereas in the preceding chapter on 'Separation' 'the elements of our stone dissevered be', in this chapter 'secret Conjunction' will join 'Natures repugnant' into 'perfect unitie'; together, these elements 'surely conjungate' (42.1). In this passage, the first verse paragraph of the chapter, we find both the words 'Conjunction' and 'conjungate'. In the next paragraph, Ripley defines conjunction as follows: 'Conjunction is nothing els / But of dissevered qualities a copulation' (42.2).[53] In the third verse paragraph of this chapter he explains that, until the time that you are cleansed from 'originall sinne', you may never begin 'true Conjunction' (42.3). Ripley's comment reflects the alchemical quest for a return to unity before the Fall. We find within the space of three verses references to conjunction, unity, copulation, sin and conjugation, the last of which can simply mean 'combined' or 'united'.[54] 'Conjugate', however, also has a grammatical meaning in Middle English referring to the formation of a verb.[55] Thus we find another example of ambiguous language, of a word with both alchemical and grammatical referents, arguably implying Ripley's desire to create a 'perfect unitie' not only of the Stone but of the text.

Norton says, 'this litille boke, the Ordynalle, / Is in Alchymye the complement of alle' (1380). 'Complement' can mean a 'completion' or a 'consummation.'[56] But 'complement' also has a grammatical sense, referring to a word or words in the predicate that refer to or describe the subject.[57] The quoted passage exemplifies grammatical complement: the phrase 'the complement of alle' is the subject complement of 'the Ordynalle'. If Norton's *Ordinal* is a complement in or of alchemy, this could suggest either that it completes alchemy or that it *is* alchemy. Similarly, in a short poem accompanying the *Compound* entitled 'Titulus operis', the function of Ripley's work is outlined:

> Here beginneth the compound of Alchymie,
> ...
> In which be declared openly
> The secrets both of Moone and Sonne,

---

53 The word 'dissevered' appears as a subject complement in the first paragraph ('elements ... dissevered be'), appearing after the noun to which it refers, and as an adjective in the next ('dissevered qualities'), appearing before the noun it modifies, but also as part of the object of the preposition 'of'. Although the repetition of 'dissevered' is not an example of paronomasia, the change in position is still interesting to note.
54 In fact, this passage from Ripley's *Compound* is the one cited in the *MED* under 'conjugat' and defined there as 'united'. Note that in Ashmole's edition of the *Compound* (in *Theatrum Chemicum Brittanicum*), 'conjugate' – without the 'n' – is used.
55 'Conjugacion' (from the same root as 'conjugate') is defined in the *MED* as the 'Stem formation (of the verb) '.
56 *MED*, definition b.
57 'One or more words joined to another to complete the sense' (*OED*). A subject complement follows a linking verb.

> How they their kinde to multiplie,
> In one bodie together must woonne. (16)[58]

'Compound' suggests two things working as a unit, whether grammatically or alchemically. They dwell in 'one bodie together' in the alchemical, hermaphroditic sense. But it is the text – the compound of words and meaning – that Ripley presents here.

The alchemical poets attempt to transcribe the creation of the Philosopher's Stone through a figurative emphasis on alchemical conjunction. Norton and Ripley continually draw attention to their written texts and to the relationship between language and alchemy. The interchange and unity of the passive and active principles are encouraged both grammatically and (in terms of alchemical conjunction) sexually. If, as Carolyn Dinshaw argues in *Chaucer's Sexual Politics*, 'literary activity has a gendered structure' in which the 'acts of writing and related acts of signifying' are masculine and, furthermore, that 'the surfaces on which these acts are performed' ('the page' and 'the text' for example) are feminine,[59] then perhaps the alchemist, in writing his text, is performing a type of alchemical conjunction in uniting the masculine and the feminine in the act of writing itself. In combination with the passive–active grammatical play, the alchemical text becomes more than an instruction manual. Norton and Ripley, in creating their written works, were *performing* conjunction. This conjunction involves something other than male–female sexual intercourse: it involves the unity of passive and active natures into one body – a metonymic icon that subverts the heteronormative (human) ideal, replacing it with a hermaphroditic (divine) union. As Menon argues, 'ignoring the rhetorical use of metonymy often goes hand in hand with ignoring nonheteronormative modes of sexuality'.[60] The possibility for sexual and gendered play within alchemical language and literature not only seduces the reader but also provides another potential site (to use Dinshaw's expression) for 'getting medieval'.[61]

---

[58] See Linden's explanatory note to 'Titulus operis' at p. 106, n. 20.
[59] Carolyn Dinshaw, *Chaucer's Sexual Poetics* (Madison, WI. 1989), p. 9.
[60] Menon, '*Richard II* and the Taint of Metonymy', 660.
[61] With my use of the phrase, I am suggesting that medieval and, in particular, Middle English alchemical literature is another body of work to which Dinshaw's theories of queer history, as they are put forth in *Getting Medieval*, could be applied.

9
Animality, Sexuality and the Abject in Three of Dunbar's Satirical Poems

ANNA CAUGHEY

IN her seminal 1980 essay *Pouvoirs de l'horreur*, Julia Kristeva identifies 'the abject' as the human reaction to a breakdown in meaning caused by the loss of distinction between the subject and the object, the interior and the exterior, or the self and the Other.[1] Her classic example of a site of abjection is that of the human corpse, which although a continuation of the dead person's corporeal presence also becomes simultaneously a marker of his or her spiritual absence, and thus must be rejected or repressed, causing the subjective experience of 'horror'.[2] Kristeva argues that human rationality necessarily involves a series of such repressions, and that the association of the human with the unrepressed thus becomes a site of potential tension. 'The abject confronts us', she suggests, 'with those fragile states where man strays on the territories of animal'.[3] This borderland between the acceptable and the unacceptable thus becomes the site of the carnivalesque, the comedic and the socially transgressive, as attested by post-medieval writers from Rabelais to Bakhtin and beyond.[4]

In the first decade of the sixteenth century, the abject was also a major concern for the poet William Dunbar, writing at the court of King James IV. Dunbar's poems are critically regarded as some of the most brilliant – and, frequently, the most offensive – writings produced in late medieval/ early modern Scotland. Many of his satirical pieces depict the court of James (who would later go on to lose his life at the disastrous Battle of Flodden) at

---

[1] Julia Kristeva, *Powers of Horror: An Essay on Abjection*, trans. Leon S. Roudiez (New York, 1982). For an earlier application of the theory of abjection to late medieval Scottish writing, see Felicity Riddy, 'Abject Odious: Feminine and Masculine in Henryson's *Testament of Cresseid*' in Sally Mapstone and Helen Cooper, ed., *The Long Fifteenth Century: Eassys for Douglas Gray* (Oxford, 1997), pp. 229–48.
[2] Kristeva, *Powers of Horror*, p. 3.
[3] Kristeva, *Powers of Horror*, p. 13.
[4] For an introductory discussion, see Andrew Stott, *Comedy* (Abingdon, 2005) pp. 83–104; Matthew Bevis; *Comedy: A Very Short Introduction* (Oxford, 2013).

play, simultaneously parodying and affirming the excesses of late medieval/ Renaissance aristocratic culture. A dance in the queen's chamber becomes an opportunity to mock the personal foibles and physicalities of the courtiers;[5] a court fool is satirized as a heroic knight,[6] and a tournament perhaps fought over one of the Moorish entertainers at James's court occasions a burlesque blazon describing the woman's African features in terms that appear grotesquely offensive to the twenty-first-century reader.[7] Relatively little concrete data on Dunbar's life remains, and his works are known primarily from a variety of miscellany and anthology sources.[8] Due to this, his poems generally do not carry authorial titles or a definite reading order – indeed, the establishment of exactly which of the surviving poems attributed to Dunbar were in fact written by him remains an issue[9] – and his biographical inferences are thus frequently problematic. Definite evidence regarding the question of whether Dunbar did or did not survive Flodden remains problematic.[10] Despite Hugh McDiarmid's assertion of *'not Burns – Dunbar'* as the foundation figure for Scottish poetry, his writing posed difficulties for nineteenth- and twentieth-century critics due to his treatment of the abject – in particular, the sexual, the scatological and the physically grotesque. Even well into the 1960s, Tom Scott described 'The Flyting of Dunbar and Kennedy' as 'the most repellent poem known to me in any language',[11] while even generally positive critics such as Ian Ross characterize Dunbar as a 'unique and disturbing presence'.[12]

[5] Designated Poem 70 by Bawcutt, see *The Poems of William Dunbar*, ed. Priscilla Bawcutt, (Glasgow, 1998), vol. 1, pp. 233–4.
[6] Designated Poem 39 by Bawcutt, see Bawcutt, *The Poems*, vol. 1, pp. 133–4.
[7] Designated Poem 28 by Bawcutt, see Bawcutt, *The Poems*, vol. 1, pp. 113–14. For further discussion of this problematic and fascinating poem, see (in reverse chronological order) David Bindman, 'The Black Presence in British Art: Sixteenth and Seventeenth Centuries', in *The Image of the Black in Western Art* ed. David Bindman and Henry Louis Gates Jr (Cambridge, MA, 2010) vol. 3, pp. 235–70; Joan Anim-Addo, 'Inventing the Self: An Introduction to the Black Woman Subject/Object in Britain from 1507', in *I Am Black/White/Yellow: An Introduction to the Black Body in Europe*, ed. Joan Anim-Addo and Suzanne Scafe (London, 2007), pp. 17–36; and Louise Olga Fradenburg, *City, Marriage, Tournament: Arts of Rule in Late Medieval Scotland* (Madison, WI, 1991), Chapter 13.
[8] These include the Bannatyne manuscript (c. 1565–68; Edinburgh, National Library of Scotland, MS Adv.1.1.6), the Maitland Folio manuscript (c. 1570–86; Cambridge, Magdalene College, Pepys Library MS 2553), the later Reidpeth Manuscript (c. 1622–23; Cambridge University Library MSS Ll.5 10) and the prints produced by Chepman and Myllar in 1508. For further discussion of the witnesses to Dunbar's work, see Bawcutt, *The Poems*, vol. 1, pp. 4–10; Catherine van Buuren, 'The Chepman and Myllar Texts of Dunbar', in *William Dunbar, 'The Nobill Poyet': Essays in Honour of Priscilla Bawcutt* ed. Sally Mapstone (Edinburgh, 2001), pp. 24–39; Julia Boffey, 'The Maitland Folio Manuscript as a Verse Anthology', in *William Dunbar, 'The Nobill Poyet'*, ed. Mapstone, pp. 40–50; Sally Mapstone, ed., *The Chepman and Myllar Prints: Digitised Facsimiles with Introduction, Headnote and Transcription*, Scottish Text Society 5th Series (Edinburgh, 2008).
[9] For further discussion of difficulties in establishing a 'Dunbar canon', see A. S. G. Edwards, 'Editing Dunbar: The Tradition', in *William Dunbar, 'The Nobill Poyet'*, ed. Mapstone, pp. 51–68.
[10] Priscilla Bawcutt, *Dunbar the Makar* (Oxford, 1999), p. 7.
[11] Tom Scott, *Dunbar: A Critical Exposition of the Poems* (Edinburgh, 1966), p. 175.
[12] Ian S. Ross, *William Dunbar* (Leiden, 1981), p. 269.

In particular, Dunbar's intermingling of the abject and the animal with praise, celebration and the use of elaborate Latin- and French-influenced diction has posed significant obstacles to coherent analysis. Antony Hasler argues that 'to attempt to produce the Dunbar canon as a ... consistent authorial project ... present[s] a scandal' and is, in effect, impossible.[13] In this essay, I will suggest that this 'scandalous' intermingling can be seen within individual poems as well as across the canon of Dunbar's works.

I will focus on three of the many poems in which Dunbar tests the boundaries between the human and the animal, the interior and the exterior, and the courtly and the obscene. It should be noted that these three poems form only a very small sample of Dunbar's dealings with the animal and the abject. In each of them he exploits what Kristeva calls the 'ambiguity' inherent in abjection: while 'we may call [abjection] a border', it in fact 'does not radically cut off the subject from what threatens it – on the contrary, abjection acknowledges [the subject] to be in perpetual danger'.[14] For Dunbar this is a danger that provides both humour and power, creating a troubling kind of enjoyment or *jouissance*, 'an ambiguous feeling pitched somewhere between pleasure and disgust'.[15] Dunbar's comic poems frequently exploit the animality – the 'state or fact of being an animal' – of their human subjects.[16] People become animals and vice versa, the physical boundaries of the body are breached by vomit, excrement and sexual congress, and various figures are threatened with ejection from the social units of the marriage, the city and the nation; yet, as I will demonstrate, Dunbar the poet draws pride and prestige from the creation of these representations, and his audience appears to have derived pleasure from them.

Perhaps Dunbar's most obvious use of the abject is seen in the poem numbered 65 by Bawcutt, and traditionally referred to as 'The Flyting of Dunbar and Kennedy' (hereafter 'The Flyting').[17] Although this poem does not deal directly with the erotic, I begin with it because it provides a useful introduction to Dunbar's treatment of the body as a site of simultaneous pleasure and horror, and to the nuanced functions of animality and abjection in his work. A 'flyting' is a verbal or written insult-battle, a term originally derived from the Old English *flītan*: 'to quarrel'.[18] The term was also applied

---

[13] Antony Hasler, 'William Dunbar: The Elusive Subject', in *Bryght Lanternis: Essays on the Language and Literature of Medieval and Renaissance Scotland*, ed. J. Derrick McClure and Michael R. G. Spiller (Aberdeen, 1989), pp. 194–208 (p. 194).
[14] Kristeva, *Power of Horror*, p. 9.
[15] Stott, *Comedy*, p. 88.
[16] 'Animality', *Oxford English Dictionary*. OED Online. September 2013. Oxford University Press. http://www.oed.com/view/Entry/7764?redirectedFrom=animality& (accessed 23 October 2013).
[17] As Bawcutt points out, 'few of the titles given to Dunbar's poems have early authority', and 'most were invented in the eighteenth and nineteenth centuries by his first editors' (Bawcutt, *The Poems*, vol. 1, p. 17). To avoid confusion in this essay, I have followed Bawcutt's convention of referring to the poems by number (assigned in alphabetical order by first line) together with the unofficial titles that are most commonly used by students and critics of Dunbar.
[18] Bawcutt, *Dunbar the Makar*, p. 222.

to informal public arguments. Although it freely employed obscene and abusive language, literary flyting also operated as a carefully constructed genre, drawing upon the French tradition of the 'sirventés-tenso'[19] and various English literary flytings[20] as well as 'the non-literary world of actual street culture'.[21] While the circumstances surrounding the composition of Dunbar and Kennedy's 'Flyting', including the extent to which it was intended as 'seriously' insulting, are not documented, it is generally perceived as 'a ritualised, literary game' rather than an expression of genuine malice.[22] Walter Kennedy, Dunbar's opponent in the match, is known to have been a graduate of Glasgow University in 1476 and the son and brother of the first and second Lords Kennedy of Dunure, Ayrshire. The fact that southern Ayrshire remained Gaelic-speaking at the beginning of the sixteenth century should be noted, as it becomes a means for Dunbar to draw comic capital from his cultural differences with Kennedy.[23] As Bawcutt argues, 'there seems to be no good reason to deny [Kennedy's] authorship' of the sections the poem attributed to him – and for the purposes of this analysis I will treat the poem *in toto* as a collaborative work.[24]

Under his three-part system of classification for Dunbar's 'modes', Jonathan Glenn positions 'The Flyting' as a 'pure vocative' poem, concerned with 'naming' and cataloguing or imprecation.[25] In this process of naming – and, more importantly, deriving power from naming – Dunbar and Kennedy each render their opponent abject by relegating him to animal status, either by directly calling him an animal ('tyk' [dog] and 'oule' [owl] are particularly popular epithets) or by comparing his behaviour to that of an animal. In total, over forty directly animal-based insults are contained within the poem, while still more refer to monsters, demons and fantastic hybrids – Kennedy theorizes that the Dunbar family is descended from the sexual union of a devil and a female bear: 'How thy forbear is come I haif a feill ... / Generit betuix ane scho beir and a deill, / Sa wes he callit Dewlbeir and nocht Dumbar' ('How your ancestor was conceived, I have a suspicion / Generated between a she-bear and a devil / So he was called "Devil-bear" and not "Dunbar"') (257–60). Similarly, Dunbar, who wishes to characterize Kennedy as an impoverished beggar, repeatedly compares him to a starving 'gled' or kite searching the landscape for food, while Kennedy condemns the castle of Dunbar by picturing it inhabited by 'Tigiris, serpentis, and taidis ... todis, wolffis, and beistis wyle' ('Tigers, serpents and toads ... foxes, wolves and cunning beasts') (287–8). Dunbar also repeatedly constructs Kennedy as the hapless victim of attack by animals, whether by alleging that he looks as though he has been pecked on

---

[19] Ross, *William Dunbar*, p. 185.
[20] Bawcutt, *Dunbar the Makar*, p. 237.
[21] Bawcutt, *The Poems*, vol. 2, p. 429.
[22] Bawcutt, *Dunbar the Makar*, p. 225.
[23] Bawcutt, *The Poems*, vol. 2, p. 427.
[24] Bawcutt, *The Poems*, vol. 2, p. 428.
[25] Jonathan A. Glenn, 'Classifying Dunbar: Modes, Manners and Styles', in *William Dunbar, 'The Nobill Poyet'*, ed. Mapstone, pp. 167–82 (p. 173).

the nose by hungry kites (52) or by constructing a fantastical set-piece in which he pictures Kennedy the Highlander being chased out of Edinburgh by jeering schoolboys and street-dogs:

> Cum thow agane to skar us with thy strais,
> We sall gar scale our sculis all the to scorne
> And stane thee vp the calsay quhair thow gais.
>
> Off Edinburch the boyis as beis owt thrawis
> And cryis owt, 'Hay, heir cumis our awin queir clerk!'
> Than fleis thow lyk ane howlat chest with crawis
> Quhill all the brachis at thy botingis dois bark.
>
> If you come again to scare us with your straws [ie. scruffy appearance]
> We shall dismiss all our schools so the pupils can scorn you,
> And stone you up the street as you leave.
>
> All the boys of Edinburgh will throng out like bees
> And cry out, 'Hey, here comes our own queer clerk!'
> Then you'll flee like an owl chased by crows,
> While all the bitches bark at your boot-heels. (214–20).

While the term 'queer' here does not yet have its modern connotations of same-sex attraction, its semantic field contains connotations of both worthlessness and oddity: it is clearly being used, together with the rest of the portrait, to reject Kennedy as Other, as not belonging to the urban landscape of Edinburgh.

The second major site of abjection in the poem is found in the aspersions that each flyter casts upon the other's ability to maintain his bodily integrity – in Kristevan terms, to defend against 'the danger to identity' that is associated with 'excrement and its equivalents'.[26] Each flyter accuses the other of being unable to control his bowels: Dunbar alleges that Kennedy is both 'countbittin' and 'beschittin' (syphilitic/impotent and covered in excrement) (239), while Kennedy's set-piece, following after Dunbar's account of his imaginary ejection from Edinburgh, features his rival suffering from a spectacular attack of sea-sickness:

> Quhen that the schip was saynit and vndir saile,
> Foul brow, in holl thou preposit for to pas.
> Thou schot and was not sekir of thy tayle,
> Beschate the stere, the compas, and the glas.
> The skippar bad ger land thee at the Bas.
> Thou spewit and kest out mony a lathly lomp
> Fastar than all the marynaris coud pomp,

---

[26] Kristeva, *Powers of Horror*, p. 71.

> When the ship was blessed and under sail,
> Foul-face, in the hold you proposed to pass the voyage,
> You vomited, and your bottom end was no more reliable,
> You be-shat the helm, the compass and the telescope.
> The captain ordered you off the ship at Bass Rock.
> You spewed and cast out many a loathsome lump,
> Faster than all the sailors could pump. (457–63)

This preoccupation with the possibility of losing control of one's digestive system also recurs in some of Dunbar's other poems, such as Poem 70 ('Ane Dance in the Quenis Chalmer'), which alludes to courtiers breaking wind during a dance, and in Poem 39 ('Schir Thomas Norny'), in which Dunbar jokingly compares the protagonist's jousting prowess to that of another who has 'befyld tua' (befouled two) saddles. Kristeva points out that loss of bodily control points out 'the objective frailty of the symbolic order':[27] in the 'Flyting' Dunbar and Kennedy jostle to push one another out of this order by symbolically depriving their opponent of control over waste, while the other poems link it with – significantly – a *reversal* or suspension of the social order as embodied in the undignified dance and the joke tournament.

Dunbar also repeatedly accuses Kennedy of being a leper: a 'La3arus, thow laithly lene tramort' ('Lazarus, you loathsome lean corpse') (161), and of living in 'Ane laithly luge that wes the lippir menis' ('a disgusting house that used to belong to the leper-men') (154). The repeated suggestion that Kennedy is dead or dying – a few lines later, he is also 'thow hungert Heland gaist' ('you hungry Highland ghost') (168) – evokes the anxiety that Kristeva identifies around the figure of the corpse: 'a body without soul, a non-body, disquieting matter'.[28] Leprosy is also profoundly abjecting in this context because it implies a lack of ability to control one's physical boundaries both in terms of having been infected with the disease itself (often perceived as sexually transmitted or connected with sexual wrongdoing, an undertone that is present in Henryson's near-contemporary *The Testament of Cresseid*) and in terms of leprosy's distressing effect on the skin as a physical boundary between the body's interior and the outside world.

Finally, both parties also invoke explicitly social boundaries in order to imagine and threaten social abjection and rejection for one another. While Dunbar pictures Kennedy being laughed out of Edinburgh, Kennedy suggests that Dunbar should leave for England where he belongs: 'In Ingland, oule, suld be thyne habitacione. / Homage to Edward Langschankis maid thy kyn' ('In England, owl, should be your dwelling-place / [Since] your ancestors made homage to Edward Longshanks') (409–10). Kennedy also mixes social and animal abjection by alluding to 'Inglise rumplis' ('English tails') (351), the

---

[27] Kristeva, *Powers of Horror*, p. 70.
[28] Kristeva, *Powers of Horror*, p. 109. See also Riddy, 'Abject odious', pp. 232–41.

Scottish legend that English people were cursed with tails.[29] In both cases, this fear of social abjection ties into Kristevan theory's concern with the 'strays and exiles and outcasts' that are inevitably created by the establishment and maintenance of social borders:[30] while Dunbar uses Kennedy's Highland ancestry and 'Erschry' (Gaelic speech) (107) as excuses to threaten him with ejection from the society of the capital, Kennedy counters by leveraging Dunbar's English-speaking Lowland ancestry into the more serious threat of ejection from the community of the nation itself.

'The Flyting' thus demonstrates some likely sites of abjection for a late fifteenth-century aristocratic Scottish audience. These include: breaches of the boundaries between human and animal (and human and demonic) behaviour; fear of the uncontrollable nature of the human body, particularly with regard to infection, emission and excrement; and fear of being pushed to the wrong side of the social boundaries delineating one's respected peer-group.

However, the question of how seriously this abjection may have been intended still remains. Another of Dunbar's poems, numbered 21 by Bawcutt and commonly known as 'The Lament for the Makaris', provides a catalogue of Scotland's greatest poets and laments the fact that they are all now dead or dying. Kennedy is included in the list:

> Gud maister Walter Kennedy
> In poynt of dede lyis veraly.
> Gret reuth it wer that so suld be:
> *Timor mortis conturbat me.* (89–92)

> Good Master Walter Kennedy
> At the point of death, in truth, lies he.
> Great pity it is that this should be:
> The fear of death disturbs me.

While critics have questioned the extent to which this poem is an exercise in self-aggrandisement – the list of Scotland's best and brightest is, after all, capped with none other than Dunbar himself – this docs not necessarily rob the expression of grief at Kennedy's death of its sincerity. It important to read 'The Flyting' as an insult competition, but a stylized one, and one that can be engaged in for the mutual profit and pleasure of the participants. In short, 'The Flyting' provides a source of *jouissance* acquired from using the confined space of the poem as a site to to 'play with' the notion of the bodily, sexually and socially abject. By labelling one another with serious forms of social abjection, Dunbar and Kennedy both exercise and 'show off' their skill with language, and work to defuse these forms of insult. Moreover, as Judith Butler points out, the act of being insulted itself can also function as a source of recognition: to be name-called is also to be *named*, and thus to be acknowledged

---

[29] Bawcutt, *The Poems*, vol. 2, p. 441.
[30] Megan Becker-Leckrone, *Julia Kristeva and Literary Theory* (Basingstoke, 2005), p. 32.

and remembered. She argues that in 'being called an injurious name, one is derogated and demeaned. But the name holds out another possibility as well: by being called a name, one is also, paradoxically, given a certain possibility for social existence.'[31]

In abjecting one another, Dunbar and Kennedy also perform a collective building-up of their fame as poets whose mutual insult-speech amuses their audience, bringing pleasure to the king and his court. By naming each other as abject outsider-figures, the poets thus paradoxically bring one another more securely *inside* the court circle regardless of the audience's decision as to 'quha gat the war' ('who got the worst of it') (554).

Poem 3, known as 'The Tretis of the Tua Mariit Wemen and the Wedo' ('The Treatise of the Two Married Women and the Widow') is perhaps even more notorious than 'The Flyting' for its use of animal-related invective, here employed in a more explicitly sexual manner. Tapping into the French tradition of the *chanson d'aventure*, the poem uses a conventional courtly setting – 'Apon the Midsumer Ewin, mirriest of nichtis' ('upon the Midsummer Eve, merriest of nights') (1) – as the occasion for the poet-narrator to overhear a conversation between the three eponymous female speakers.[32] The poem also blends elements of the *chanson de mal marieé*, the *demande d'amour* and the *planctus*, humorously destabilizing the latter by building the narrative around the complaint, not of an absent lover, but of a *present* husband.[33] The poem opens with the image of a narrator who walks within a classic *locus amoenus* '[b]esyd ane gudlie grein garth full of gay flouris' ('beside a goodly green garden full of gay flowers') (3), enjoying 'the sugarat sound' ('the sweet sound') (7) of the birdsong and 'the savour sanative of the sueit flouris' ('the wholesome smell of the sweet flowers') (8). Coming across a walled garden, he conceals himself behind the wall to hear the speech of 'thre gay ladeis' with 'tressis so glitterit as the gold' ('three beautiful ladies with hair glittering as brightly as gold') (17–19), and is quickly surprised by their distinctly uncourtly conversation.

The company consists of two married women and a widow, who are freely passing around 'ryche wynis' (rich wines) (35) and exchanging confidences. Each of the married women has a complaint to make about her husband: one is a traditional *senex amans*; 'ane wallidrag, ane worme, ane auld wobat carle' ('a miserable creature, a worm, an old woolly bearded caterpillar of a man') (89) whose physical grossness and unwanted sexual attentions disgust his young wife, while the other is a lecher who spreads his sexual favours too thinly among the women of the town, like a 'dotit dog that damys on all bussis / And liftis his leg apon loft thoght he nought list pische' ('stupid dog that pees on all the bushes / And lifts his leg up high although he doesn't need to piss')

---

[31] Judith Butler, *Excitable Speech: A Politics of the Performative* (London, 1997), p. 2.
[32] Bawcutt, *The Poems*, vol. 2, p. 284.
[33] Maureen Fries, 'The "Other" Voice: Woman's Song, Its Satire, and Its Transcendence in Late Medieval British Literature', in *Vox Feminae: Studies in Medieval Woman's Song*, ed. John Plummer (Kalamazoo, MI, 1981), pp. 155–78 (p. 168).

(186–7). As in 'The Flyting', this poem gives us the human-as-the-animal: husbands become worms, scorpions, seagulls, slugs, male cats and more. In total, the poem contains over twenty direct comparisons of people to animals, and the vast majority of these are derogatory in nature. Similarly, uncontrolled elimination (here a conflated urination/ejaculation) once more becomes a troubling site of breached borders between the inside and the outside of the body, mixed with animalization in the image of the dog. Again, as in 'The Flyting', demonic images are also introduced, as the first husband is compared to 'hiddowus Mahone' ('the hideous Devil') (101), 'auld Sathan' ('old Satan') (102), a 'bogill' ('an evil spirit') (111) and 'Belӡebub' (Beelzebub) (112).

However, these descriptions of the male characters also implicate the female speakers through their own use of the language of the abject, which appears particularly jarring alongside their conventional physical beauty. The poem's combination of the courtly and the obscene is particularly discomforting as it disrupts any notion of Dunbar's work as featuring 'three styles: high, low and plain' with easily marked distinctions from poem to poem.[34] Following Bakhtin's theory of the carnivalesque, Deanna Evans perceives the poem as a comic dramatization of the seven deadly sins in which 'women, rather than men, complain of marital woe and sexual dissatisfaction'.[35] However, given that these women are constructed by a male poet, the question of the legitimacy of their complaints becomes pertinent. Ross argues that the widow, in particular, is depicted as 'wanton of manners', and that the women's conduct reveals another side to the 'green and gold world of womanly and natural beauty' presented in the poem's opening stanzas, one that is 'unlovely and bitter'.[36] A. C. Spearing argues that the poem reveals 'not the truth about women but the truth about the nature of male fantasy about women',[37] and other critics have joined him in this reading of 'The Tretis' as a traditional 'cleric's revenge'.[38] Bawcutt, on the other hand, points out the tension between the apparent and the actual in the poem, suggesting that the relation of the courtly setting to the women's lewd discourse is 'teasing and enigmatic', not 'simply a shocking contrast between ideal beauty and ugly actuality'.[39] Maureen Fries follows this, arguing that Dunbar's characterization of the women's simultaneously abject and abjecting voices simply reflects the fact that women's speech 'is essentially

---

34 John Corbett, 'Aureation Revisited: The Latinate Vocabulary of Dunbar's High and Plain Styles', in *William Dunbar, 'The Nobill Poyet'*, ed. Mapstone, pp. 183–97 (p. 183). It should be noted that Corbett lists these simplistic distinctions in order to deconstruct them.
35 Deanna Delmar Evans, 'Dunbar's *Tretis*: The Seven Deadly Sins in Carnivalesque Disguise', *Neophilologus* 73 (1989): 130–41 (131).
36 Ross, *William Dunbar*, p. 219.
37 A. C. Spearing, *The Medieval Poet as Voyeur: Looking and Listening in Medieval Love-Narratives* (Cambridge, 1993), p. 266.
38 Bart Veldhoen, 'Reason versus Nature in Dunbar's "Tretis of the Twa Mariit Wemen and the Wedo"', in *'And Never Know the Joy': Sex and the Erotic in English Poetry*, ed. C. C. Barfoot (Amsterdam, 2006), pp. 49–64 (p. 63).
39 Bawcutt, *The Poems*, vol. 2, p. 284.

Other to the orthodoxy of male-voiced love lyric'.[40] This is particularly the case given that the courtly imagery appears not only at the poem's opening but also at its close, as the narrator returns to describing the beauty of the scene while the women perform 'danceis full noble' until 'the morow myld' ('noble dances until the mild morning') (511–13). Fries argues that the dichotomy between the narrator's diction and the women's speech is 'more than clever paradox or poetic conceit: [it] suggest[s] that, when men and women speak of love, they may (literally) not be talking the same language'.[41]

It is worth noting at this point that, unlike 'The Flyting', not all comparisons of humans to animals in 'The Tretis' are negative in nature. Early in the poem, the First Wife animalizes both men and women to present a surprising image of gender equality and sexual freedom. She suggests that wild birds have a better system for managing sexuality than do humans:

> God gif matrimony wer made to mell for ane ȝeir!
> It war bot merrens to be mair, bot gif our myndis pleisit:
> It is agane the law of luf, of kynd, and of nature,
> Togidder hairtis to strene, that stryveis with vther:
> Birdis hes ane better law na bernis be meikill,
> That ilk ȝeir, with new ioy, ioyis ane maik
>
> God, if only matrimony was made to mix [two people] for [only] a year![42]
> It's just a vexation for it to be longer, unless our minds desire it,
> It is against the law of love, of instinct and of nature,
> To restrain two hearts together that strive with each other.
> Birds have a better law than men, by a long way,
> That each year, they make joy with a new joy [i.e., a new partner].
> (56–61).

This image re-emphasizes the positive potential of sex as a distinctly animal desire, but one that is also 'of kynd and of nature', an idea that is revisited in the horse imagery that I shall discuss below.

The Widow also animalizes *herself* when describing her system for managing her second husband: she 'to flyte wes als fers as a fell dragoun' ('was as fierce in arguing as a deadly dragon') (342). This speech does play into medieval misogynist discourse regarding women's obstreperousness – it is possible that Dunbar intends the reader to laugh *at*, rather than *with*, the character. However, given that the statement is offered within the context of relating a verbal victory, it also carries overtones of pride – we are reminded of the Wife

---

[40] Fries, 'The "Other" Voice', p. 156.
[41] Fries, 'The "Other" Voice', p. 157.
[42] Here the word 'gif' could translate as either 'if' or 'give': an alternative translation might thus be 'God grant that matrimony were made to mix for a year!' It is worth noting that when translating Dunbar's Older Scots vocabulary into modern English, it is at times difficult to convey the ambiguity that he frequently exploits for comedic and/or disturbing effect: where possible, I have flagged these ambiguities in the translations given below.

of Bath's equally difficult-to-read self-identification as a 'leonesse' (*Wife of Bath's Prologue* 637). The moment is particularly ambiguous given the value that we know Dunbar places on flyting as a source of prestige and strength. The Widow further states that in the past she 'prunʒa plesandly in precius wedis' ('preened myself pleasantly in expensive clothes') (374) and 'payntit me as a pako' ('painted myself as a peacock') (379), again tapping into anti-feminist images, but doing so in a way that is presented as triumphalist; a few lines later, she is 'a papingay' (a brightly coloured parrot) while her defrauded husband is comically 'a plukit herle' (a plucked heron) (382). This linking of animal nature with power in marriage is generalized to all the women when the Widow advises her companions on the way to conceal an animal/abject mind within a saintly exterior in marriage. Cheerfully inverting the injunction of Matthew 10.16 to be 'wise as serpents and harmless as doves'[43] she blurs species boundaries still further with two lewd puns on 'tailis'/tails/tales:

> Thought ʒe be kene, inconstant, and cruell of mynd.
> Thought ʒe as tygris be terne, be tretable in luf,
> And be as turtoris in your talk, thought ʒe haif talis brukill.
> Be dragonis baitht and dowis ay in double forme,
> And quhen it nedis ʒow, onone note baith ther stranthis.
> Be amyable with humble face, as angellis apperand,
> And with a terrebill tail be stangand as edderis.

> Though you be bold, unfaithful and cruel-minded.
> Though you be fierce as tigers, be biddable in love,
> And be as turtle-doves in your talk, though you have fragile 'talis'[44]
> Be both dragons and doves in double form,
> And when you need to, then practise both their strengths.
> Appear as amiable, with a humble face, as angels,
> And with a terrible tail, sting as sharply as adders. (260–66).

If husbands are caterpillars, dogs and scorpions, wives must embrace their own animal natures in order to match them. Although Dunbar is again tapping into anti-feminist rhetoric here, this is a particularly enjoyable moment given that, as Bawcutt points out, he may also be appropriating or parodying elements of the branch of Scottish conduct literature directed towards women that appears in at least two fifteenth-century texts concerned with behaviour and conduct.[45]

As Edwina Burness notes, the association of human beings with horses is a recurrent theme for Dunbar, and the horse imagery in 'The Tretis' is particularly

---

43 Bawcutt, *Dunbar the Makar*, p. 335.
44 Here meaning either sexual parts or, as Bawcutt suggests, a pun on *tales*, narratives (Bawcutt, *The Poems*, vol. 2, p. 291).
45 Bawcutt, *The Poems* vol. 2, p. 285.

complex.⁴⁶ Both husbands and wives are presented in equine terms, invoking the biblical image of the 'yoke of marriage' as well as 'the folkloric image of sex as ploughing'.⁴⁷ However, the question of who should 'ride' whom is reversed by the Widow. Evoking the image of Aristotle and Phyllis, she describes her dead husband as a horse whom she would have ridden harder, were it not for social disapproval: 'as a best I broddit him ... / I wald haif riddin him to Rome with raip in his heid / Wer not ruffill of my renovne and rumour of pepill' ('As a beast I goaded him / I would have ridden him to Rome with a rope around his head, / Would it not have caused people to spread rumours about me') (330–2).⁴⁸ However, a few lines later *she* is the horse, rebelling against the bit and bridle in a moment of explosive orality: 'I wald na langar beir on bridill bot braid vp my heid. / Thar myght na molet mak me moy na hald my mouth in' ('I would no longer bear the bridle, but tossed up my head / There might no bit make me meek nor hold my mouth in [check]') (348–9). After literally and metaphorically spitting out the bit, the Widow then announces her dominion by reclassifying her husband as a horse again: 'Than said I to my cummaris in counsall about, / "Se how I cabeld ȝone cout with a kene brydill"' ('Then I said to my women friends in counsel with me, / "See how I tied up that colt with a keen bridle!"') (353–4). Similarly, when the First Wife is fantasizing about the possibility of choosing a new husband each year, she imagines a young, eager stallion or ox 'And quhen I gottin had ane grome, ganest of vther, / ȝaip and ȝing, in the ȝok ane ȝeir for to draw' ('And when I had found a fellow, better than the others, / Eager and young, to draw in the yoke for a year') (78–9). Here the 'yoke of marriage' is once again reconnected to the idea of 'ploughing' as sexual intercourse, suggesting the animalized fantasy husband-figure as a source of crude pleasure. This complicates the idea that men are simply 'degraded ... [to] beasts of burden' in the poem:⁴⁹ by presenting herself as an unbridleable horse and her husband as a horse that can be 'cabeld ... with a kene brydill' the Widow suggests that animalization is a nuanced process that cannot always be read as simple abjection, while the First Wife's animal fantasy refers to sexual prowess rather than the capacity to bear burdens. It may be positive to be a horse oneself – if one is a sufficiently untameable one – and characterizing one's prospective husband as a biddable or sexually eager horse may be a description given approvingly.

The simplest conclusion to be drawn may then be that by acknowledging the animal/abject within both the wives and their husbands Dunbar leaves us with sympathy for both sides – or neither. However, the poem's weaving-together of the abject and the aureate is in fact significantly more

---

46 Edwina Burness, 'Dunbar and the Nature of Bawdy', in *Bryght Lanternis*, ed. McClure and Spiller, pp. 209–20 (p. 213).
47 Burness, 'Dunbar and the Nature of Bawdy', p. 213.
48 A story that is known to have been circulating in fifteenth-century Scotland, as it appears in Gilbert Hay's 1460 *Buik of King Alexander þe Conquerour*.
49 Bawcutt, *The Poems*, vol. 2, p. 285.

complicated. As Joanne Norman suggests, 'The Tretis' sets up 'courtly and anti-courtly codes ... in a dizzying dialectic' in the women's speeches[50] – a dialectic which is ultimately subverted by the narrator's return to courtly imagery at the poem's conclusion.[51] By re-establishing standard courtly diction as though the previous comic subversion had not taken place, the poem forces us to accept that neither the goldenness nor the filth represents the speakers' 'true' selves: rather, we are led to the knowledge that human women – and human men – must live within both registers simultaneously. In the same way, Dunbar's use of both positive and abject animal imagery resists any possibility of reading the poem as a simple condemnation of sexuality as the 'animalistic' underside of courtly convention. Lois Ebin suggests that the poem maintains a tension between aureate diction and bawdy language throughout, 'the aureate inflating or enhancing its object, the bawdy dehumanising or reducing it to an animal level'[52] – yet this animal level is obviously pleasurable both for the characters and the audience. This is reflected in the narrator's concluding statement to the reader: by asking '[q]uhilk wald ʒe waill to ʒour wif, gif ʒe suld wed one?' ('which would you marry if you had to choose one?') (530), he slyly insinuates that *all* possible wives carry the potential for such behaviour.

In the poem that begins 'This hindir nycht in Dumfermeling', numbered 76 by Bawcutt and titled 'The Wowing of the King quhen he wes in Dumfermeling' in the Bannatyne manuscript ('The Wowing'), Dunbar further mixes the abject with the courtly.[53] The poem ostensibly relates a tale that the narrator has heard of recent carryings-on in Dunfermline, a town across the Firth of Forth north of Edinburgh. 'This hindir nycht in Dumfermeling' ('The other night in Dunfermline') (1), the narrator explains:

> To me was tawld ane windir thing:
> That lait ane tod wes with ane lame
> And with hir playit and maid gud game,
> Syne till his breist did hir imbrace
> And wald haif riddin hir lyk ane rame,
> And that me thocht ane ferly cace.
>
> To me was told a wondrous thing,
> That lately a fox was with a lamb,
> And played with her, and made great games,
> Then to his breast he embraced her,
> And he would have ridden her like a ram,
> And that I thought a strange situation. (2–7)

---

50 Joanne S. Norman, 'William Dunbar, Grand Rhetoriquer', in *Bryght Lanternis* ed. McClure and Spiller, pp. 179–93 (p. 189).
51 John Burrow, 'William Dunbar', in *A Companion to Medieval Scottish Poetry*, ed. Priscilla Bawcutt and Janet Hadley Williams (Cambridge, 2006), pp. 133–48 (p. 143).
52 Lois Ebin, 'Dunbar's Bawdy', *The Chaucer Review* 14:3 (1980): 278–85 (285).
53 Bawcutt, *The Poems*, vol. 2, p. 469.

In addition to the animal nature of the main figures, the image of sex as 'riding' seen in the 'The Tretis' is revisited, as is the intermingling of courtly 'game' and sexually explicit imagery. The fox in this poem – 'ane lusty, reid haird lowry' ('a lusty, red-haired crafty creature or Lawrence, "fox"') (16) – is read by critics such as Ridley and Ross as a possible allusion to the charming, playful but heavily womanizing young James IV, who is depicted in many of his portraits with long reddish-brown hair.[54] As a candidate for the 'lamb', Ross puts forward Janet Kennedy, the woman with whom James began an affair in 1498–99, and the mother of three of his eight illegitimate children, citing the fact that Kennedy 'was about to be married to Archibald Bell-the-Cat, Earl of Angus, when James took her as his mistress',[55] corresponding to the lamb's condition as one who has 'nevir trespast' (31) at the beginning of the poem.[56] However, it should be noted that critical opinion is divided on this subject: Lyall points out that 'the association of the poem with the king ... is not proven',[57] while Bawcutt notes the 'unsolved problems in identifying the fox with James IV',[58] including the mildly disparaging nature of the animal association and Henryson's prior use of 'fox' as a label for 'treacherous nobles or unprincipled churchmen' in his *Morall Fabillis* – although she does conclude that 'Dunbar probably alludes to some contemporary sexual scandal' the precise nature of which remains unknown.[59]

The description of the assignation between the fox and the lamb operates in courtly terms: the traditional red-and-white colouring associated with female beauty is evoked when we are told that 'The tod wes reid, the lame wes quhyte' ('the fox was red, the lamb was white') (22), while later the fox is compared to the successful male lover '[q]uhen men dois fleit in ioy maist far' ('when men float in joy most fair') (50). Delicately, the narrator states that he will not 'lesingis put in vers / Lyk as thir iangleris dois rehers' ('put slanders in verse / like the gossips rehearse') (42–3) – however, the 'game' between lamb and fox becomes increasingly sexually explicit:

> Quhen licht wes owt and durris wes bard
> I wait nocht gif he gaif hir grace,
> Bot all the hollis wes stoppit hard,
> And that me thocht ane ferly cace.
>
> When lights were out and doors were barred,
> I don't know if he showed her any mercy,

---

[54] It is worth noting, however, that the title is only found in the Bannatyne MS, and may have been given by Bannatyne rather than being authorial.
[55] Ross, *William Dunbar*, p. 168.
[56] For further discussion of James IV's relationship with Kennedy, see Ishbel C. M. Barnes, *Janet Kennedy, Royal Mistress: Marriage and Divorce at the Courts of James IV and V* (Edinburgh, 2007), pp. 17–54.
[57] R. J. Lyall, 'William Dunbar's Beast Fable', *Scottish Literary Journal: A Review of Studies in Scottish Language and Literature* 1:1 (1974): 17–28 (25).
[58] Bawcutt, *The Poems*, vol. 2, p. 470.
[59] Bawcutt, *The Poems*, vol. 2, p. 470.

> But all the holes were stopped hard,
> And that I thought a strange situation. (46–49)

The poem also emphasizes the fact that the lamb consents, or at least makes no objection, to this encounter: 'scho schup nevir for till defend hir' ('she never tried to defend herself') (27), and 'this innocent ... tuke hert that scho wes handlit fast / And lute him kis hir lusty face' ('this innocent ... took heart that she was held fast / And let him kiss her [pleasant, beautiful or lustful – all meanings seem intended here] face') (31–3). Shortly afterwards a wolf appears to interrupt the 'play'; this figure can be read as either an angry husband/lover[60], perhaps evoking the traditionally adulterous nature of the *paramour* relationship, or an equally angry father-figure.[61] The narrator relates how the wolf 'ombesett the hous / Vpoun the tod to mak ane chace' ('besieged the house / to chase out the fox') (53–4). Unable to escape, and unnerved by the howling of the wolf:

> This wylie tod plat doun on growf,
> And in the silly lambis skin
> He crap als far as he micht win
> And hid him thair ane weill lang space.
>
> This crafty fox crawled down on the ground,
> And in the innocent lamb's skin,
> He crept as far as he could get,
> And hid himself there for a good long time. (58–61)

On the crudest level, this image may simply convey sexual penetration: the fox 'crept inside' the lamb, then remained quiet and hoped not to be discovered. However, Bawcutt glosses the moment in a more threatening manner: 'the image here is peculiarly sinister, and implies ... that the fox has killed the lamb' and has *climbed inside her empty skin* to hide there, conflating sexual 'consumption'/consummation with a literal gustatory consumption.[62] This is reinforced, as Bawcutt points out, by the earlier use of 'morsall of delyte' to describe the lamb in line 23, combining 'the literal sense, "small mouthful of food", with the metaphorical sense, "pretty young woman"' and the poem's later use of 'strikkin' in line 66, with a double meaning of '"struck", "killed" and "copulated with"'.[63] The poem concludes with the unhappy wolf returning to his den, forced to accept 'the secound place' ('second place') (68) as either lover or hunter – exactly which remains unclear. Disturbingly, we are given no information as to whether the lamb emerges from the encounter alive.

Dunbar furthers our sense of ambivalence in the poem's refrain: a 'ferly case' can be translated, as I have given it above, as a 'strange', 'astonishing'

---

[60] Barnes, *Janet Kennedy, Royal Mistress*, p. 14.
[61] Scott, *Dunbar: A Critical Exposition of the Poems*, pp. 214–15.
[62] Bawcutt, *The Poems*, vol. 2, p. 471.
[63] Bawcutt, *The Poems*, vol. 2, p. 471.

or 'wondrous' event or situation, but the word is derived from the Old Norse *ferligr*, 'monstrous', and its semantic field also includes connotations of monstrosity or unnaturalness.[64] The poem maintains a sense of instability throughout: are we to perceive these animal sex acts as shameful, menacing, comic, satisfying, or all of the above? Despite the fox's glossy coat and the lamb's innocent beauty, abjection is introduced both by the transgressive nature of the 'ferly' interspecies sex and by the disturbing questions we are left with regarding exactly to what extent the borders of the lamb's body have been breached by the fox's 'creeping inside'. Again, this is reminiscent of Kristeva, who reminds us that it is not necessarily 'lack of cleanliness or health that causes abjection but what disturbs identity, system, order', and 'what does not respect borders, positions [and] rules'.[65]

Ross suggests that the poem is moralistic in intent: 'the point of the joke would be to awaken shame in the King when he was made to view his animal-like antics, and to encourage him to maintain a consciously rational existence.'[66] Similarly, Florence Ridley characterizes the tone as one that 'teases' the king when he 'gets caught' in illicit sexual escapades.[67] However, this sits uneasily with Dunbar's position as a servitor to the king and a member of his court – as Edwards comments, those of his poems that 'appeared in print during his lifetime did so under the auspices of James IV's own printers', and many of his poems speak directly to James and to his queen, Margaret.[68] While Dunbar does playfully satirize the king and court's excesses in burlesques such as Poem 28, it appears somewhat unlikely that he would produce a poem deliberately shaming or condemning the monarch for his sexual escapades – although Ridley's assessment of 'teasing', in the most light-hearted sense of the word, may be closer to the mark. Describing Dunbar's petitionary poems, which are gathered in the Maitland Folio,[69] Hasler notes that this manuscript context 'suggests circulation within a small court coterie',[70] meaning that the poems were 'written to amuse an audience to whom the poet was familiar'.[71] 'The Wowing' appears in the Maitland Folio poem (it also appears in the Bannatyne and Reidpeth manuscripts).[72] Combined with its tone and content,

---

64 'Ferly', *Dictionary of the Scots Language/Dictionar o the Scots Leid*, ed. Susan Rennie (Dundee, 2004).
65 Kristeva, *Powers of Horror*, p. 4.
66 Ross, *William Dunbar*, p. 168.
67 Florence H. Ridley, 'Scottish Transformations of Courtly Literature: William Dunbar and the Court of James IV', in *The Expansion and Transformation of Courtly Literature*, ed. N. B. Smith and J. T. Snow (Athens, GA, 1981), pp. 171–84 (p. 173).
68 Edwards, 'Editing Dunbar: The Tradition', p. 51.
69 See note 8 above.
70 Antony Hasler, *Court Poetry in Late Medieval England and Scotland: Allegories of Authority* (Cambridge, 2011), p. 64. See also Priscilla Bawcutt, 'The Earliest Texts of Dunbar', in *Regionalism in Late Medieval Manuscripts and Texts: Essays Celebrating the Publication of A Linguistic Atlas of Late Medieval English* (Cambridge, 1991), pp. 183–98.
71 Hasler, *Court Poetry*, p. 64.
72 See footnote 8 above for details of these manuscripts: note that the poem is incomplete in Reidpeth (Bawcutt, *The Poems*, vol. 2, p. 470). It is worth observing here that the poem's

it is tempting to suggest that it was intended to circulate on an intimate level, and perhaps to function as an inside joke for a small-scale audience familiar with the events to which it alludes.

Lyall and Bawcutt[73] both suggest that the poem 'belongs to the genre of beast-fable',[74] perhaps following the example of Dunbar's recent predecessor Henryson, whose beast-fables questioned and satirized aspects of fifteenth-century Scottish society. However, as Ridley comments, the poem 'scarcely fits the fable genre':[75] if 'The Wowing' carries a moral, it is a dark and obscure one. Moreover, while the motif of a 'wolf in sheep's clothing' is relatively common in Aesopic literature, 'the *fox* in a lamb's skin is a rarer and almost exclusively Scottish phenomenon'.[76] It also appears in the poem 'The Thre Prestis of Peblis' and on two other occasions in Dunbar, most notably in 'The Tretis' in which the Widow admits that 'As foxe in a lambis fleise fenye I my cheir' ('like a fox in a lamb's fleece, I pretend to be sorrowful') (423) when considering male admirers in church. To this end, as Bawcutt suggests, the less overtly moral and more 'trickster'-focused French *Roman de Renart* provides a more useful context for this poem than the moralistic Aesopic tradition.[77] The *Roman de Renart* and its descendants were circulating in Scotland at the end of the fifteenth century and may have been drawn upon by Henryson for a number of his *Morall Fabillis* such as 'The Fox and the Wolf', 'The Trial of the Fox', 'The Fox, the Wolf and the Husbandman' and 'The Fox, the Wolf and the Cadger'. This alternative tradition, less rigidly moral than the Aesopic beast-fables and more akin to the *fabliau*, frequently features sympathetic 'trickster' fox protagonists whose schemes to win food, social advantage and prestige are successful and go unpunished by the story's conclusion. As in many Reynardian fables, while the tone of 'The Wowing' is comic and grotesque, it is not at all clear that we are being encouraged to view the fox as a purely negative figure. Indeed, the narrator praises his craftiness and blazons his virility and masculine physical attributes:

> The tod wes nowder lene nor skowry.
> He wes ane lusty, reid haird lowry,
> Ane lang taild beist, and grit with all.

presence in the Bannatyne manuscript (c. 1568) and the Reidpeth manuscript (begun 1622) may suggest a wider circulation.

73 Priscilla Bawcutt, '"Nature Red in Tooth and Claw": Bird and Beast Imagery in William Dunbar', in *Animals and the Symbolic in Mediaeval Art and Literature*, ed. L. A. J. R. Houwen (Groningen, 1997), pp. 93–105 (p. 102).
74 Lyall, 'William Dunbar's Beast Fable', 26.
75 Florence H. Ridley, 'The Treatment of Animals in the Poetry of Henryson and Dunbar', *The Chaucer Review* 24:4 (1990): 356–66 (360).
76 Lyall, 'William Dunbar's Beast Fable', 24.
77 Bawcutt, *The Poems*, vol. 2, p. 469. For further information on the *Roman de Renart*, see R. Anthony Lodge and Kenneth Varty, *The Earliest Branches of the Roman de Renart* (Louvain, 2001); J. R. Simpson, *Animal Body, Literary Corpus: The Old French 'Roman de Renart'* (Amsterdam, 1996) and Alison Williams, *Tricksters and Pranksters: Roguery in French and German Literature of the Middle Ages and the Renaissance* (Amsterdam, 2000).

> The fox was neither lean nor scruffy.
> He was a lusty, red-haired Lawrence,
> A long-tailed beast, and large all over. (15–17)

Although we begin to perceive the 'playing' of the fox and the lamb as less courtly and more carnal as the poem goes on, there still seems little evidence that we are encouraged to see the fox as the butt of a 'joke' or the subject of shame. Rather, the use of animal sexuality, in all its explicitness and violence, becomes a source of dark *jouissance* in which we are encouraged to share from the fox's perspective:

> He held hir till him be the hals
> And spak full fair, thocht he wes fals,
> Syne said (and swoir to hir be God)
> That he suld nocht twich hir prenecod.
> The silly thing trowd him, allace.
>
> He held her to him by the neck,
> And spoke very fairly, though he was false,
> Then said (and swore to her by God)
> That he would not touch her 'pincushion',
> The [foolish/innocent] thing believed him, alas. (36–40)

Although he is depicted as both lecherous and deceitful, it is clear that the laugh in this passage is at the expense of the lamb, for whom 'silly' takes its full semantic range of 'innocent', 'hapless', 'helpless', 'deserving pity', 'feeble-minded',[78] rather than on the lecherous fox who wants to 'touch' her transparently euphemistic 'pincushion'. The fox functions as a sexual 'trickster' whose exploits are to be admired by the narrator and audience, even as his moral transgressions are noted. In 'The Flyting', Dunbar and Kennedy raised their real-life social prestige as poets by play-acting at reducing one another to animals in their public contest of words. Here, whether the fox is actually James IV or another contemporary 'lady-killer', Dunbar appears to be elevating the social prestige of the figure he pretends to chastise for a 'crime' that the audience is in fact invited to wink at. 'Having' the lamb, in whatever sense we choose to take the word, is an amusing trick that the hero has succeeded in getting away with rather than a subject for genuine reproach.

Whether Dunbar is animalizing his opponent in 'The Flyting', depicting the animal side of human sexuality in 'The Tretis' or playing out the disturbing bestial sex of the 'The Wowing', one constant theme in his portrayal of the animal abject emerges. This is, in Bawcutt's words, 'a strong sense of parity between animals and humans', in which we learn that 'Man, rather than [being] a being of a higher order ... is involved in the same natural cycle'.[79]

---

78 'Sely', *Dictionary of the Scots Language/Dictionar o the Scots Leid*.
79 Bawcutt, 'Nature Red', pp. 104–5.

While some critics have read this as a revelation of horror, arguing that it is 'not only degrading, but also [conveys] a quality of sinfulness and depravity',[80] for Dunbar and his intended circle of readers it is clearly also a source of power and pleasure. C. S. Lewis famously characterized the human being as 'an animal which finds its own animality either objectionable or funny'[81] – but in the poems examined here these are not two separate possibilities, but an ambivalent and indivisible whole. Animal nature and the abject self are clearly presented as abhorrent – yet we are also repeatedly invited to enjoy both the characters' abjection and our own disgust at its presentation. In Dunbar's satirical poems, as in so many comedic texts ancient, medieval and modern, 'the moment you are most like an animal is also a moment in which you will find a way to understand yourself as more than that':[82] perhaps, indeed, the moment at which you will find yourself most fully human. For Dunbar, the act of seizing or conveying social, verbal and sexual power is rooted in an acknowledgement of the pleasures and horrors of the body – and ultimately, in an acceptance of the animal nature of the self.

---

[80] Veldhoen, 'Reason versus Nature', p. 61.
[81] C. S. Lewis, *Miracles: A Preliminary Study* (1947; London, 2001), pp. 206–7; the connection here is drawn from Bevis, *Comedy*, p. 24.
[82] Bevis, *Comedy*, p. 28.

10
The Awful Passion of Pandarus

CORY JAMES RUSHTON

THERE was a time when all good and alert critics, according to E. Talbot Donaldson, were supposed to be in love with the heroine of *Troilus and Criseyde*. Gretchen Mieszkowski, writing on Donaldson's important and compelling criticism, addresses this oddity:

> Is Donaldson's criticism dated? Surely some of it is. When he writes in *Chaucer's Poetry* that Criseyde 'has almost all the qualities that men might hope to encounter in their first loves', I, for one, hear the white-picket-fences of the 1950s translated into a critical position. This is the Donaldson who told graduate students that no woman could understand *Troilus and Criseyde* because the experience of the poem required falling in love with Criseyde.[1]

Leaving aside Donaldson's apparent dismissal of same-sex attraction, further leaving aside the privilege on display, try replacing 'falling in love' with lust, 'their first loves' with the first girl who lets them get to fourth base. At that point, we might be nearer to an understanding of Pandarus than most criticism has previously allowed: for the possessiveness of Donaldson is a milder, partly because it is extra-diegetic, form of the possessiveness of Pandarus. Donaldson argues that the reader must 'skate over' the scene in which Pandarus visits Criseyde in bed, the morning after she first sleeps with Troilus, otherwise said reader will 'end up in some very cold, very dark water'.[2] To interpret would be to risk drowning. Worse than that, Donaldson also notes Pandarus's Anteus-like ability to elude or escape 'Every wrestling hold known to criticism',[3] but I will not attempt to pin Pandarus down here. Something might happen, given his tendency to seduce critics of all stripes. And I will not insist, as nobody now insists, that we love Criseyde (although we are perhaps supposed to sympathize

---

[1] Gretchen Mieszkowski, '"The Least Innocent of all Innocent-Sounding Lines": The Legacy of Donaldson's *Troilus* Criticism', *The Chaucer Review* 41:3 (2007): 299–310 (307).
[2] E. Talbot Donaldson, *Chaucer's Poetry* (New York, 1958), pp. 284–5.
[3] Donaldson, *Chaucer's Poetry*, p. 285.

with her, either because Chaucer wants us to do so, or because we live in a post-feminist age, or both). However, I will argue here that part of Chaucer's method, regardless of where our rational and emotional sympathies should lie, is to make us feel complicit in the actions of Pandarus, and thus complicit in his desires: the issue is not the lovableness of Criseyde, but her fuckability.

When Troilus and Criseyde make love for the first time, the famous passivity of the former is played to good effect against the timidity of Criseyde. Pandarus links his happiness with that of the lovers early in the text, even before he approaches Criseyde: once the lovers are united, he promises, 'we may ben gladed alle thre' (I. 994). His constant proximity to the lovers betrays a possibly voyeuristic interest; critics have been unable to agree on whether he leaves the room at all when the lovers first make love. Criseyde, staying at her uncle's house to avoid going home in bad weather, is alarmed at the 'sodeyn comynge' of Troilus to her room (through a secret door), even though he is on his knees beside her bed in a posture of courtly submission, almost presented as an offering (III. 953–9). Pandarus is needed to negotiate power between two individuals who seem utterly incapable of doing it for themselves, and the reader is likely reminded that these negotiations have always been partially a show put on for Pandarus himself, who busies himself with reading an 'old romaunce' by the fire as he waits for things to heat up (III. 978–80). The foreplay of Troilus and Criseyde is sweet, but embarrassing – or is it embarrassing, but sweet? – as Troilus faints with emotion, and must be hauled 'aswowne' into his beloved's bed. When her kisses wake him up, his first words indicate that he does not know where he is or what Criseyde is doing (III. 1119–24). She wonders, and many readers wonder with her, '"Is this a mannes game?"' (III. 1126).[4] Pandarus decides that light is not conducive to whatever game this is, and takes away the candle (III. 1135–41); he is still there a few lines later, when he encourages Troilus not to faint again (III. 1188–90). Criseyde shows real anxiety (or, perhaps, arousal – or both) when Troilus at last embraces her: 'Right as an aspes leef she gan to quake' (III. 1200–1).

Pandarus's motivations in acting as Troilus's agent are thinly sketched: love of his friend, a desire for his niece which can only be enacted vicariously, an unsuccessful love affair of his own which prompts a kind of empathy in him: 'That Pandarus, for al his wise speche, / Felt ek his part of loves shotes keene' which make 'his hewe a-day ful ofte greene' (II. 57–60). Earlier, he had told Troilus that there is someone he loves 'best, and that me smerteth sore' (I. 667). Criseyde refers to this mysterious lover in another moment full of ambiguity. When he asks whether the book she's reading is about love, she replies: '"Uncle," quod she, "youre maistresse is nat here"' (II. 98). Everyone has a good laugh, which sounds both arch and knowing: the book is about Thebes, that famous city destroyed by incest and patricide (II. 99–102). Pandarus

---

[4] Cory James Rushton, 'Sexual Variations', in *A Cultural History of Sexuality in the Middle Ages*, ed. Ruth Evans (Oxford and New York, 2012), pp. 81–100 (pp. 96–7).

dismissively states that he knows all about Thebes, and suggests that Criseyde dance with him to celebrate springtime: to '"don to May som observaunce"' (II. 111–12). This love affair may or may not actually exist: critics seem entirely divided on whether Pandarus is actually in love with someone or not, and if he is in love with someone, if that someone is Criseyde. Fehrenbacher reads Criseyde's response as a joking attempt to 'restore a sense of propriety, to deflect such desire, by emphasizing their blood relationship' before referring to Thebes' history of 'incestuous desire in its most unpalatable and destructive form'.[5] Even if there is some other woman whose love is denied to Pandarus, the glancing manner in which it is invoked and then dismissed from the narrative depends on the tradition of the domina-mistress going back to Republican Rome. In fact, as Marilynn Desmond reminds us, it goes back specifically to Ovid, whose satiric manual for the pursuit of sex includes almost contrary advice: sometimes you need to force a woman and sometimes you need to pretend to debase yourself, depending on circumstances that include, among other factors, her social rank.[6] Chaucer only needs to invoke the idea of the unattainable to simultaneously invoke the idea of attainment by force, the erotics of the situation fully dependent on various competing social conventions. Pandarus thinks of his lady, whoever she is, as something which gives him pain, but that line of thought leads inexorably to a plan which calls for the manipulation and seduction of (another, or the very same?) lady.

Something clearly causes Pandarus to sleep badly the night before he is to begin the winning of Criseyde, something to do with that mysterious, unexplained love that fills him with woe:

> So shop it that hym fil that day a teene
> In love, for which in wo to bedde he wente,
> And made, er it was day, ful many a wente. (II. 61–3)

He moves from the restless night to the day's specific activity through a mythologically significant bird's song:

> The swalowe Proigne with a sorrowful lay,
> Whan morwen com, gan make hire waymentynge,
> Whi she forshapen was; and evere lay
> Pandare abedde, half in a slomberynge,
> Til she so neigh hym made hire cheterynge
> How Tireux gan forth hire suster take,
> That with the noyse of hire he gan awake (II. 64–70)

Pandarus is immediately prompted into activity by the swallow's song, remembering the 'gret emprise' he has undertaken on behalf of Troilus; he examines

---

5 Richard W. Fehrenbacher, '"Al that chargeth nought to seye": The Theme of Incest in *Troilus and Criseyde*', *Exemplaria* 9:2 (1997): 341–69 (363).
6 Marilynn Desmond, *Ovid's Art and the Wife of Bath: The Ethics of Erotic Violence* (Ithaca, NY, and London, 2006), pp. 41–6.

his horoscope which gives him confidence that the time is right, and the narrator asks the two-faced god Janus, here the god of entrances, to guide him in his task (II. 71–7).

The poem suggests elsewhere, obliquely, that Pandarus has fantasized about Criseyde. When she is forced to stay the night in a room at his house, Pandarus reveals that he has a trap-door which allows him access to that room; startled by his sudden appearance beside her bed, he warns her not to call for her servants. If she does, '[t]hey myghte demen thyng they nevere er thoughte' (III. 763). Evan Carton draws out the implications: 'Pandarus' intimation is clear: what the attendants have never thought before but might now imagine is incest. He, evidently, has imagined it.'[7] Pandarus might well indulge himself some eight hundred lines later, the scene in which the narrator tells us that he cannot tell us about what happens (III. 1555–82, quoted below). Carton argues that the narrator leaves so much to the reader's imagination, so explicitly, that the reader becomes 'responsible for the meaning he produces':

> if the possibility is to be realized, we must realize it in our reading. But, in the instant that we do, we (like Pandarus) strip ourselves of our last defense, the vicariousness of our involvement, and come face to face with the thoroughness of our complicity in all that has occurred.[8]

Perhaps Chaucer is questioning standard gender or sexual stereotypes here: Criseyde, famous example of infidelity, is pushed into a relationship with Troilus and perhaps with her uncle, and is then forced into a camp of foreigners, where she finds protection with another lover, the implication being that she is also forced then.

Pandarus's early morning visit to Criseyde's post-coital borrowed bed has been read in disturbing ways, but perhaps more surprisingly it has also been read innocently:

> And ner he com, and seyde, 'How stant it now
> This mury morwe? Nece, how kan ye fare?'
> Criseyde answerde, 'Nevere the bet for yow,
> Fox that ye ben! God yeve youre herte kare!
> God help me so, ye caused al this fare,
> Trowe I,' quod she, 'for al youre wordes white.
> O, whoso seeth yow knoweth yow ful lite.'
>
> With that she gan hire face for to wrye
> With the shete, and wax for shame al reed;
> And Pandarus gan under for to prie,
> And seyde, 'Nece, if that I shal be ded,

---

[7] Evan Carton, 'Complicity and Responsibility in Pandarus' Bed and Chaucer's Art', *PMLA* 94:1 (1979): 47–61 (56).
[8] Carton, 'Complicity and Responsibility', 58.

> Have here a swerd and smyteth of myn hed!'
> With that his arm al sodeynly he thriste
> Under hire nekke, and at the laste hire kyste.
>
> I passe al that which chargeth nought to seye.
> What! God foryaf his deth, and she al so
> Foryaf, and with here uncle gan to pleye,
> For other cause was ther noon than so.
> But of this thing right to the effect to go:
> Whan tyme was, hom til here hous she wente,
> And Pandarus hath fully his entente. (III. 1562–82)

Criticism has been divided in reading this scene: innocent word play or something altogether more sinister? Criseyde's blushing could be an understandable reaction to Pandarus's knowledge of her newly active sex life and nothing more, especially given very different ideas about privacy in the fourteenth and twenty-first centuries. But there are curious markers of discomfort everywhere, not just in Chaucer's bantering refusal to gossip (III. 1577) or the irony of comparing whatever happens here to the crucifixion of Christ (III. 1578): the arm, thrust under Criseyde's neck and compared to a sword (III. 1574–6), the groping under the sheets (III. 1572); or Criseyde's playing with her uncle because there was no other possible response (III. 1579–80), and Pandarus achieving 'fully his entente' (III. 1582). One would have to work hard to avoid the strong implication of impropriety, even assault.

Critics have been generally up to the task of working hard to avoid exactly those implications Chaucer seems to have intended, sometimes through outright denial but at other times through a refusal to make any kind of claim at all except for the saving throw of twentieth-century criticism, ambiguity: as Barry Windeatt contends, 'baseness remains an implication' and not a certainty. The editor of the *Riverside Chaucer*, the standard student Chaucer experience, writes that the accusation of seduction or rape here is 'baseless and absurd'.[9] John Burrow argues that whether Chaucer intended it or not, this scene cannot go 'untouched by suggestions of avuncular or vicarious eroticism; but they are offered as *signa reconciliationis*, and it is as such that Criseyde happily accepts them'.[10] Mieszkowski briefly rehearses the case against Pandarus, citing first Donaldson ('the least innocent of all innocent-sounding lines' in a 'delightful scene'), then four critics writing between 1968 and 1971, followed by more elaborate arguments by Carton in 1979 and Richard Fehrenbacher in 1997.[11] Chaucer knew his craft enough that he could have avoided all hint of impropriety had he wanted; and it is important to note that Chaucer did not find this scene in Boccaccio, although Spearing is entirely right to remind us that most or even all of Chaucer's audience would not have read or known

---

9 Fehrenbacher, '"Al that chargeth nought to seye"', 342.
10 J. A. Burrow, *Gesture and Looks in Medieval Narrative* (Cambridge, 2002), p. 125.
11 Mieszkowski, '"The Least Innocent of all Innocent-Sounding Lines"', 306.

Boccaccio.[12] Whatever it is that this scene says about Pandarus, and about his relationship with his niece, Chaucer clearly presents us with a suggestive scene, one that simultaneously sets off alarm bells and throws sound-muting pillows over them. His insistence that he will 'passe al that chargeth nought to seye' sounds suspiciously like other medieval writers faced with the reality of incest. Are we to read Criseyde as the victim of Pandarus's inappropriate attentions?

Why do so many of the 'innocent' readings of this passage start to look more like a Pythonesque 'nudge-nudge, wink-wink'? Fehrenbacher notes that the 'shotes keene' of Pandarus's affair sound suspiciously reminiscent of the moment when Troilus is 'Right with hire [Criseyde's] look thorugh-shoten and thorugh-darted' (I. 325).[13] Fehrenbacher concludes by refusing to 'assert that Pandarus's mentions of an unnamed love throughout the text are to be taken as veiled references to Criseyde; rather it is to suggest that in the economy of love in which Pandarus participates, desire itself is a much more unstable thing than it represents itself to be – to the point that it may even transgress that economy's own barriers'.[14] The 'dreamy vision of incestuous rape', on Fehrenbacher's account, allows Pandarus to participate in a discourse that allows incestuous desire by paradoxically forbidding it.[15]

Criseyde's fear at the moment of the consummation of the affair with Troilus is perhaps not unwarranted, at least as far as the narrator is concerned; he has only just drawn a parallel between sexual activity and the hunt: 'What myghte or may the sely larke seye, / Whan that the sperhauk hath it in his foot?' (III. 1191–2). In the narrator's view, Criseyde has no more choice in this matter than a songbird in the claws of a raptor. This invocation of the hunter/prey relationship to describe sexual seduction and foreplay is not unique in the Middle Ages, nor is it unknown in subsequent centuries. In *Sir Gawain and the Green Knight* (also fourteenth-century), Gawain finds himself confronted in bed, naked, by the unnamed lady of the castle. Social awkwardness quickly becomes something else. She tells Gawain that he is 'tan astyt' (quickly caught), and that she intends to bind him in his bed (1208–11). She is flirtatious and playful, and her language of capture is the language of bondage, sadomasochism's kinder, gentler cousin; the courtly context and the magic of the Green Knight and the goddess Morgan le Fay cannot make this erotic moment look entirely foreign to the reader. Indeed, the moment does not fully work if the erotic potential is not acknowledged; otherwise it is simply inept hosting. Nor does it seem unlikely that morning is the best time to seduce a visiting knight, just as morning is the time when Pandarus lies half-awake in bed, dreaming of a Philomela who shades imperceptibly into Criseyde. There is a certain kind of energy at work in the morning, and in both texts that energy

---

[12] A. C. Spearing, *Textual Subjectivity: The Encoding of Subjectivity in Medieval Narratives and Lyrics* (Oxford, 2005), pp. 85–6.
[13] Fehrenbacher, '"Al that chargeth nought to seye"', 361.
[14] Fehrenbacher, '"Al that chargeth nought to seye"', 361.
[15] Fehrenbacher, '"Al that chargeth nought to seye"', 361–2.

asserts itself as the language of capture and containment, and ultimately of use. Pandarus will drive the deer, Criseyde – the prey – right towards the bow of Troilus (II. 1535).[16]

As Marilynn Desmond has argued, Foucault's assertion that sexual sadism only becomes possible in the eighteenth century is accurate in its 'historically specific' form, but 'a cultural fantasy of power erotics as the triumph of delirium and desire emerges in the high Middle Ages', specifically in the 'proliferation of texts and images of the ancient philosopher Aristotle mounted and ridden by a woman'.[17] Desmond argues that this image percolates through European literature in the Old Woman of the *Roman de la Rose*, who suggests that a certain young man has a mouth too tender for the bridle (thereby implying that bits sometimes belong in human mouths); or in Gower's version of the story of King Cyrus dominated by the 'goodly lok', a glare perhaps, of the woman Apemen.[18] Desmond argues that while the image of Aristotle ridden 'encodes a misogynist anxiety regarding female sexuality, it nonetheless designates sexual agency as separate from masculinity, and in the process it highlights the erotic value of sexual difference in medieval cultures', a distinction between an erotic power-reversal and the 'erotic violence ... most evident in marital violence, a form of intimate violence that enacts masculine dominance'.[19] This is not to say that the same theme – the eroticism of humiliation or helplessness, of captivity – could not be found earlier. Two stories in Jerome's *Life of Paul* involve beautiful young men tied up and either covered in honey or fondled by courtesans.[20] In these cases, the eroticism is partially found in a reversal of the normal power hierarchy, a playing with the physical and social differences between medieval men and women. If we are meant to see the taking of Criseyde as potentially erotic, even if we are then meant to critique that eroticism, it would seem that the idea of the female as powerful courtly domina is itself ripe for reversal. As Robert Mills has argued, cases in which female saints are the object of potentially titillating bondage and sadism are not hard to find, but these by definition do not involve the construct of courtly love.[21] Chaucer plays most explicitly with the gap between courtly love and male aggression.

There is at least some manuscript proof for readers using medieval texts for erotic purpose, even if we avoid Dante's famous scene of Paolo

---

16 Carton comments on the line: 'Book II concludes with the planning and execution of Pandarus' plot to bring about a meeting between the lovers or, as Pandarus puts it, to drive the deer to Troilus' bow' (p. 54). Of course, they are not lovers yet, a curious moment for the sceptical Carton.
17 Desmond, *Ovid's Art and the Wife of Bath*, pp. 13–14.
18 Desmond, *Ovid's Art and the Wife of Bath*, p. 27.
19 Desmond, *Ovid's Art and the Wife of Bath*, p. 28.
20 Virginia Burris, 'Queer Lives of Saints: Jerome's Hagiography', *Journal of the History of Sexuality* 10:3–4 (2001): 450–2; Rushton, 'Sexual Variations', pp. 97–8.
21 Robert Mills, *Suspended Animation: Pleasure, Pain, and Punishment in Medieval Culture* (London, 2005), pp. 106–44.

and Francesca condemned to the inferno for reading about and imitating Lancelot and Guinevere's affair. Andrew Taylor has noted the existence of two marginal glosses in the Osborn manuscript of Gower's *Confessio Amantis*: one, a pointing hand, appears on folio 114v (5.6177) just when Neptune thrusts his hand between the thighs of Cornix, whom he wishes to rape; the other, the phrase 'here is the tale' appears at folio 137v (6.1977), when the sorcerer Nectanabus fools Queen Olympias into sleeping with him. The marks clearly exist 'to facilitate finding the passages again so that they [the readers] may do so vicariously'.[22] If one anonymous reader can show a prurient interest in a text ostensibly meant to warn such readers away from lust, Pandarus goes much further – and he will do so partially on the reader's behalf. His question concerning Criseyde's book of Thebes – whether it is about love – was answered negatively: it was about history, about destruction, about incest. But Pandarus had already dismissed that difference as no difference at all; indeed, his very question might seem the lingering effect of his morning arousal.

The story of Procne, Philomela and Tereus is a dark one, partially retold from Ovid's original by Chaucer himself in his *Legend of Good Women* (a collection of short poems extolling the virtues and tragic ends of a number of heroines from Greek mythology and Roman history). Tereus is Procne's husband, and is charged with bringing her sister Philomela for a visit. Instead, Tereus rapes her and cuts out her tongue – hence perhaps the dual meaning of the lines in *Troilus*. The swallow Procne's chattering concerns 'How Tereus gan forth hire suster take' (II. 68–9); the *Legend*'s Procne both convinces Tereus to accompany Philomela for a visit (*LGW* 2260–5) and weeps when she hears the story of the rape (2379–80). To take Philomela is both to accompany her on her journey and to rape her. Philomela tells her story in a tapestry, which Procne reads. Ovid's sisters avenge their injuries by killing Procne's child and feeding him to Tereus, and all three are turned into birds by the gods: Procne into a swallow and Philomela a nightingale (Chaucer leaves the revenge out of his version).

The swallow's song has been variously interpreted, and it is possible that Pandarus does not even understand what he hears – that it is the narrator who provides the mythological background, and thus perhaps an interpretation of events which Pandarus would not recognize.[23] Mudrick argues that the nightingale's song serves to provide Pandarus with a 'lonely recognition of his own failure' as a lover and further 'of his looming treachery to Criseyde which, in a dream, the universal poignance of the myth dims somewhat and makes more

---

[22] Andrew Taylor, 'Reading the Dirty Bits', in *Desire and Discipline: Sex and Sexuality in the Premodern West*, ed. Jacqueline Murray and Konrad Eisenblicher (Toronto, 1996), pp. 280–95 (p. 284).

[23] Indeed, sometimes a nightingale can simply be a nightingale, or a stand-in for the male poet and not the female victim of sexual violence. See Wendy Pfeffer, *The Change of Philomel: The Nightingale in Medieval Literature* (New York, 1985), especially Chapter 7 (pp. 157–68).

endurable'.[24] The problem, if we accept that Chaucer is too early for free indirect discourse, is to determine the nature of the narrator: bumbling incompetent at a distance from Chaucer the poet, or Chaucer himself, with the fissures and cracks of his attempt to wrestle with the past still showing? Perhaps it is one of Derek Brewer's 'multiplicity of narrative viewpoints' which 'appear to surge up and fall away' throughout the text.[25] Certainly, when Criseyde is considering Troilus's love at the middle of the book, she too hears a nightingale's song, which the narrator implies might be 'yn his bryddes wyse, a lay / Of love' – in any event, the prettiness of the bird's song cheers Criseyde, prompting her to fall into a sleep, subsequently having the famous dream of the bone-white eagle painlessly ripping her heart from his chest, and replacing it with his own, 'with herte left for herte' (II. 918–31). The pattern reverses Pandarus's experience: a dream followed by a nightingale's song, now the song prompting a dream. Both involve the invocation of mythological, sexual violence. The songs, and the myths they represent, have some real diegetic effect, reminding both listeners of the painful possibilities inherent in sexual love, pushing them towards consummation (of lust, of elaborate plans). In both cases, the songs assert first the coercive nature of the Ovidian erotic hunt, and then the gender roles meant to be played in that hunt: Criseyde reacts passively to the events of her dream; Pandarus is spurred to begin the seduction which the dream-assault parallels.

These quick glimpses of mythological sexual violence and incest are clearly meant to comment on the action of *Troilus and Criseyde* precisely because they seem to prompt or shape the narrative itself. Mudrick further reminds us that whatever specific mythological or thematic meanings are held by these birdsongs, the birds are still birds: 'The nightingale and the swallow, cut off from Criseyde's yearning and from Pandarus's premonition of ruin and dishonor, go on singing somewhere nevertheless, intact and unheard'[26] Still, Procne's song undeniably introduces an ominous note into Criseyde's story. The exact nature of this ominous note understandably eludes definition – ambiguity again. One of Pandarus's harshest critics, Jane Chance, will only say that the reference to Philomela is one of many that 'undercut the intentions and roles of Pandarus'.[27] Carolyn Dinshaw notes that the birdsong 'haunts' Chaucer's text, and that the latter's sorrowful song 'reminds Pandarus to begin the wooing of Criseyde'.[28] Indeed, for Chance, Criseyde is like

---

[24] Marvin Mudrick, 'Chaucer's Nightingales', *The Hudson Review* 10:1 (Spring, 1957): 88–95 (91). Mudrick further reminds us that whatever specific mythological or thematic meanings are held by these birdsongs, the birds are still birds: 'The nightingale and the swallow, cut off from Criseyde's yearning and from Pandarus' premonition of ruin and dishonor, go on singing somewhere nevertheless, intact and unheard' (92).
[25] Derek Brewer, 'Presidential Address: The Reconstruction of Chaucer', *Studies in the Age of Chaucer* 1 (1984): 3–19 (14). Discussed in Spearing, *Textual Subjectivity*, p. 75.
[26] Mudrick, 'Chaucer's Nightingales', 92.
[27] Jane Chance, *The Mythographic Chaucer: The Fabulation of Sexual Politics* (Minneapolis and London, 1995), p. 124.
[28] Carolyn Dinshaw, *Chaucer's Sexual Poetics* (Madison, WI, 1989) pp. 81–2.

Philomela to some extent: specifically in that 'she will be "seduced", in a manner of speaking, by her relative and 'guide', her older, presumably wiser *em* Pandarus'.[29]

It may reward us to think further on the nature of traps themselves, using Rey Chow: 'the trap, by virtue of its binary operation (open or shut), is a line of pressure, constraint, and blockage. Before the prey is caught, the trap lies in waiting, carrying the potentiality of the hunter's imaginary like a blueprint.'[30] Pandarus arranges his trap for Criseyde down to the minutest details, even intervening when the tableau threatens to fail of its promise: he is an artist of the trap, his art a central component of the poem's conflation of narrative, destiny and reputation. Following Derrida, Chow notes that the 'trap may therefore be analogized or approximated to a hinge or pivot, around which multiple planes rotate in perpetual slippage from one another, in such ways as to conjoin mobility with enclosure, and alterity with capture ... The missing link is the prey's experience of *being* captured.' The moment of capture changes both the prey and the trap itself: the trap is fulfilled, but because the past and present actions of the prey must now be read as part of the trap, 'the prey's existence renders the trap more than just the elegant design understood from the sovereign command perspective of the hunter, who can henceforth no longer monopolize the terms of the interaction'.[31] Criseyde disrupts the clean linearity of the trap by refusing to talk the language of flirtatious hunting (and later by slipping through the trap, albeit because she is then caught in another conflicting trap), but she is nonetheless still opened up for sexual use: her erotic encounter with Troilus prompts a further erotic encounter with Pandarus, a sharing of prey. To risk an even more disturbing line of argument, if this was a hunt for the benefit of Troilus, we should recall that medieval hunting is a group activity, and the prey was historically divided amongst all who brought it down. Pandarus is a hound taking his portion.

But there are, too, traps which intersect and disrupt the poem's other traps. This is a poem set within the long, dire consequence of mythology's most famous capture/abduction, that of Helen (of Troy, but of course fundamentally and obviously *not* of Troy – that's rather the point). The exchange of Criseyde for Antenor is a direct result of Troy's situation, and at the same time 'exemplifies patriarchal culture's usual policy of "trafficking in women"'; like most women in this kind of culture, Criseyde's 'fortunes – including her literary and ethical fortunes – are subject to very specific and identifiable threats: she represents a mere currency of exchange in the masculine political economy, rather than a moral agent ... estranged, seduced, exchanged,

---

[29] Chance, *The Mythographic Chaucer*, p. 123.
[30] Rey Chow, *Entanglements, or Transmedial Thinking about Capture* (Durham, NC, and London, 2012), p. 46.
[31] Chow, *Entanglements*, p. 46.

isolated, and betrayed by men.'³² But it is interesting how Criseyde's being seduced and Criseyde's being exchanged are more than simply past-tense verbs in a list; they are diametrically opposed. If Criseyde is exchanged politically so that she can be returned to her father, she is no longer available to those who planned to and succeeded in capturing her for sex. The makers of the political trap, the Trojan parliament, are completely unaware of the other trap they are disrupting, and further may not know they are springing a trap at all. They do not see Criseyde as prey, but as game piece. The exchange of Criseyde for Antenor is not a matter, or simply a matter, of an ethical versus an unethical possibility, although Hector's famous insistence that 'We usen here no wommen for to selle' in Troy (IV. 182) sets up those terms. Instead, the poem contradicts Hector not just in that Troy actually does sell women, but also in suggesting that the real conflict concerns use-value: it is not that Troy should not exchange or sell women, but that the trade itself makes no sense. Criseyde cannot fight in battle or provide counsel as Antenor can, nor can Antenor fulfil the role of heteronormative sexual partner. The poem insists that they are made for different things (although, as the critical tradition of the poem has revealed, they are both known for their betrayals). This helps contextualize Criseyde's intense loneliness in the Greek camp, as she cannot fulfil the role the trade has made for her; Diomedes, on this account, is a kind of perverse salvation, returning her to an emotional and physical position she understands. Therefore, I see a distinct conflict in poem not only between private love and public need, or courtly love and a more direct exchange of women, but between the public life of women – their social participation – and their purpose in the bedroom. The conflict is between kinds of use, and Chaucer makes it perfectly clear that this one bad exchange between unlike objects stands in for a greater problem with exchange full stop.

But there is a further trap, in which Criseyde changes the hunter's intention precisely when we recall that she herself is prey and trap: Troilus is the proud peacock whose arrogance towards lovers causes the God of Love to seek vengeance (I. 183–210). The instrument of that vengeance is Criseyde, who stands alone and attempts to be unobtrusive yet still catches the arrow-shot eye of Troilus 'thorugh a route' (I. 271–3). The poem's first glance at Criseyde is just before the punishment of Troilus. Under a 'cloude blak' thanks to the departure of her father Calchas, Criseyde tries to stay out of the way:

> And yet she stood ful lowe and stille allone,
> Byhynden other folk, in litel brede,
> And neigh the dore, ay undre shames drede,
> Simple of atir and debonaire of chere (I. 177–80)

---

[32] J. Allan Mitchell, 'Criseyde's Chances: Courtly Love and Ethics about to Come', in *Levinas and Medieval Literature: The 'Difficult Reading' of English and Rabbinic Texts* (Pittsburgh, 2009), pp. 185–206 (p. 190).

Surrounded by 'many a lady fressh and mayden bright' (I. 166), Criseyde should blend in, but does not – because she has been selected as the instrument for the humbling of Troilus, the 'lasshe ... of the longe whippe' for 'proude Bayard' (I. 218–20). Cupid is not merely the figure who causes one to love, he also controls how and when: 'as hymselven liste, he may yow bynde' (I. 256). Troilus acknowledges the specifics of this after his song:

> And to the God of Love thus seyde he
> With pitous vois, 'O lord, now youres is,
> My spirit, which that oughte youres be.
> Yow thanke I, lord, that han me brought to this.
> But wheither goddesse or wommman, iwis,
> She be, I not, which that ye do me serve' (I. 421–6)

The 'this' of 424 is paratactically the 'She' of 426: the specific service Cupid requires is to or through Criseyde. The punishment aspect is obvious, given the eventual fate of Troilus, seeking death after losing her first to politics and then to another lover.

There is a further, metatextual wrinkle. Cupid is also the in-text instigator of the *Legend of Good Women* project, in which blameless women suffer at the hands of bastards and cads. This, too, is a punishment. Now, it is 'Chaucer' who is punished (not by means of Criseyde, but because he wrote about Criseyde): 'Hast thow nat mad in Englysh ek the bok / How that Crisseyde Troylus forsook' (*LGW* G. 264–5). The sentence is that Chaucer must write stories of good, faithful women; one of these stories is that of Philomela and her sister. But since the stories in the *Legend* all involve romantic love and/ or sexual violence, the project itself raises questions. In the case of Tereus and Philomela, is Cupid not somehow responsible for the lust that enters Tereus at the sight of his innocent sister-in-law (2289–93)? Philomela had been completely innocent, her only crime being beauty itself. Criseyde had tried to be unobtrusive but was nonetheless noticed: not just by Troilus, but by Cupid.

In the *Memorable Thoughts of Socrates*, Xenophon reports the philosopher's thoughts on beauty, specifically the beauty of an Athenian courtesan, Theodota.[33] When he hears people talking of her beauty, Socrates decides he had better go see her for himself; his group finds her posing for a painting, apparently a frequent occurrence. After considering her 'at leisure', when the painter finishes Socrates asks a question:

> Do you think we are more obliged to Theodota for having afforded us the sight of her beauty than she is to us for coming to see her? If all the advantage be on her side, it must be owned she is obliged to us; if it be on ours, it must be confessed that we are so to her.[34]

---

[33] Xenophon, *The Memorable Thoughts of Socrates*, trans. Edward Bysshe (New York, 2009), pp. 116–18.
[34] Xenophon, *The Memorable Thoughts of Socrates*, p. 117.

Socrates concludes that the woman benefits from praise itself, and then from the social effects of praise, but that the viewer benefits from a new desire 'to enjoy the things we have seen. We go hence with souls full of love and uneasiness; and from this time forward we must obey Theodota in all she pleases to enjoin us.'[35] This is not, of course, an example of courtly love, but it mines the same territory: the question of the gaze and where power lies within it, the idea of beauty as something to be obeyed, the uncomfortable link between love and uneasiness.

Theodota is a courtesan who make a living through her beauty; the conversation in Xenophon turns to the ideal of friendship because to gaze, and then to speak of what one saw, is to advertise by word of mouth. Criseyde and Philomela are not Theodotas. Criseyde desires neither the gaze of strangers nor their advertising; Philomela is a complete innocent, who suffers private rape as a result of a man's gaze. It might perversely be their very reticence and innocence that prompt the sexual violence both suffer. When Christine de Pizan engaged with the infamous Roman legend of the rape of Lucretia, she first uses Lucretia's experience to illustrate that women do not want to be raped.[36] That point seems obvious to us now, although it may have seemed less so in 1405. Her subsequent re-invocation of the story is more germane to our purpose, as she essentially argues that innocence carries its own sense of frisson:

> Most notably, I could tell you about various saints of paradise whom men lusted after specifically for their purity. This also happened to Lucretia, whose rape I recounted to you earlier. It was because of her exemplary virtue, not simply her beauty, that Tarquin fell for her.[37]

Tarquin is 'so impressed by her integrity, her simple and laudable conduct, as well as her modest bearing, that he conceived a burning desire for her'.[38] Christine posits that 'modest bearing', far from being a defence against male sexual aggression, can be a spur to lust just the same as its opposite. She argues that this should not prevent a woman from cultivating modest virtues; indeed, she oddly introduces the example of Lucretia to prove that many men find virtue attractive. The problem still looks very much like a catch-22.

Chaucer's Criseyde, as we saw, first appears as a modest, unglamorous face in a crowd, the kind of face that should not attract young Troilus's attention. She does so not despite her attempts to hide in plain sight, but because of them. Chaucer repeats the detail of her widow's black clothing not as an ironic counterpoint to her beauty, but as a central component of her attractiveness: Criseyde is attractive because she is not looking to attract,

---

35 Xenophon, *The Memorable Thoughts of Socrates*, p. 117.
36 Christine de Pizan, *The Book of the City of Ladies*, trans. Rosalind Brown-Grant (Harmondsworth, 1999), p. 147.
37 Christine de Pizan, *The Book of the City of Ladies*, p. 190.
38 Christine de Pizan, *The Book of the City of Ladies*, p. 191.

which makes her a more exciting prospect. She can be plucked, trapped, a worthier prize because she is so unlikely, a traitor's daughter mourning the death of an undiscussed husband. Criseyde, in fact, understands that she was trapped long before Troilus begins play-acting at the exchange of power on the night of their consummation. She simply did not see the precise nature of the trap, or the trap after that. The critical truism is that this poem reveals courtly love as an illusion, a dangerous social conceit at best, a lie men and women tell to themselves to mask the essentially brutalist nature of lust (all bird-of-prey metaphors and arrows). Pandarus's final assertion, that he will hate Criseyde eternally for her betrayal (V. 1731–43), is the act of a man who feels every bit as betrayed as his poor friend Troilus: he finally argues only that Criseyde ought to be taken 'fro this world' (V. 1742–3).

11
Invisible Woman: Rape as a Chivalric Necessity in Medieval Romance

AMY N. VINES

IT has long been a commonplace in criticism of medieval romances that acts of masculine prowess in chivalric situations, such as jousts, tournaments, and battles, are often enacted across the 'terrain' of women's bodies.[1] Whether fighting other men for the rights to a woman's body (and potentially the dowry and lands that accompany it), or actually performing or threatening acts of violence in the form of rape or abduction, the movement and exchange of women and the male physical aggression that surrounds and often penetrates their bodies are fundamental aspects of the socialization that solidifies individual knightly identity in the Middle Ages.[2] These acts of prowess, centralized around women's bodies, afford men the right to participate in the systems of chivalric and cultural exchange necessary for social advancement. Although the act or threat of rape is often the narrative hub around which knightly action rotates in medieval romances, in many of these texts this

---

[1] Jamie Friedman, 'Between Boccaccio and Chaucer: The Limits of Female Interiority in the Knight's Tale', in *Grief, Guilt, and Hypocrisy: The Inner Lives of Women in Medieval Romance Literature*, ed. Jamie Friedman and Jeff Rider (New York, 2011), pp. 203-22 (p. 204).

[2] For more on the legal and cultural distinctions between rape and *raptus* in the Middle Ages, see Corinne Saunders, *Rape and Ravishment in the Literature of Medieval England* (Cambridge, 2001), Kathryn Gravdal, *Ravishing Maidens: Writing Rape in Medieval French Literature and Law* (Philadelphia, 1991), Elizabeth Robertson and Christine M. Rose, eds, *Representing Rape in Medieval and Early Modern Literature* (New York, 2001), Shannon McSheffrey and Julia Pope, 'Ravishment, Legal Narratives, and Chivalric Culture in Fifteenth-Century England', *Journal of British Studies* 48 (October 2009): 818-36, Caroline Dunn, 'The Language of Ravishment', *Speculum* 86:1 (January 2011): 79-116 and her *Stolen Women in Medieval England: Rape, Abduction, and Adultery, 1100-1500* (Cambridge, 2013). Saunders's study is an excellent source of information on medieval social and legal understandings of rape; she suggests that modern readers need to recognize 'the broader definition of the crime in the medieval period – a definition that incorporates the ideas of rape, abduction, and enforced marriage, and is now best suggested by the less specific term "ravishment"' (p. 4). In this essay, I will limit my examination to acts of rape, or forced coitus, rather than abduction and other facets of the broader category of *raptus*.

aggression takes place outside the main plot of the story and is committed by men other than the romance hero. In her well-known and indispensable study on rape in medieval literature and law, Katherine Gravdal writes that rape – either attempted or enacted – comprises 'one of the episodic units used in the construction of a romance';[3] it is a narrative building block, part of the romance genre's very DNA. These acts of masculine aggression against women, she continues, provide the opportunity for the heroes of these romances, such as Lancelot, Yvain, and even Arthur himself, to augment their own chivalric reputations; indeed, because the rapes take place primarily in the past tense and outside the narratives' main action, the audience is encouraged to 'ignore the physicality of rape and its literal consequences' and, instead, focus on the acts of chivalry that seek to avenge the trespasses.[4] Gravdal's argument, however, is based on the assumption that the rape and the chivalric feats that follow are two distinct sets of actions performed by two different people: the rapist and the hero-knight. The reprehensible act of one provides the catalyst for the laudable reparations of the other.

But how do we address romances where the rapist is also the heroic figure of the text, when the rape *itself* is the act that both inaugurates and cultivates the hero's knightly reputation? Such texts ask the audience to engage in a different – and, potentially, more problematic – type of moral reflection on chivalric codes than Gravdal suggests. Although the trope of rape in medieval romances doubtlessly exposes the violence toward women inherent in romantic love and the performance of chivalry, it is not typically considered to be constitutive of or even necessary to knightly development. In this essay, I will examine several depictions of rape perpetrated by the primary heroic characters in romance narratives to suggest that the act of rape is in many cases a foundational aspect of establishing masculine chivalric identity. These depictions of rape are inceptive moments, I argue, often preceding important stages of martial and social development for the knight. However, because these acts occur primarily at the beginning rather than at the conclusion of romances, they are often dismissed as challenging and problematic moments of weakness to overcome through the fine-tuning of the knight's chivalric process, not as fundamental and, indeed, necessary to his knightly identity. One of the reasons rape is often overlooked as a constitutive element of chivalry is that it is typically depicted

---

3   Gravdal, *Ravishing Maidens*, p. 43.
4   Gravdal, *Ravishing Maidens*, p. 43. Gravdal offers several examples of Chrétien de Troyes's tendency to elide the immediate representation of rape in his works, including Yvain's belated but successful intervention in the threatened rape of the daughter of one of his relatives in *Le Chevalier au Lion* (pp. 47–8). Although Gravdal's discussion centres around Chrétien de Troyes's romances, the connections she identifies between rape and chivalry have been profitably expanded to other medieval narratives as well. See, for example, Corinne Saunders's articles, 'A Matter of Consent: Middle English Romance and the Law of *Raptus*', in *Medieval Women and the Law*, ed. Noël James Menuge (Woodbridge, 2000), pp. 105–24, and 'Woman Displaced: Rape and Romance in Chaucer's *Wife of Bath's Tale*', in *Arthurian Literature* 13, ed. James P. Carley and Felicity Riddy (Cambridge, 1995), 115–31.

as socially aberrant, the 'act of base men',[5] and a violation of the chivalric code. It is a crime with a victimized woman whose presence (however fleeting and abstractly rendered in some cases) necessitates reparative acts on the part of the offending knight.[6] Although the woman's victimization in such narratives causes the rapist-knight to endure various punishments, such as social ostracism and the threat of death, these acts of physical and social penance inevitably offer him the opportunity for chivalric advancement. I will begin this essay with a brief examination of two traditional rape scenes in medieval English and French romances: Chaucer's *Wife of Bath's Tale* and the story of Gawain and the Pucelle de Lis in the Old French Continuation of *Perceval*. In each of these very different romance narratives, the acts of rape are mediated by various reparative undertakings on the part of the knights. The audience's attention is guided towards these demonstrations of social and chivalric restitution in an effort to sever the uncomfortable connection between the rape acts and the advancement and success enjoyed by all the rapist-knights at the end of these romances.

However, in several romances where rape is orchestrated and staged by the heroine, the female body is not presented as victimized and, thus, the audience's attention is drawn to the male body performing the act of forced coitus, rather than reparative chivalric feats. Many critics have noted the subtle eroticism and titillation that acts of sexual aggression or voyeurism afford to the audience of such medieval romances.[7] Yet the moments of sublimated eroticism that are perfunctorily depicted and quickly abandoned in favor of the knightly reparative tasks that must follow in cases of actual rape can be explored more fully in representations of staged rapes in which the woman is the *agent provocateur* rather than the victim. Placing the emphasis on the eroticized performance of male aggression in these orchestrated encounters and revealing that reparative acts are unnecessary for the 'rapist' knight to advance socially enable us to more easily understand how a socially and legally aberrant act like rape can be constitutive of knighthood. Thus, after my discussion of the traditional rapes in the *Wife of Bath's Tale* and the *Perceval* Continuation, I will turn to one of the most intriguing examples of a staged rape found in late medieval romance. In the fifteenth-century Middle English version of *Partonope of Blois*, the mechanism of the staged rape is laid bare, made so obvious that the audience must explore the act in all its aggressive eroticism. The heroine's body is not victimized; indeed, through her mastery of necromancy Melior is not even visible until far into her romantic relationship with Partonope. Rather, it is the young man's acts of sexual aggression and his demonstration of physical masculine prowess

---

[5] Gravdal, *Ravishing Maidens*, p. 44.
[6] In the Chrétien romances Gravdal examines, these reparative acts are taken up by the hero-knights, such as Lancelot and Arthur, rather than the rapists or sexual aggressors themselves.
[7] See, for example, Gravdal, *Ravishing Maidens*, pp. 44–5 and A. C. Spearing, *The Medieval Poet as Voyeur: Looking and Listening in Medieval Love Narratives* (Cambridge, 1993), especially pp. 1–25.

(at least as he experiences it) that begin his knightly development immediately after the supposedly forced act of coitus. Without the victimized female body, there is no need for reparative action, and, thus, the staged rape reveals that male sexual aggression is foundational to chivalric identity even if it is normally obscured by the intervening process of restitution.

The *Wife of Bath's Tale* includes one of the most notorious and heavily debated instances of rape in medieval literature. Although there are several analogues to the Wife's story of the loathly lady, such as *The Weddynge of Sir Gawen and Dame Ragnell* and *The Marriage of Sir Gawain*, the rape scene is Chaucer's unique addition to the narrative, and is potentially related to the discussions about women's *maisterye* pursued in the Wife's *Prologue*.[8] Suzanne Edwards notes that the rape scene has become an 'interpretive crux' for much of the criticism on the *Tale* because it 'refuses the ambiguities that characterize the medieval legal regulation of sexual violence'.[9] In the thirteenth and fourteenth centuries, when acts of forcible coitus and abduction with or without the woman's consent were often difficult to distinguish in legal documents and literary representations, the knight's taking of the woman's maidenhead 'maugree hir heed / By verray force'[10] is undeniably an act of sexual violation.[11] While much recent scholarship on the rape in the Wife's *Tale* focuses on Chaucer's representation (both realistic and idealized) of fourteenth-century rape law, my brief discussion of the text here will concentrate primarily on the knight's trajectory and development throughout the narrative. I suggest that the rape, which is swiftly committed and then, arguably, transformed into a reclamation of the rapist for the 'honour of women',[12] is actually not completely rewritten or forgiven, but is rather simply moved beyond by the knight's reparative process and incorporated into the larger lessons and development of chivalry. It is a subtle distinction, but an important one for my argument. The rather unorthodox knightly errand on which the rapist embarks at the beginning of the *Tale* does function as the

---

[8] The body of criticism on rape in Chaucer and late medieval literature and culture is too large to review fully in this essay. However, for particularly thorough discussions of the *Tale* and issues of consent, see Christine M. Rose, 'Reading Chaucer Reading Rape', and Monica Brzezinski Potkay, 'The Violence of Courtly Exegesis in *Sir Gawain and the Green Knight*', both in *Representing Rape*, ed. Robertson and Rose, pp. 21–60 and pp. 97–126. Other important feminist readings of the *Tale* include Carolyn Dinshaw, *Chaucer's Sexual Poetics* (Madison, WI, 1989), especially pp. 113–31; Angela Jane Weisl, '"Quiting" Eve: Violence Against Women in the *Canterbury Tales*', in *Violence Against Women in Medieval Texts*, ed. Anna Roberts (Gainesville, FL, 1998) pp. 115–36; Jill Mann, *Geoffrey Chaucer* (Atlantic Highlands, NJ, 1991); and Elaine Tuttle Hansen, *Chaucer and the Fictions of Gender* (Berkeley, CA, 1992).
[9] Suzanne Edwards, 'The Rhetoric of Rape and the Politics of Gender in the *Wife of Bath's Tale* and the *1382 Statute of Rapes*', *Exemplaria* 23:1 (Spring 2011): 3–26 (3).
[10] Larry D. Benson, ed., *The Riverside Chaucer* (Boston, 1987), III. 887–8. All subsequent references to this edition will be cited by fragment and line number within the text.
[11] In addition to Edwards, 'The Rhetoric of Rape', 4, see also Christopher Cannon, 'Chaucer and Rape: Uncertainty's Certainties', in *Representing Rape*, ed. Robertson and Rose, pp. 255–79 (p. 267).
[12] Saunders, 'Woman Displaced', p. 130.

vehicle for his rehabilitation and provides the Wife with the opportunity to explore more fully the possibilities of female *maisterye*; yet at the core of this learning process and the knight's social and chivalric transformation lies an act of rape. This instance of forced coitus is an aberrant act both socially and legally, and, thus, it necessitates the rapist's immediate reparative quest to find out what women most desire. But the rape, I argue, is foundational to how the knight will advance in the chivalric system: from an unnamed Arthurian knight to the husband of a beautiful and noble wife. The rape, although briefly and almost mechanically narrated in the *Tale*, provides the grist for the chivalric mill, an inceptive moment from which all his future knightly success flows.

From the *Tale*'s first lines in which the Wife establishes the nostalgic setting in 'th'olde days of the Kyng Arthour' (III. 857), the narrative asserts the intimate connections between rape and chivalry. In this seemingly playful bygone age, when the 'elf-queene, with hir joly compaignye / Daunced ful ofte in many a grene mede' (III. 860-1), there is also the possibility that incubi will lie with young maidens. However, we soon realize that the true danger to women in the Wife's nostalgic vision of the past actually stems from Arthur's court and, indeed, is intimately tied to Arthur's own history. Arthur is the product of a questionable sexual encounter between his mother, Igerne, and his father, Uther Pendragon, who has been transformed by Merlin into the likeness of her husband; Gravdal notes that 'from the earliest stages of courtly romance, the character of Arthur is linked with the narration of rape' in Geoffrey of Monmouth's story of Arthur's revenge against the Mont St Michel giant, who attempted to rape Helena, the niece of Duke Hoel, to death.[13] Thus, the setting of the Wife's *Tale* – both its landscape and sovereign – is saturated with references (some more oblique than others) to rape.

After the knight 'rafte[s]' the young woman's 'maydenhed' (III. 888), he is placed on trial in Arthur's court, where he is sentenced to death only to have that doom postponed for a year and potentially commuted upon the queen's intervention. As the knight embarks upon his life-saving errand, the narrative moves from legal realism into the realm of fantasy, a world in which the knight's reputation may not only be rehabilitated, but augmented by a year-long journey.[14] Saunders remarks that the workings of providence are prominent during the year's errand for the knight: 'the underlying pattern is

---

[13] Gravdal, *Ravishing Maidens*, p. 42. See Part Seven of Geoffrey of Monmouth's *Historia Regum Brittaniæ* in which he relates the story of Helena's abduction (*The History of the Kings of Britain*, ed. and trans. Lewis Thorpe (New York, 1966), pp. 237-41). Although the young woman dies before the giant can rape her, the giant turns his physical desire on her nurse and rapes her repeatedly until Arthur kills him.

[14] See Corinne Saunders's reading of the trial scene's realistic portrayal of legal procedure in fourteenth-century England ('Woman Displaced', pp. 125-6). Although the scene doubtlessly represents an idealized trial where the most severe punishment for the offence of rape – death – is meted out, she notes that the people's broad condemnation of the act of rape in making a clamourous 'pursuite' (III. 890) to Arthur 'recalls the rarely-pursued legal possibility of community indictment in the fourteenth century' ('Woman Displaced', p. 125).

that of the chivalric quest, in which the knight meets with *aventure* as he rides, apparently aimlessly but guided by destiny through unknown lands.'[15] Yet, she notes, rather than go through the forests and other natural boundaries which traditionally mark one realm from another in romance texts, the rapist-knight explores through towns and cities, seeking everyday people rather than exotic encounters. As the knight meets different women throughout his journey, Saunders suggests, his 'specialized' quest becomes a penitential act of desperation as he repeatedly questions each woman in turn: 'he seketh every hous and every place / Where as he hopeth for to fynde grace / To lerne what thyng wommen loven moost' (III. 919–21). Each compulsory interview becomes a re-enactment of the moment when he forced his own desires upon a woman 'maugree hir heed' (III. 887). The knight must force himself into the position of supplicant – he must hear the woman's desires before acting, whether it is attempting to engage with her further or moving on.

Though the knight's journey is doubtless a penitential act in part to make reparations for the rape, the sheer repetitive nature of these almost identical interactions with women connects very closely with the formula of more traditional, non-reparative chivalric errands. One need only recall Lancelot's numerous encounters and battles with unnamed sentries and guards throughout Chrétien de Troyes's *Le Chevalier de la Charette*, each one only slightly different from the one before, yet all contributing to the knight's aggregate chivalric worth.[16] Although the knight in the Wife's *Tale* spends a year asking the same question and cannot 'fynde in this mateere / Two creatures accordynge in-feere' (III. 923–4), his attempts at thoroughness allow the Wife to provide readers with an indication of the breadth and variety of female desire; the options run the gamut from 'richesse' to 'lust abedde', to be both 'wydwe and wedde' (III. 925–8). The significance of this exercise to the knight's rehabilitation, of course, lies in the asking, the acknowledgement that women may not all have the same desires, but that they have them; they are not simply 'mayde[s] walkynge hym biforn' to whom he can help himself (III. 886). At this point in the narrative, the knight does not seem to have internalized these lessons – if, indeed, he ever does – but his journey, while retaining the element of knightly *aventure* Saunders suggests, particularly in his chance meeting with the dancing ladies and the old hag in the forest, is also predicated on the important element of repetition in chivalric errands, the hammering home of key lessons that the hero does not necessarily master the first time.

When the knight meets the old woman and reluctantly becomes her husband and a student of her moral curriculum, it actually indicates the continuation of a common knightly process in romance rather than an abandonment of this aspect of the genre. The hag, who will become the beautiful, faithful wife at the end of the story, leads the young man through the next logical portion of

---

[15] Saunders, 'Woman Displaced', p. 127.
[16] We may also consider the famous three hunts and three kisses sequence in *Sir Gawain and the Green Knight* to be a version of this motif of repetition in chivalric journeys.

his knightly errand: to understand that 'gentillesse', and all of the potential attractiveness and success that the characteristic implies in the chivalric society in which the knight operates, lies in one's deeds rather than one's rank.[17] The knight's final acquiescence to the hag's desire – 'as yow liketh, it suffiseth me' (III. 1235) – marks what Saunders has termed a 'rewrit[ing]' of the act of rape so that the audience may be better able to 'accept the final transformation of the old loathsome hag into a beautiful young woman'.[18] Yet what has continued to trouble critics about the end of this *Tale* is the fact that, regardless of the knight's intervening quest to discover women's desires and his eventual acceptance (sincere or otherwise) of the hag's *maisterye*, he is still a rapist who is not punished, but is ultimately rewarded for his crime. He not only keeps his life, but ends his journey like all other successful knights in romance literature: with a marriage to a beautiful, noble woman and all of the cultural and social prestige that attends it. Given the notable similarities between the knight's reparative errand in the *Wife of Bath's Tale* and the trajectories of other romance heroes, such as Lanval or Yvain, it becomes clear that rape or other acts of male physical aggression against women are not simply rewritten or forgotten in the process of rehabilitating certain knights, but are actually constitutive of knightly development in many cases. Not every romance hero is a rapist, of course, but in many romances, the rapist can become the hero.

In the case of the anonymous Old French First Continuation of Chrétien de Troyes's *Perceval*, however, it is actually a well-known romance hero – Gauvain – who is the rapist. In this short section of a much longer text on the Grail Quest, Gauvain's sexual transgression against the Pucelle de Lis tarnishes his existing impressive chivalric reputation for only a short time.[19] Although Gauvain's rape of the woman does not inaugurate his chivalric development, as it does with the anonymous Arthurian knight in the *Wife of Bath's Tale*, and (as I will discuss further below) Partonope of Blois, it does advance his knightly standing in significant and unique ways. At the end of this episode, Gauvain

---

[17] For more on the role of women as teachers and patrons of young knights in medieval romance, see Amy N. Vines, *Women's Power in Late Medieval Romance* (Cambridge, 2011).
[18] Saunders, 'Woman Displaced', p. 127.
[19] For a discussion and modern edition of all the Continuations of Chrétien's *Perceval*, see vol. 1 of William Roach, ed. *The Continuations of the Old French Perceval of Chrétien de Troyes*, 4 vols (Philadelphia, 1949-83). There are four Continuations of Chrétien's *Perceval*, and many scenes of the original are reworked multiple times by various continuators. Versions of the incident between Gauvain and the Pucelle de Lis are included no fewer than four times in both the First and Fourth Continuations. For an excellent study of the revisionary impulse in the *Perceval* Continuations, see Matilda Tomaryn Bruckner's *Chrétien Continued: A Study of the Conte du Graal and Its Verse Continuations* (Oxford, 2009), and Thomas Hinton, *The Conte du Graal Cycle: Chrétien de Troyes' Perceval, The Continuations, and French Arthurian Romance* (Cambridge, 2012). In this essay, I am concerned primarily with the interactions between Gauvain and the Pucelle de Lis in the First Continuation, and particularly with the rehearsal of the encounter at the end of the Continuation. R. E. Bennett refers to the episode I discuss here as *The Rape*, and differentiates the section from the first version of the same encounter with the Pucelle de Lis, called *The Seduction*, in the First Continuation of Chrétien's *Perceval* ('The Sources of the "Jeaste of Syr Gawayne"', *Journal of English and Germanic Philology* 33:1 (January 1934): 57-63 (59-60)).

gains a young son (begotten with the Pucelle during the encounter five years earlier), and a loyal and powerful retainer (the Pucelle's brother, Bran de Lis), both of which are significant elements of chivalric advancement that are direct consequences of the knight's act of forced coitus.

In a notable departure from most representations of rape in medieval romance, the First Continuation's depiction of the encounter is extremely detailed, both in terms of Gauvain's desire for the Pucelle in the moment and in his description of the violation to his uncle, Arthur, five years later.[20] There is a surprising difference between the initial description of the circumstances of Gauvain's encounter with the Pucelle at the beginning of the First Continuation and the subsequent rehearsal of the meeting – what Bruckner calls the 'travestied retelling'[21] – over six thousand lines later. In the first meeting, the Pucelle seduces Gauvain, expressing her desire openly and repeatedly; in Gauvain's recollection of the encounter to Arthur several years later, however, the knight 'unexpectedly transforms a tale of female desire into a story of rape'.[22] While there has been significant debate among critics about the reasons for the continuator's revisions, I will concentrate my argument on the second *Rape* narrative.[23] The nature of the narrative change suggests that the continuator deliberately sacrifices representations of female desire in order to construct a chivalric masculine identity predicated on the knight's violent domination of a woman's body. This revision serves the critical purpose of forcing the reader to examine the often uncomfortably close connections between chivalric heroism and sexual aggression in medieval romance.

According to the *Rape* version of the encounter, when Gauvain sees the Pucelle asleep in her pavilion, he confesses that

> de s'amour si espris fui,
> Ne me poi tenir d'acoler
> La rien que tant pooie amer,
> Ne de li baisier dolcement

---

[20] The entire episode of *The Rape* in the First Continuation is told in retrospect; five years after the initial encounter between Gauvain, the Pucelle de Lis, and her brothers and father (related in *The Seduction*, lines 2546–3145 in Roach's edition), Gauvain, Arthur and the other knights of the Round Table arrive at Bran de Lis's castle during the Grail Quest. When Gauvain notices where he is and realizes that he is honour-bound to fight the Pucelle's brother to the death, he confesses the entire encounter to Arthur in *The Rape* episode.

[21] Bruckner, *Chrétien Continued*, 109.

[22] Bruckner, *Chrétien Continued*, 107.

[23] In addition to Bruckner's discussion of the Pucelle de Lis episode revisions in Chapter Two of *Chrétien Continued*, see Jean Frappier, 'Le personnage de Gauvain dans la *Première Continuation de Perceval (Conte du Graal)*', *Romance Philology* 11 (1958): 331–44; Pierre Gallais's "Gauvain et la Pucelle de Lis' in *Mélanges de linguistique romance et de philologie médiévale offerts à M. Maurice Delbouille*, 2 vols (Gembloux, 1964), 2: 207–29 and *L'imaginaire d'un romancier français de la fin du XIIe siècle: Description raisonée, comparée et commentée de la Continuation-Gauvain (Première suite du Conte du Graal de Chrétien de Troyes)*, 4 vols (Amsterdam, 1988–89), 4: 2261–64; and Keith Busby, *Gauvain in Old French Literature* (Amsterdam, 1980), pp. 160–70 and p. 238, n. 22.

> such feeling sprang up from love of her
> That I could not stop myself from taking her into my arms,
> I could do nothing to prevent my great love for her,
> Nor from gently kissing her.[24]

Indeed, Gauvain's thorough description of the lady's body seems to be an attempt to explain his carnal desire, if not to excuse it: 'les oex li baisai et le vis, / Qui plus ert blans que flor de lis, / Et puis la bouche et puis la fache' ('my eyes kissed and saw her / Who was whiter than a *fleur de lis*, / And then [her] mouth, and then [her] face') (10037–9). Gauvain's extended explanation of his motivations is matched, however, by the Pucelle's explicit and repeated objections to his advances. When his sweet kisses initially awaken her, she cries out, 'Diex! qui est ce lez moi? / Ce n'est pas mes freres, ce croi' ('God! Who is this next to me? / It is not my brothers, I believe') (9995–6). To his rather cheeky reply – 'Pucele, non; mais vostre amis' ('Maiden, no, but your friend') (9998) – the Lady soberly chides him for his impertinence, saying that she has never had an 'amis', 'et grand vilonnie feroit / Qui d'amistié m'aparleroit' ('and you have done a great villainy / To speak so to me of friendship') (10001–2). The lady even warns Gauvain of the potential consequences of his actions, claiming that her family is comprised of wise and worthy knights, and that her father 'molt ert iriez, s'ara raison, / S'il vos trove en son paveillon' ('would be greatly angered, with good reason, / If he found you in his pavilion') (10013–14). The more appropriate course of action, the Pucelle suggests, would be to wait and to be greeted honourably by her family; such a reception would only augment the chivalric reputation of a knight already so 'pros et renomez' ('brave and renowned') (10029) as Gauvain. The lady's plea for Gauvain to abandon this potential (and soon to be actual) rape seems intended to help him to avoid having to undergo reparative acts afterward.

Yet the Pucelle's appeals to Gauvain's more chivalric nature go unheeded. Gauvain later confesses to Arthur that

> si grant oltrage fis
> Qu'a force la despucelai,
> Ainc por son plorer nel laissai.
> Et el faisoit un doel si grant
> Que ainc a nule rien vivant
> Ne vi si grant doel demener.
>
> I did such great outrage
> In forcing her deflowerment,
> Never ceasing for all her cries.

---

[24] Roach, *Continuations*, vol. 1, lines 9987–91. Further citations from this source will be cited parenthetically within the text. I would like to thank Melissa Ridley Elmes for her assistance with the translation of the Old French romance.

> And I did her such great sorrow
> That nothing can ever surpass it,
> I have never seen such great sorrowing. (10042–7)

Her face, which was once so attractively lily white, is now coloured with 'ire [anger],' 'angoisse [anguish],' and 'dolor [pain]' (10049). The Pucelle's repeated cries and resistance draw her brother and his men into the pavilion. When Gauvain's act of rape is discovered, the Pucelle's challenge to her brother to avenge her violation begins the series of reparative acts that Gauvain must endure in order to repair his compromised reputation:[25]

> qui m'ostera
> Cest chevalier qui m'a honie?
> Frere, nel vos celerai mie;
> Jamais ne viverez nul jor
> Que n'i aiez honte et dolor,
> Qu'el mont n'a terre ne contree
> Ou je soie mais honoree.
> Biax dols chiers frere, ore est alez
> Li biens qui m'estoit destinez.
>
> who will rescue me [from]
> This knight who has ruined me?
> Brother, I will hide nothing from you;
> You will never live another day
> When you will not feel shame and sorrow,
> In this world [there is] neither land nor country
> Where I will [not] be badly honored.
> My noble, sorrowful dear brother, now is gone
> The good for which I was destined. (10066–74)

With its emphasis on traditional modes of combat between a knight and a challenger, the reparative process in the *Perceval* Continuation is not as unique as the knight-rapist's errand in the *Wife of Bath's Tale*. Yet Gauvain's challenge follows a repetitive structure similar to that found in Chaucer's narrative, and, ultimately, the knight benefits from the rape act in comparable ways. In her analysis of the *Jeaste of Sir Gawain*, a fifteenth-century Middle English romance that combines elements of both the *Seduction* and *Rape* narratives in the Old French *Perceval* Continuation, Sarah Lindsay discusses what she reads as the discordant use of both masculine fighting and exhibitions of prowess and Gauvain's attempt to make amends without fighting, a tactic she identifies as a more feminine mode of reconciliation.[26] Although Lindsay's argument

---

[25] This moment in the Continuation's *Rape* narrative corresponds to the trial scene in the *Wife of Bath's Tale* where Guinevere sends the rapist-knight on his errand to establish what women truly want. See also Thomas Hahn, 'Introduction', in *The Jeaste of Sir Gawain* in *Sir Gawain: Eleven Romances and Tales* (Kalamazoo, MI, 1995).

[26] See Sarah Lindsay, 'Chivalric Failure in *The Jeaste of Sir Gawain*', *Arthuriana* 21:4 (2011):

focuses primarily on the much later Middle English text, the tension between combat and amends is present to an extent even in the Old French version. In the *Rape* retelling of the First Continuation, when Gauvain is confronted by each of the Pucelle's two brothers and her father in turn, he repeats an offer to marry the woman he has raped; the first attempt to make marital amends for his transgression is directed at the lady herself, addressing her perversely as 'my sweet friend' ('Dolce amie bele') (10134):

> Je sui Gavains, li niez Artus;
> El mont n'a home qu'il aint plus.
> Lealment vos di et otroi
> Ja n'arez a seignor for moi,
> Se vos le volez otroier;
> Ci sui toz pres del fiancier.
>
> I am Gauvain, nephew of Arthur,
> The world has no man more chivalric [than me].
> Loyally I tell you and consent,
> I would not have to be forced by a lord,
> If you also wanted to consent to it,
> To become affianced. (10137–42)[27]

There are several interesting aspects of Gauvain's proposals in this narrative. The entire *Rape* episode is related as a confession of Gauvain's wrongdoing to his uncle, King Arthur, five years after the attack. Throughout his relation of these events, both the sexual transgression and the subsequent slaying of the lady's kinsmen, Gauvain's tone is one of sheepish desperation. He admits to the king that he lost his mind and his nobility during the rape: '[Ja] congioit / La riens que mes cuers plus amoit' ('I took leave of / The things dearest to my heart') (10015–16). Yet during his admission of even the most egregious sexual trespasses and his unsuccessful attempts to repair them, Gauvain repeatedly reminds Arthur that he is the king's nephew – 'Gavains vostre niez' (10253) – just as he declared his name and his relationship to Arthur during his initial marriage proposal to the Pucelle. Although Gauvain acknowledges to an extent that his forcible sexual encounter with the lady is a crime requiring some form of restitution (even a hastily constructed marriage proposal), he also suggests that a rape act is part of his chivalric identity, for 'el mont n'a home qu'il aint

---

23–41. Lindsay asserts that the *Jeaste*'s emphasis on the possibility of 'non-prowess-based forms of reconciliation' (25) reflects the fifteenth century's methods of managing rape that involved verbal negotiations and financial compensations for the loss of virginity (28).

27 Gauvain repeats a version of this offer before he battles her father (10251–4) and her second brother, Bran de Lis (10346–8). Bran admits that, had he been the first to discover Gauvain and his sister, he would have accepted Gauvain's offer of marriage to her. However, because Gauvain has slain his brother and father in the intervening fights, he cannot accept the offer now and save face (10349–64). Bran's suggestion of amenability to Gauvain's reparative proposal foreshadows the actual reconciliation that will occur between the two knights at the conclusion of the *Rape* episode.

plus' ('the world has no man more chivalric') (10138). By consistently invoking his uncle's name, Arthur becomes at once the *de facto* arbiter of chivalry and a legitimizer of rape.

Lindsay reads Gauvain's attempts to forestall combat with the Pucelle's male relatives as an indication that 'Gawain holds a view of chivalry that encompasses not only prowess but also the ability to create lasting relationships and effect reconciliation through verbal and legal means'.[28] Although she places these combative and verbal modes of reconciliation at gendered odds in her analysis of the *Jeaste* and its sources, in the *Perceval* Continuation both of these reparative methods function together. Gauvain's repeated attempts to persuade the male members of the de Lis family that he is Arthur's nephew, that the rape was committed by the epitome of Arthurian chivalry, and that they should accept his proposals in order to avoid being slaughtered by him in hand-to-hand combat land on deaf ears. The reticence of the de Lis men, however, does outline a tension between an over-masculine reliance on combat to the exclusion of Gauvain's enlightened possibility for non-violent interactions. Their reluctance to accept Gauvain's peaceful proposal forces the knight into the mode of reconciliation through multiple combats. Yet these battles with the de Lis men soon become victories for Gauvain as he slays the Pucelle's brother and father for seeking revenge; Gauvain fights the final brother, Bran de Lis, but both men are wounded and they postpone the fight until they meet again. Even before the final positive outcome of Gauvain's post-rape reparative process, which will occur five years later, the knight's reputation has already been bolstered by his success on the battlefield and the subtle connections he continues to draw between his inherent chivalry and his connection by birth to King Arthur.

The final resolution to the *Rape* episode in the *Perceval* Continuation solidifies the chivalric benefit of Gauvain's reparative quest, but also underscores the fact that the social and cultural rewards the knight reaps are first and foremost the results of a rape. After confessing all the events of his previous encounter with the de Lis family five years earlier, Gauvain reveals that they have now arrived by chance at Bran de Lis's castle. Once the Pucelle's brother realizes that Gauvain has returned, the two knights renew their aggressions with the intent of fighting to the death. The Pucelle, who has remained with her brother since her initial violation, has borne Gauvain's child; upon learning that Gauvain and Bran de Lis are fighting, the lady sends the young boy to intervene:

> Fix, proiez vostre pere
> Qu'il ait merchi de vostre mere,
> Qu'il laist por Dieu que il n'ochie
> Mon frere, plus l'aim que ma vie.

---

[28] Lindsay, 'Chivalric Failure in *The Jeaste of Sir Gawain*', 25.

> Son, ask your father,
> If he would have mercy on your mother,
> For God's sake, do not kill
> My brother, [who is] more loved than my life. (11041–4)

When the boy stands between his uncle and father, pleading for the end of the slaughter of the Pucelle's family, Arthur intervenes and stops the battle. In her brief discussion of the Continuation's ending, Lindsay asserts that the 'beneficial relationships [that] form among all the characters' is the result of successful verbal and legal intervention.[29] While it is ultimately the cries of the young boy rather than the blows of the sword that end the battle and begin the knights' reconciliation, this non-prowess-based resolution is only possible because of the rape Gauvain committed. The presence of the boy – the product of this sexual violation – will bring tangible chivalric benefits to Gauvain as well. After Arthur incorporates Bran de Lis and his men into his retinue,[30] an act that adds to Gauvain's honour as much as Arthur's and Bran's, the Pucelle's brother publicly forgives his sister's attacker for all his previous transgressions:

> Sire Gavain,
> Toz mautalens vos pardonrai
> Et d'ore en avant vos serai
> Amis de foi et de corage;
> Ja nel lairai por nul damage
> Que m'aiez fait ça en arriere.
>
> Sir Gauvain,
> I pardon you all your wrongs
> And we will be friends in faith and courage;
> I will not hold you accountable for any damages
> You committed in the past. (11129–34)

Like the knight-rapist's trespass at the end of the *Wife of Bath's Tale*, Gauvain's rape of the Pucelle de Lis is absolved because of female intervention and mercy, in this case, by the victim herself. At the conclusion of this episode, a retelling of a sexual encounter that began with such an egregious and detailed act of forced coitus, the offending knight not only acquires the fealty of the victim's brother and his men, he also gains a son, who is often identified as Gingalain or Le Bel Inconnu, the hero of the romance *Lybeaus Desconus*.[31] The particular success Gauvain enjoys in this romance is the direct result of his rape of the Pucelle,

---

29 Lindsay, 'Chivalric Failure in *The Jeaste of Sir Gawain*', 29.
30 '[I]l n'est pas drois / Que vos ja mes hom deveignois, / Ains vos ferai tot lige homage. / Mais vers moi erent en ostage / Li per de la Table Roonde / Que sont li plus proisié del monde.' ('It is not right / That you never become my men, / From now on, you will come from a great lineage / You are my host, / A peer of the Round Table / Which is the greatest esteem in the world' (11107–12). Bran de Lis also swears fealty to Gauvain: 'homage li fist de ses mains / Ilueques mesire Gavains' ('he did homage by hand / Now to Sir Gauvain' (11143–4).
31 See Lindsay, 'Chivalric Failure in *The Jeaste of Sir Gawain*', 40 n. 20.

despite the intervening reparative acts of prowess and honourable verbal negotiation. Thus, Gauvain's particular happy ending suggests that rape is a necessary and integral part of his chivalric development.

While the direct relationship between rape and knightly advancement can often be obscured in many romances through the subsequent performance of other chivalric activities, in romances where the rape scene is staged by the woman who is raped and in which there is no need for a reparative process, it becomes far more obvious that forced coitus and chivalry can be mutually constitutive. As I have discussed elsewhere, the rape in the fifteenth-century romance *Partonope of Blois* is orchestrated by the heroine specifically for the knightly benefit of the young hero.[32] In my previous work on *Partonope*, I consider only briefly what I would like to expand on further here: the possibility that a fundamental aspect of establishing chivalric identity is male sexual aggression against women. Gravdal notes that in medieval chivalric literature 'from the notion of strength, manliness, and bravery, we move to the knight's striving after heroism, and then to the idea of forced coitus'.[33] This trajectory of masculine force – from the battlefield to the bedroom – is reversed in *Partonope*; the act of forced coitus Partonope believes he has committed is the inceptive act that paves the way for later public fame through acts of chivalry and prowess.[34] As with the rape in the *Wife of Bath's Tale* and Gauvain's transgression with the Pucelle de Lis in the Continuation of *Perceval*, it is the placement of this scene at the beginning of Partonope's narrative that suggests it is essential to the knight's subsequent journey and development. Whereas Chaucer's and Chrétien's texts move quickly beyond the genuine rapes in favour of narrating the reparative process of fighting or errantry which will ultimately serve the knights well, in *Partonope of Blois* there is no female victim to tend, no crime for the hero to avenge. Indeed, there is almost no female body at all, for throughout this critical scene in *Partonope* (and indeed through the first year of their relationship), Melior remains invisible to her lover. Thus, the audience has no other object to occupy its attention in this encounter except Partonope's body committing the act of masculine aggression; the knight's future chivalric success is based in large part on the confidence and self-assertion he gains from it. Rape, in this text, bolsters rather than harms the knight's reputation.

Representing rape as staged in *Partonope*, and in other romance narratives as well,[35] serves two purposes: it makes the act of masculine sexual aggression more palatable to the audience, and highlights the erotics of the rape scenario that may be elided or suppressed to a degree in cases of actual forced coitus.[36]

---

[32] See Vines, *Women's Power*, especially pp. 85–114, for a reading of the performative politics in the consummation scene of *Partonope of Blois*.
[33] Gravdal, *Ravishing Maidens*, p. 3. Saunders also discusses the 'predatory male ethic created by warfare' (*Rape and Ravishment*, p. 13).
[34] Vines, *Women's Power*, pp. 97–8.
[35] See also the staged rape scene in Chrétien de Troyes's *Le Chevalier de la Charrette*.
[36] This is not to say that actual rape may not have an erotic valance in literature.

Yet the fact that *Partonope*'s staged consummation scene includes only one visible body – that of the man – has implications for how rape may be read as a fundamental first act of knighthood. With the embodied, solely masculine performance of rape in *Partonope of Blois*, we move beyond the often obscured, briefly rendered descriptions of sexual attacks in other romances and receive a detailed physical account of the act: one that the audience knows is consensual but that the knight believes is a rape. In this way, the author can explore the erotics of rape 'safely', free from the expectations of the social and legal repercussions that follow.

Many critics, such as Sarah Stanbury and A. C. Spearing, discuss the significance of sight to medieval theories of desire and power. In recent years, scholars have begun to revise the notions, largely inherited from film theory, that associate the gaze with masculine dominance and the object of the gaze with passive femininity.[37] However, more than the vexed dynamic of masculine gaze on female object which often accompanies readings of erotic scenes in medieval romance,[38] the relationship between public and private spaces as the locus for specific acts of male chivalric development is particularly relevant to the ways in which *Partonope* reveals the fundamental place of rape in this system. Traditional acts of masculine prowess – tournaments, battles, hand-to-hand combat – occur in full view of the public; indeed, they depend upon the audience's corroboration for their validity. The knight's progress throughout the romance landscape is marked at each juncture by some form of public acknowledgement.[39] However, sexual acts – both forced and consensual – remain largely the realm of private experience in romance narratives, with poets relying primarily on innuendo or brevity in their descriptions. When these acts are exposed, it is typically through public outcry, as in the case of the people's juridical 'clamour' in the *Wife of Bath's Tale* or the family's accusation in the *Perceval* Continuation, or it is the result of audience voyeurism. In his study of medieval voyeurism, Spearing characterizes the act of translation (in this case of Old French romances into Middle English narratives) as a highly intrusive one: 'the English poet opens up [the French source's] private

---

37 In her excellent study of medieval visuality, Sarah Stanbury discusses the historical limitations of visual theories, such as Freud's and Foucault's, that rely primarily on gendered metaphors ('Regimes of the Visual in Premodern England: Gaze, Body, and Chaucer's *Clerk's Tale*', *New Literary History* 28 (1997): 261–89). She questions the validity of reading a medieval gaze as phallic on a paradigmatic female body when 'the central body in that system of representation is not female at all', but rather male: Christ (266). Ultimately, Stanbury suggests, object relations theory provides a more appropriate paradigm for understanding medieval visuality, positing a gaze that is 'independent of gendered prohibitions and distinctions' (268).
38 See in particular Spearing's discussion of *Partonope* in *The Medieval Poet as Voyeur*, especially pp. 140–54.
39 Here we may recall the fortunate 'crowding' that tends to occur around Lancelot's various chivalric activities in Chrétien's *Le Chevalier de la Charrette*; even his notorious leap into the cart, ostensibly witnessed in the moment only by the dwarf and Gawain, is quickly advertised and evaluated throughout the kingdoms of Logres and Gorre.

spaces, enables us to follow him into them, and thereby intensifies the privacy he violates.'[40] Spearing's discussion of translation here can be extended to understanding intrusive visuality in romances as well. Much as the audience is complicit in exposing the 'private spaces' of the translated text, the audience's gaze also participates in the act of male sexual aggression it witnesses; we are implicitly called upon to ratify or reject the act just as we must determine the knight's worth based on his performance in a tournament.

As Stanbury and others have noted, private spaces, such as the bedroom,[41] the lonely riverbank and the isolated pavilion, often allow for the most fetishized and erotic exposures of the female body.[42] In these moments of penetrating voyeurism, the fetishized pieces of women's bodies – the breast, the braid, the patch of skin – become the target of erotic desire (the knight's and the audience's) and, ultimately, the site at which prowess and future chivalric success are determined. Friedman notes that a necessary precondition for achieving masculine connection and development in medieval romance is depicting a female body 'vacated of its interiority' or made 'spectral'.[43] Although Friedman's use of the term spectral refers to Chaucer's reticence to describe Emelye's naked body during her ritual bathing in the Temple of Diana,[44] I would like to discuss the more literal and complete 'spectrality' of Melior's body in *Partonope of Blois*.

In the lengthy bedroom interactions between Partonope and Melior, there is never a portion of her body available for the audience's or the knight's gaze; her body cannot be eroticized because it is not visually present.[45] But that does not mean that the sexually provocative aspects of such a unique encounter are not included. Focusing rather on the eroticism of hearing and touching, Spearing reads Partonope's participation in this scene as a 'solitary dreamlike journey ... a quest into the mysterious, archaic depths of "female sexuality"'.[46] Perhaps because he is invested in the masculine, penetrating gaze so prominent in traditional readings of medieval romances, Spearing seems to categorize a non-visually based intimate encounter between a knight and a woman as an 'exploration of feminine darkness'.[47] Yet for all the overwhelming, all-encompassing (yet non-visual) femininity Partonope may experience in this scene, the

---

[40] Spearing, *The Medieval Poet as Voyeur*, p. 141.
[41] See Leitch, 'Enter the Bedroom', this volume, p. 39.
[42] See Stanbury, 'Regimes of the Visual', 309, and Friedman, 'Between Boccaccio and Chaucer', p. 221 n. 34.
[43] Friedman, 'Between Boccaccio and Chaucer', p. 215. In this article, Friedman discusses Chaucer's treatment of Emelye in the *Knight's Tale*.
[44] Friedman, 'Between Boccaccio and Chaucer', p. 203.
[45] After their initial consummation scene and after her explanation of the significant power under which she brought him from France to Chef d'Oire to be her lover, she informs Partonope that he will have fulfillment of her in every sense but sight: 'In kyssynge, in felynge, and in all þat may be plesyre, / ... / Safe onely syghte[,] desyre þat noghte of me' (1800–2).
[46] Spearing, *The Medieval Poet as Voyeur*, p. 144.
[47] Spearing, *The Medieval Poet as Voyeur*, p. 149.

encounter is still a representation of one of the most penetrating acts of male sexual aggression.

Ironically, however, the staged rape scene in this romance begins with the young knight lying in a state of debilitating fear in 'þe chamber all derke.'[48] The poet emphasizes Partonope's lack of experience (sexual and otherwise), making him seem like a frightened young child rather than a potential aggressor:

> for fere he dryste not ryghte well slepe,
> He was In better poynte to wepe
> Thys lay he stylle all in a traunse;
> He was a-ferde of some myschaunse. (1174-7)

Finally, with a 'herte fulle nere quappynge' (1180), he hears a footstep in the room and begins to regret that he was ever 'of woman bore' (1186). After Melior climbs into bed with Partonope, both characters lie silently in bed out of fear and shame; the poet takes the opportunity to investigate their individual desires during this critical moment in the narrative. On the one hand, Melior debates the social acceptability of her actions, for although she is 'so yonge for to lese' her 'maydenhode' (1218), she is

> þynkyng howe sh[e] myghte endure
> Euer of hym to haue plesauns;
> For she wyth-owten varyauns
> Purposyed euer to be hys. (1227-30)

Of course, the comical element of the scene lies in the fact that, while Melior believes that 'she haþe in here bedde / A lusty man' (1215-16), Partonope worries that she is an 'Illusione / Off þe deuylle and of conivrysone' and he 'Dare ... not speke In no wyse' (1284-6).

The impasse of his fear and her reticence to seem too eager could continue indefinitely; indeed, the poet makes a lighthearted comment about the need to get the ball rolling, so to speak: 'Lette se nowe ho can beste deuyse / Þes tweyne to make a-quentyd to be' (1287-8). Yet the innocence of the author's remark masks a much darker reality; they will become 'a-quentyd' not through family members or at a chaperoned social event, but through an act of staged rape, one that will act as the critical first step in the trepidatious knight's chivalric development. As Partonope gains confidence in this bedroom scene through the physical aggression he displays, so too will he gain the confidence to assert his will publicly on the battlefield and in court.[49] The point at which

---

[48] *The Middle English Versions of Partonope of Blois*, ed. A. Trampe Bödtker, EETS, e.s. 109 (London, 1912), line 1172. Further references to this source will be cited by line number within the text.

[49] This change in Partonope's ability to perform the public duties of the nobility is tied directly to the consummation scene. Before he arrives in Chef d'Oire, Partonope participates in a boar hunt with his uncle, the King of France. Although the young man does slay a boar,

Melior 'streyght forþe here legge, and happed to ffele, / ... / Off þys wofulle Partonope' (1298–300) is the moment that the spell of fear and hesitance Partonope has been under is broken, and he begins his repetitive physical striving for his goal: consummation. At every new physical frontier he reaches – her foot, unseen but felt; her side, 'so softe, so clene [that] Plesaunce had hym ouer-come / [and] all hys wyttes were fro hym nome' (1537–9) – the lady orders him out of her bed in no uncertain terms. Although she does not scold him loudly, 'for þer shulde be / No grete a-ffray' (1308–9), she does threaten him repeatedly with death if her men find him there. Far from the frightened child who initially occupied her bed, Partonope is now comforted to know that 'hyt was ne deuelle ne no ffynde' (1345), but 'hyt was a woman, what euer she were' (1349). Yet along with this realization comes a desire to push the physical and personal boundaries Melior attempts to establish:

> Alle-þo she had spoke be-fforne
> Wordes of malys and cruelte,
> Yette fully trusteth and howpeth he
> That he shalle haue of hyr fulle grace.
> And þer-wyth-alle he þynketh to enbrace
> Thys ffayre lady in hys armes too. (1356–61)

Indeed, over the course of the poet's lengthy description of this sexual choreography, it seems to be precisely her words of 'malys and cruelte', her repeated rejections of his advances, that incite Partonope's desire and galvanize him toward committing rape. It is immediately after her final refusal – 'For þe loue of Gode, I praye yowe lette be' (1561) – that the knight begins to rape her:

> And wyth þat worde a-none ganne he
> In hys armes her faste to hym brase.
> ...
> And her legges sh[e] gan to knytte,
> And wyth hys knees he gan hem on-shote. (1562–6)

Although she protests even during the encounter, crying 'Allas!' (1564) and 'Syr, mercy!' (1567), Partonope 'wolde not lefe ne be þer-by; / For of her wordes toke he no hede' (1568–9).

The way in which the poet renders this scene is startling in its inclusion of details not found in other rape scenarios in medieval romances. Aside from the standard brief references to the knight forcefully 'embracing' his victim and

> prompting Clovis to exclaim, 'thys was welle don, as of a chylde … He ys ryghte lyke to ben a man' (556–9), Partonope soon becomes separated from his hunting party and is frightened of the 'wylde and wodde bestes' (662) who might devour him in the forest. After his arrival in Melior's kingdom and the aggressive beginning of their sexual relationship, however, the 'chylde' (705) becomes a 'yong man' (2071) under Melior's influence and tutelage. The rest of Partonope's time in this magical kingdom is spent hunting and engaged in other noble pastimes; when he finally returns to France, he will lead an army to purge his native country from Saracen invaders.

'raft[ing]' her maidenhead (both of which are also included in *Partonope*), the rapes in other narratives move the audience's attention swiftly beyond these forced sexual encounters to concentrate on the victim's explicit, if ineffectual, objections (as in the *Perceval* Continuation) and on the reparative act that will ostensibly offer a modicum of justice to the victim and will certainly rehabilitate the knight's somewhat tarnished reputation. Yet in *Partonope*, we are asked to linger over the violation itself, concentrating not so much on the invisible legs she 'knytte[s]' together to thwart his aggression, but on the knight's very visible knees which attempt to 'on-shote' her legs to gain better access to her body. Partonope's own erotic physicality in this scenario is notable; he not only 'rafte' her virginity through his act of forced coitus, but he also 'geffe her hys' (1571), suggesting a mutual, if forced, physical transgression has occurred. Once the initial rape has taken place, the poet notes that they 'Entergamynyd' (1572), or played sexual games with one another for a time. For Partonope, this sexual play is exciting, for 'suche a game a-fore he neuer a-sayde' (1573). Melior, however, is 'alle dysmayde / Off her-selfe' (1574–5) and is 'sore and also wery' (1581). Despite the audience's undoubted knowledge that the scene was organized and put in motion entirely for Partonope's benefit, it is still quite shocking to witness how quickly the frightened boy becomes the sexually aggressive man with little or no active encouragement. Partonope in particular experiences the rape as a new 'game' he can play at will, a game that will prepare him for success in the future 'games' of chivalric prowess that require the same perseverance and single-mindedness that the staged rape did with Melior. With his initial victory over a resistant woman in the bedroom completed, Partonope's fledgling chivalric cachet increases exponentially under Melior's keen patronage. Because this sexual encounter was a staged rape for the knight's benefit rather than an actual instance of forced coitus, such as in the *Wife of Bath's Tale*, there are no reparative journeys or errands to mitigate the scene's erotic potency or to obscure its role as fundamental to knightly development.

I do not intend to suggest that a rape must occur in a medieval romance in order for chivalric development to take place; in many cases, as Saunders suggests, rape and abduction 'function as emblems of villainy, placing the knight outside the strictures of chivalry, and providing a focus for the defence of the chivalric ideal'.[50] This essay, however, examines how our understanding of chivalry is altered when the act of villainy is committed by a knight from *within* the established and central court system. Such a possibility makes it necessary to divert the audience's attention away from the rapes and towards the reparative acts of social penitence and chivalric prowess. This diversion, I argue, is part of the process of recasting the acts of sexual deviance in medieval romances as *external* to chivalry, attempting to make them *not* indigenous to

---

[50] Saunders, 'A Matter of Consent', p. 119. Saunders also notes that 'actions of *raptus* are frequently associated with the heathen and hostile world beyond the court, a world where no legal and chivalric structures exist to defend women from the action of *raptus*' (p. 116).

the knightly code. Yet even in romances where rape is not present, hints of sexual aggression toward women remain, committed by young knights and often written off as innocent foolishness.[51] Reading all sexual misconduct, from the innocent yet unwanted kiss to the more overt acts of forced coitus in romances such as *Partonope*, the *Wife of Bath's Tale* and the Old French *Perceval Continuation*, exposes some very uncomfortable possibilities about the fundamental place of male sexual aggression in the implicit expectations of medieval chivalric behaviour.

---

[51] See, for example, the fifteenth-century Middle English romance *Blanchardyn and Eglantine*, translated by William Caxton. In this text, the young, virtually untested hero is advised to steal a kiss from 'lorguilleuse damours', or the Proud Lady of Love (William Caxton, *Blanchardyn and Eglantine*, ed. Leon Kellner, EETS e.s. 58 (London, 1890), p. 35). His advisor warns that, at first 'hit shall tourne for pryde of her, tyl a grete displeasire vnto her, and shal be therof wors apayed more than reason requyreth. But care you not for that' (p. 39). After Blanchardyn is successful in his 'entrepryse' (p. 40), the Lady is furious to have 'thus sodaynly [been] kyst of a man straunger out of her knowledge' (p. 43). Although her will and, potentially, her reputation have been violated in this seemingly innocent act, the poet is careful to gloss over Blanchardyn's act of aggression as 'a thynge of nought' (p. 43) and, ultimately, depicts the kiss as a remedy for the Lady's 'pryde dampnable' (p. 38). When Blanchardyn sets out to kiss the Lady, he is motivated almost exclusively by the 'promesse' he made to the older knight that he would 'brynge [to] an ende the werke that he hath vndertaken, that is to wyte, to kysse the proude mayden in amours' (p. 40). Thus, we see how even 'innocent' acts of physical aggression against women are woven into the fabric of chivalric development.

Notes on the Contributors

Aisling Byrne is Fitzjames Research Fellow in Old and Middle English at Merton College, Oxford. She has published on topics such as feasting and the supernatural in Arthurian romance and on textual transmission between medieval England and Ireland.

Anna Caughey is Fellow in Old and Middle English at Keble College, Oxford. Her research interests are centred on masculinity, aggression and warfare in late medieval Britain, with a focus on knighthood and chivalry. She has recently published short articles on virginity and sexuality in Malory, forgiveness in Scottish romances and the Scottish Alexander the Great tradition.

Kristina Hildebrand teaches English Literature at Halmstad University, Sweden. She is the author of *The Female Reader at the Round Table* (2001). Her other research interests include ethnicity, gender and disability in medieval texts. She is currently working on a study of the forger Charles Bertram.

Amy S. Kaufman is Associate Professor of classical and medieval literature and feminist theory at Middle Tennessee State University. She is Director of Conferences for the International Society for the Study of Medievalism and the author of a number of articles on women in medieval literature and neomedievalism in contemporary culture.

Yvette Kisor is Associate Professor of English at Ramapo College, New Jersey. She has published articles on a range of medieval and post-medieval literary topics, ranging from *Beowulf* and medieval romance, to Tolkien and the Twilight novels.

Megan G. Leitch is Lecturer in Middle English Literature at Cardiff University. She has published articles in journals including *Medium Aevum*, *The Chaucer Review*, and *Arthurian Literature*, and her book *Romancing Treason: The Literature of the Wars of the Roses*, is forthcoming with Oxford University Press. Her current project is a study of sleep and its spaces in the pre-modern English imagination.

Cynthea Masson works in the English Department at Vancouver Island University where she teaches a variety of writing and literature courses. Her PhD (McMaster University) focused on medieval literature and the rhetoric of mysticism. Her research and publications are in two primary areas: Medieval

Studies and Whedon Studies. She is the co-editor of *Reading Joss Whedon* (2014). Her fiction includes *The Elijah Tree* (2009), a novel that combines theories of medieval mysticism with contemporary issues of faith and sexuality. She is currently working on her second novel, *The Alchemists' Council*.

Hannah Priest is a research fellow at the University of Manchester. She has recently edited *She-wolf: A Critical History of Female Werewolves*, forthcoming from Manchester University Press, and is the author of several articles on intersections of sex, violence and monstrosity in both medieval romance and contemporary speculative fiction.

Samantha J. Rayner is Director of the Centre for Publishing at University College London. She teaches and writes on publishing and book-related topics, as well as medieval and Arthurian texts. She is the author of *Images of Kingship in Chaucer and his Ricardian Contemporaries* (2008) as well as chapters and articles relating to Malory and more recent Arthurian retellings. She is currently working on a book about Arthurian paratexts with Leah Tether.

Robert Allen Rouse is Associate Professor at the University of British Columbia, Vancouver. He is the author of *The Idea of Anglo-Saxon England in Middle English Romance* (2005), and publishes widely on medieval literature and culture.

Cory James Rushton is Associate Professor of English at St Francis Xavier University in Nova Scotia. He is the co-editor of *A Companion to Medieval Popular Romance*, with Raluca Radulescu (2009), *Disability and Medieval Law: History, Literature, Society* (2013), and two volumes on zombies and popular culture, with Christopher Moreman (2011). In addition to numerous essays on Malory and Middle English romance, he has a forthcoming book on ethnic factionalism and empire in the *Morte Darthur*.

Amy N. Vines is Associate Professor of Medieval Literature at the University of North Carolina at Greensboro. She is the author of *Women's Power in Late Medieval Romance* (2011), as well as several articles on medieval patronage, Hoccleve, and medieval lyric poetry. She is currently working on her second book, *Teaching Chivalry: The Context of a Medieval Ideal*, which examines the role of women and domestic didacticism in the construction of chivalric identity in a variety of medieval genres.

Index

abjection, 127
Accolon, Sir, 19, 25
adultery, 15–16
Agravayne, Sir, 20
Alan of Lille
   Plaint of Nature, 118–19, 122
alchemy, 111–26
Allman, W. W., 6, 27, 29
Andreas Capellanus, 5, 74, 86–87
Archibald, Elizabeth, 21
Armstrong, Dorsey, 14, 16, 21
Arundel, Thomas, 70
Ascham, Roger, 13
Aude, 5
Augustine, Saint, 7, 101, 115

Bawcutt, Priscilla, 129, 130, 135, 137, 143, 144
Benson, David, 13
Bersani, Leo, 6
Berthelot, Anne, 64
Bevis of Hampton, 93
Blamires, Alcuin, 29
Boholm, Åsa, 121
Breunis sans Pité, Sir, 14, 18
Brewer, Derek, 155
Bruckner, Matilda Tomaryn, 168
Bruhn, Mark J., 112, 117, 123
Bunt, G. V. H, 85, 96
Burness, Edwina, 137
Burrow, J. A., 77, 83, 151
Butterfield, Ardis, 76, 80

Carton, Evan 150, 151
Chance, Jane, 155
Chaucer, Geoffrey
   Canon's Yeoman's Tale, 112

General Prologue, 2
Legend of Good Women, 154, 158
Merchant's Tale, 27–37
Miller's Tale, 6
Prioress' Tale, 2
Sir Thopas, 99
Troilus and Criseyde, 69, 147–60
Wife of Bath's Prologue and Tale, 2, 137, 163, 164–67
Chrétien de Troyes
   Le Chevalier de la Charette, 166
   Eric et Enide, 6
Christine de Pizan, 5, 157
Chow, Rey, 156
Copeland, William, 41
Cowell, Andrew, 121, 123
courtly love, 4–5
   as a fetish, 40 n. 3
Crocker, Holly, 35

Damyan, 27–37
Dante Alighieri, 153–54
Daenerys Targaryen, 7
De Pascalis, Andrea, 111
Derrida, Jacques, 156
Desmond, Marilynn, 149, 153
Dinshaw, Carolyn, 126, 155
Donaldson, E. Talbot, 27, 147
Dunbar, William, 127–45
   The Flyting, 129–33, 144
   The Lament for the Makaris, 133
   The Tretis of the Tua Mariit Wemen and the Wedo, 134–39
   The Wowing of the King in Dunfermline, 139–45

Ebin, Lois, 139

Edwards, Suzanne, 164
Elaine of Astolat, 19, 87
Elaine of Corbenic (Carbonek), 19, 47–49, 55–56, 61, 62, 91
Eliot, T. S., 35, 70
eroticism,
   and animals, 127–45
   and the body, 29–37
   and class, 4
   and gaze, 27–28
   and gender, 4
   and heteronormativity, 3–4
   and nakedness, 55–67
   and sin, 4
   of stabbing, 27
   of women, 27–37
   and voyeurism, 148
Evans, Deanna, 135
Everest, Carol, 33

Fabliau (genre), 31
Fairy lovers, 99–110
Fehrenbacher, Richard, 151–52
Fisher, John, 69
Foucault, Michel, 3, 7, 153
Floris and Blancheflour, 44, 94
Floire et Blanchefleur, 95
Freud, Sigmund, 30
Fries, Maureen, 135–36
Froissart
   Le Joli Buisson de Jonece, 76

Game of Thrones (HBO Cable Television Series), 1, 6–7
Gaheris, Sir, 20, 25
Galahad, 61
Gareth, Sir, 19, 20, 25, 49–50
Gaunt, Simon, 95
Gawain, Sir, 20, 25
Geoffrey of Monmouth, 165
Glenn, Jonathan, 130
Gower, John
   Confession Amantis, 69–83, 153–54
   Mirour de l'Omme, 69
   Vox Clamantis, 69

Gravdal, Katherine, 162–63, 165, 174
Grosz, Elizabeth, 30
Guerin, Victoria, 15
Guillaume de Lorris, 74
Guinevere, 2, 4, 14, 17–18, 20–25, 47–49

Hagen, Susan, 30
Hanks, D. Thomas, 6, 27, 29
Hansen, Elaine Tuttle, 29, 35
Hares-Stryker, Carolyn, 87
Hasler, Antony, 129, 142
Henryson, Robert, 140, 143
   Testament of Cresseid, 132
Hilberry, Jane, 112
Hopkins, Amanda, 55, 59–60
Horn Childe and Maiden Rimnild, 43–45
Hotchiss, Valerie, 93, 94
humours, 34

Igrayne, Duchess of Cornwall, 14–19
Immram Brain (The Voyage of Bran), 101–2
incest, 148–49
Islam, 1
Isolde, 4

Januarie, 27–37
Jeaste of Sir Gawain, 170, 172

Karras, Ruth Mazzo, 89
Kelly, Kathleen Coyne, 8
Kennedy, Walter, 130, 132
Khal Drogo, 7
King Arthur, 15–18, 20–21
Kristeva, Julia, 127, 129, 142
Kyng Horn, 42–45

Lacan, Jacques, 30
Lamorak, 4, 18, 25
Lancelot, Sir, 2, 14, 20–25, 47–49, 55–58, 61, 62, 91
Lancelot-Grail cycle, 57–58, 60–62, 66–67
Landavale, 60
Legenda Aurea, 90

Leupin, Alexandre, 115–16, 120
Lewis, C. S., 79, 145
Lindsay, Sarah, 170–73
Lot of Orkney, 16–17
Lyall, R. J., 140, 143
Lybeaus Desconus, 173
Lyonesse, Dame, 19, 49–50
Lyonors, 16

Malory, Sir Thomas, 2, 13–25, 55–67, 91
   and bedrooms, 47–51
   and love, 13–14
   and Pentecostal Oath, 14, 17
Marchaut
   Voir Dit, 76
Marie de France
   Bisclavret, 97
   Graelent, 106
   Lanval, 7, 100, 103–6
Martin, George R. R., 1–2, 6–7
masculinity, 13–25
May, 27–37
McCracken, Peggy, 93
McDiarmid, Hugh, 128
medievalism, 1–8
Meleagant, Sir, 14, 18, 25
Melusine, 51–52, 107
Menon, Madhavi, 112, 126
Merlin, 15
Mieszkowski, Gretchen, 147, 151
Mills, Robert, 153
Mitchell, J. Allan, 157
Mordred, 16, 20–21
Morgan le Fay, 14, 18–19, 63, 152
Morgause, 4, 18, 20
Morte Darthur, see Malory, Sir Thomas
Mudrick, Marvin, 154–55

necrophilia, 14
Niebrzydowski, Sue, 29–30
Nicholson, Peter, 82
Norman, Joanne, 139
Normington, Katie, 93
Norton, Thomas
   Ordinal of Alchemy, 111–26

Palomides, Sir, 19
paraphilia, 3
Partonope of Blois, 163, 174–80
Patterson, Lee, 118
Pellinore, King, 16–17
Perceval, Old French First Continuation, 163, 167–74
Perkins, David, 3
Pratchett, Terry, 75
Prisciani regula, 2
Pugh, Tison, 7
Pulp Fiction (Film), 1
Putter, Ad, 77, 78–79, 93–94

rape, 1, 45, 154, 159, 161–80
Ridley, Florence, 140, 142
Ripley, George
   Compound of Alchemy, 111–26
Roberts, Gareth
   The Mirror of Alchemy, 116, 120
Rochester, John Wilmot, Earl of, 74–75
Roman de Silence, 92
Romance of the Rose, 72, 76, 153
Romans of Partenay, 52
Ross, Ian, 128, 140, 142
round table, 18, 20
Rouse, Robert Allen, 34, 75

Sailor Moon, 4
Salisbury, Eve, 69
Saunders, Corinne, 100, 165–67
Schiff, Randy, 92, 96
Schueler, Donald, 69
Scott, Tom, 128
senex amans, 28
Shahar, Shulamith, 75
Siege of Jerusalem, 59
Sir Degaré, 106
Sir Gawain and the Green Knight, 45–47, 152
Sir Launfal, 60, 106
sodomy, 1
Song of Ice and Fire (Series of Novels), 1, 6–7
Song of Roland, 5
space, 39–53, 175–77

Spearing, A. C., 135, 151, 175–76
Squire of Low Degree, 39–41
Stanbury, Sarah, 175–76
Stevens, Martin, 31

Taylor, Andrew, 27–28, 30, 154
Thomas of Erceldoune, 107
Tin, Louis-George, 4
Tochmarc Étaíne (The Wooing of Étaín), 101–2
Torre, Sir, 17
Tristram, Sir, 18

uncanny, 7
Uther Pendragon, 15, 18–19

Wade, James, 100, 102–103

Wars of Alexander, 59
Watt, Diane, 69, 82
Weiss, Judith, 88
werewolves, 85–98
Wetherbee, Winthrop, 82
William of Palerne, 85–98
Windeatt, Barry, 151
Wogan-Browne, Jocelyn, 90
Worde, Wynkyn de, 41

Xenophon, 158–59

Yde at Olive, 92
Yvain and Gawain, 88

Žižek, Slavoj, 5, 7, 30

www.ingramcontent.com/pod-product-compliance
Lightning Source LLC
Chambersburg PA
CBHW070806230426
43665CB00017B/2510